THE JACKSON COUNTY REBELLION

THE JACKSON COUNTY REBELLION

A Populist Uprising in Depression-Era Oregon

Jeffrey Max LaLande

Oregon State University Press   Corvallis

Library of Congress Cataloging-in-Publication Data

Names: LaLande, Jeffrey M., author.
Title: The Jackson County Rebellion : a populist uprising in depression-era
    Oregon / Jeffrey Max LaLande.
Other titles: Populist uprising in depression-era Oregon
Description: Corvallis : Oregon State University Press, 2023. | Includes
    bibliographical references and index.
Identifiers: LCCN 2022059680 | ISBN 9780870712296 (trade paperback) | ISBN
    9780870712302 (ebook)
Subjects: LCSH: Jackson County (Or.)—History—20th century. | Populism—
    Oregon—Jackson County. | Good Government Congress—History. | Banks,
    Llewellyn A., 1870–1945. | Fehl, Earl H., 1885–1962. | Ruhl, Robert, 1880–
    1967. | Political corruption—Oregon—Jackson County—History—20th
    century. | Oregon—Politics and government—1859-1950. | Jackson County
    (Or.)—Biography.
Classification: LCC F884.J14 L35 2023 | DDC 979.5/27—dc23/eng/20230118
LC record available at https://lccn.loc.gov/2022059680

♾ This paper meets the requirements of ANSI/NISO Z39.48-1992
(Permanence of Paper).

Oregon State University
OSU Press

Oregon State University Press
121 The Valley Library
Corvallis OR 97331-4501
541-737-3166 • fax 541-737-3170
www.osupress.oregonstate.edu

For Vicki

The exhuming of buried reputations and the revivifying of dead causes is the familiar business of the historian, in whose eyes forgotten men may assume as great significance as others with whom posterity has dealt more generously.

—Vernon L. Parrington, *Main Currents in American Thought*

Contents

Illustrations

Preface

During the Great Depression, economic distress and social unrest gave rise to various populistic political movements in the United States. This was especially true in rural sections of the country. Three notable examples—each of them tinged with violence—include the 1931 Iowa Cow War, the 1933 Wisconsin Milk Strike, and the 1932–1936 Farmers' Holiday movement of the upper Midwest and northern Great Plains. In Jackson County, Oregon, discontented citizens—many of them from rural areas—joined an insurgent movement known as the Good Government Congress. Under the charismatic leadership of wealthy orchardist and newspaper publisher Llewellyn A. Banks, the movement challenged the local urban elite for control of county government, and it threatened to spread beyond Jackson County.

In its attempt to effect political change, the Good Government Congress used demagogic and inflammatory newspaper rhetoric, mass demonstrations, recall elections, and economic boycotts to mobilize support. Southern Oregon's turmoil during the years 1932 and 1933—dubbed the "Jackson County Rebellion" by prominent newspaper editor Robert Ruhl—included electoral fraud, intimidation, and violence. However, the rebellion, which gained widespread state, regional, and even national attention, ended with the insurgents defeated. The outbreak may have helped, in some minor fashion, inspire Sinclair Lewis's 1935 novel, *It Can't Happen Here.*

During the height of the Jackson County Rebellion, opponents characterized the movement as "radical" or "Bolshevik"; after its defeat, they described it as "fascist." This account of the Jackson County Rebellion examines newspaper accounts, personal interviews, official correspondence, personal papers of major participants, criminal investigatory files, and trial transcripts. The rebellion's roots lay in a forty-year-long local tradition of agrarian insurgency, beginning with the People's, or Populist, Party of the 1890s. The local Populist movement helped establish an enduring, endemic tradition of backcountry resentment and political action directed at the area's urban elite. Jackson County's powerful Ku Klux Klan of the early 1920s, which thrived on similar populistic sentiments, was another factor in this long-standing

tradition. The tumultuous Jackson County Rebellion of the 1930s was merely
the insurgency's final and most dramatic episode.

Some readers of this book may be struck—as I have been during the
course of writing it—by the parallels between political events in Depression-
era southern Oregon and the divisive, turbulent national politics of the
twenty-first century.

Acknowledgments

Although the result of this project reveals a history of political conflict and social strife, my research effort has been met with kindness and cooperation at every turn. I am thankful to the many people who have helped during the preparation of this study. The late Richard Maxwell Brown gave consistently insightful advice as I began this project years ago. His suggestions were always on the mark. So too were the those of William G. Robbins as I brought the project to a close. I am in their debt.

My research benefited in crucial ways from assistance given by staff members of the following institutions: the Beinecke Library of Yale University, the Jackson County Archives, the Jackson County Library, the Knight Library of the University of Oregon, the Medford Irrigation District, the Medford *Mail Tribune*, the Oregon Historical Society, the Oregon State Library in Salem, the Southern Oregon Historical Society, the Hannon Library of Southern Oregon University, and the State of Oregon Archives.

In addition to the helpful people at those institutions, many other individuals contributed to the project in a wide range of direct ways: Kay Atwood, Ruth Banks, Cecile Baril, John Billings, Todd Carney, Dunbar Carpenter, Jane Carpenter, Lida Childers, Frances Port Clark, Harlan Clark, Scott Clay, Larry Deckman, Bob Dickey Jr., Linda Dodds, Pam Ferrara, Richard Frey, Otto Frohnmayer, Sam Harbison, Sloan Heermance, Jack Hollenbeak, Dean Orlando Hollis, Hannah Horn, Dan Hull, Donald Husband, Peggyann Hutchinson, James Johnson, Marianne Keddington-Lang, George Kramer, Jon Lange, Gerald Latham, Kira Lesley, Glen Love, Jack Maddex, Barbara Mahoney, Alicia Ruhl McArthur, Alice and Larry Mullaly, Jay Mullen, Cathy Noah, LaVerne Norman, Marjorie O'Harra, Jeff Ostler, Elton Petri, Peter Sage, Arthur Schoeni, Gordon Stanley, Kevin Talbert, Jay Taylor, Rich Thelin, Ben Truwe, Louise Wade, Sue Waldron, Lee Webb, Jan Wright, and Emil Zimmerlee.

It has been a genuine pleasure to work with the staff of Oregon State University Press—Marty Brown, Kim Hogeland, and Micki Reaman—who helped bring this book into print. I am also very grateful to copyeditor Susan Campbell.

The ongoing support of friends and colleagues in Oregon and elsewhere has been important to this undertaking, as was the generosity of my late parents, Al and Georgia LaLande. Central to its completion has been the advice and encouragement of my life partner, Vicki Fox.

1

Jackson County Rebellion:
The View from New York City

In March 1933, American writer Sinclair Lewis—then residing in New York City—was at the height of his fame. Lewis, whose novels of the 1920s brilliantly portrayed complacency and philistinism in small-town America, received the Nobel Prize for literature in 1930, the first American to be honored. His often-caustic comments on the absurdities of the national scene found wide play in the press.

By the early 1930s, a rising sense of panic had replaced the smugness of the 1920s—a decade when America's large corporate businesses had held immense (and largely unquestioned) sway over the federal government and the nation's economic policies. With unemployment skyrocketing and bank failures spreading, news about social and political upheavals growing out of the Great Depression filled the pages of New York papers in March 1933. In a much-publicized nationwide radio address that month, Senator Huey Long warned of revolution unless America's wealth was redistributed.[1] Sinclair Lewis may have listened to the popular Louisianan's admonition that day, perhaps thinking that if anyone would lead a revolution's charge it might be Senator Long himself. It is also likely that Lewis, an alert observer of American politics, would have read a front-page article that appeared that same day, March 17, in the New York *Herald Tribune*, headlined "'Law and Order' Champion Held in Slaying of Oregon Constable." The brief piece described turmoil and tragedy in distant Jackson County, Oregon, where Llewellyn A. Banks, the embattled leader of a local insurgent political movement, had fatally shot a law officer sent to arrest him. The *New York Times* carried the same story, reporting that the Oregon State Police stormed "the barricaded house" of Banks.[2] Senator Long's prophecy may have gained added credibility by this echo from the distant provinces.

Sinclair Lewis left New York in April 1933 for a tour of Europe. There, economic depression swelled that continent's rising tide of fascism, suggesting to him the dark new direction that revolutionary change could take. Back in New York the following spring, Lewis no doubt read with interest the *Times'*

May 8, 1934, front-page story about that year's Pulitzer Prize awards; eight years earlier, already enjoying renown as a novelist, Lewis had created a sensation when he refused the Pulitzer committee's prestigious award. His first item of interest probably would have been the 1934 award for "best novel," which went to a Georgia author's portrayal of a nineteenth-century backwoods family, her first novel and a work that was not destined to endure as a classic.[3]

However, a special sidebar article in the *Times*, featuring the Pulitzer's journalism award for "meritorious public service," told a story that would have been of more interest to Lewis. Titled "Newspaper Fought Rise of 'Dictator,'" it described the 1933 events in southern Oregon's Jackson County, wherein Medford newspaper editor Robert W. Ruhl crusaded against a takeover of local government by armed supporters of would-be dictator Llewellyn Banks.[4] Ruhl, who described the episode as the "Jackson County Rebellion," was lauded by the Pulitzer committee as the voice of reason, and as a brave editor who withstood boycott and personal threats in his fight against political extremism.

Political extremism, especially the potential for an American fascism, was on the minds of liberal intellectuals like Sinclair Lewis that year. Huey Long was on the rise as a populist messiah; Father Charles Coughlin, the "radio priest" who would soon support a fascist solution to the nation's economic woes, enjoyed immense popularity. When Lewis's wife, journalist Dorothy Thompson, returned from a visit to Nazi Germany in 1934 filled with foreboding, the novelist began writing *It Can't Happen Here*, a novel about the rise of a fascist dictatorship in America.

If Lewis read about the Jackson County affair and the crusading Oregon editor's resulting Pulitzer Prize award, as reported in the New York newspapers, the news story may have contributed—at least in a small way—to Lewis's conceptualization of an incipient American fascism in his best-selling 1935 novel, *It Can't Happen Here*.[5] The hero of the tale is, like Jackson County's Robert Ruhl, a small-town newspaper editor who refuses to be intimidated by totalitarian bullies. *It Can't Happen Here* remained popular during the 1930s, and the phrase "it can't happen here" became an enduring American touchstone for extremist, authoritarian threats to American democracy.

The tumult in southern Oregon provides a significant case study, portraying the threats to democracy characterized in Sinclair Lewis's novel. Aside from its possible role as at least one of a number of events that inspired Lewis's novel, the Jackson County episode is also an important example of political insurgency and social turmoil in the Depression-era United States.

Historians have described the months of late 1932 and early 1933 as the "winter of despair." The Republicans' New Era lay in tatters, and Franklin Roosevelt's New Deal was then only a campaign promise. That winter was a time of unprecedented economic crisis in America. One historian of the Depression, the late Bernard Sternsher, recorded very few instances of violent protest across the nation during the period, fewer than twenty. Historian John Garraty allows that "there may have been many more." Historians have ignored the southern Oregon outbreak of 1932–1933, when Jackson County citizens became galvanized into advocating direct action. Demagogic leaders encouraged violence and channeled popular discontent into a grassroots movement of political extremism, one that ultimately ended in violence.[6]

The Jackson County Rebellion began with the formation of a movement called the Good Government Congress. Led by wealthy orchardist and newspaper owner Llewellyn Banks and newspaperman Earl Fehl, the Good Government Congress coalesced around populist resentments—fueled by repeated allegations of corruption and conspiracy on the part of the local political establishment.[7] The movement's crusade pitted "have-nots" against "haves," the rural hinterland against the urban elite. The movement's leaders—Banks and Fehl—used mass meetings, inflammatory newspaper rhetoric, recall campaigns, and economic boycott to mobilize support among rural and working-class citizens. The Good Government Congress employed electoral fraud and the threat of violence to effect political change.

The Good Government Congress movement resulted not only from the Depression's severe economic distress. Jackson County's rebellion dated from a local tradition: a heritage of agrarian unrest and political rancor. Southern Oregon's People's Party movement of the 1890s and the area's Ku Klux Klan's activities of the 1920s illuminate an ongoing struggle of rural-based insurgency against the region's commercial and political establishments. This long history of rural resentment contributed to the events of 1932–1933. In addition, southern Oregon's legacy of insurgent politics owed much to the nation's longer-yet tradition of backcountry social and economic rebellion. Rural protests, characterized by uprisings against the perceived wrongs of near or distant elites, marked American history from the colonial period through the early twentieth century.

Trading the spatial distance of a contemporary observer like Sinclair Lewis for the temporal distance of the historian, the view of the Jackson County Rebellion as a direct outgrowth of the Great Depression still holds. But first, it is important to examine the episode's historical taproot, following the pattern of previous conflicts in southern Oregon long before Huey Long or Sinclair Lewis came onto the national scene.

2
Southern Oregon, A Place Apart

The political history of southern Oregon has long been significantly different from that of the rest of the state. Among other distinctions, by 1930 the region's populace had earned a well-deserved reputation among other Oregonians for political discontent and turmoil, stemming from a decades-long tradition of political dissension and insurgent movements that would culminate dramatically in the Jackson County Rebellion of 1932–1933. This tradition first took root in the area's fertile ground of nineteenth-century agrarian discontent and political factionalism. These factors continued to play out well into the twentieth century.

Gestating during the region's participation in the widespread Populist Revolt of the 1890s, dissension persisted in southern Oregon through the early twentieth century, erupting with particular ferocity in Jackson County during the rise of the Ku Klux Klan in the early 1920s. This persistent strain of disgruntlement and protest culminated with a near-insurrection during the onset of the Great Depression. From the 1890s into the 1930s, local demagogues, aided by strident newspaper editors, emerged to play important parts in the region's politics. So too did several exuberantly strident newspapermen. In all of this, southern Oregon's unique political history also reflected broader trends taking place elsewhere in the country during periods of economic stress.

Before exploring, in this chapter, how the region's political tradition developed, it is necessary to place southern Oregon—Jackson County in particular—within its wider geographic and historical setting.

THE WILD, WILD SOUTH

As a geographic and historic region, now-capitalized "Southern Oregon" is a long-used proper noun referring to Oregon's southwestern interior. The term first came into use during the 1850s, when most White settlers within the bounds of Oregon Territory lived west of the Cascade Range, in the Willamette Valley. East of the Cascades lay a vast semiarid country, much of it dominated by sagebrush, that would not begin to "settle up" until the 1860s–1870s. The portion of Oregon commonly considered as "western Oregon," situated entirely west of the Cascades' crest, encompasses about one-third of the state's present area. In 1850, the overwhelming majority of western Oregon's White settlers lived in the Willamette Valley, a place that many of them considered to be synonymous with what they thought of *as* Oregon. In contrast, southern Oregon in that same year had yet to receive its first influx of non-Native settlers. (Today, the southern Oregon region is usually considered to include Douglas, Josephine, and Jackson Counties; some definitions include the coastal counties of Coos and Curry as well.)

Composed of rugged, heavily forested mountains with deep river canyons, the area contained a few fertile valleys, although much smaller in size than the Willamette. For years, Native people who inhabited the region had been contesting entry by White travelers, thereby acquiring the name *les coquins* (rascals, or rogues) from the brigades of French-Canadian fur trappers who passed through in the 1830s. In the central portion of what became Jackson County, steep terrain gives way to gentle valley lands. The Rogue River Valley, which includes the extensive Bear Creek Valley, experienced a major land rush of White farmers that began suddenly after 1851. Spurred by the generous land-claim provisions of Congress's 1850 Oregon Donation Land Act, many would-be farmers came west to southern Oregon directly from the states of the Upper South and the Ohio River Valley, arriving in southwestern Oregon via the Applegate Trail. Other newcomers migrated southward after a few years' residence in the Willamette Valley.[1]

Coinciding with the land rush of the early 1850s, gold discoveries in the Siskiyou Mountains of southwestern-most Oregon resulted in a rapid northward extension of California's gold rush. This gold frenzy was without precedent in Oregon. With a population dominated by young, single men, the early mining period contributed to southern Oregon's distinctive reputation: up to that point, Willamette Valley farmers and merchants had considered the Rogue River country as an isolated, much wilder part of Oregon.

By 1856, the three counties that today make up the core of southern Oregon had been established: Douglas County, which embraces the Umpqua River watershed, in the north; Josephine County to the southwest, occupying the most rugged portion of the Siskiyou Mountains; and Jackson County, southeast of Douglas, abutting the California border and extending, west to east, from the Siskiyou Mountains to the Cascade Range. Among these counties, Delaware-sized Jackson County, established in 1852 and named for the nation's seventh president, possessed three major geographic blessings that gave it primacy: more easily accessible gold deposits than elsewhere in the region; the fertile Bear Creek Valley; and that valley's location—situated between the Siskiyous to the west and the Cascades to the east, directly on a gentle section of the main travel route between California and the Willamette Valley. Because of these factors, Jackson County steadily became the wealthiest and most populous county in southern Oregon. It has remained so to the present day.

*　*　*

Southern Oregon's Rogue River War, a series of bitter clashes between Indigenous populations and White miners and farmers between 1851 and 1856, was the only conflict of its kind to occur anywhere west of the Cascade Range in Oregon. During the 1840s, White American farmers had enjoyed a remarkably peaceful settling of the Willamette Valley, due to the terrible toll of mortality in the 1830s on the area's Indigenous people from various diseases brought by White newcomers. The 1851–1856 conflicts further marked the southern portion of western Oregon as a challenging and potentially dangerous place to settle. Although US Army soldiers participated in the conflicts, much of the fighting (including massacres of women and children) was done by volunteer militia units composed of local miners and farmers, some of whom, to the disgust of Oregon's federal Indian Agent Joel Palmer, baldly referred to themselves as "exterminators." The Rogue River War ended with what can only be described as an ethnic cleansing. Surviving Native people were marched to the Coast Reservation, located far distant from their homeland in southern Oregon.[2]

Yet another difference between the region and the Willamette Valley/ lower Columbia River section of Oregon was its domination by a greater percentage of settlers who came from the Upper South, or from the lower tier of the Midwest that had been heavily settled by people of southern political and social values. These agricultural immigrants, most of them staunch Democrats, also dominated in the older Oregon settlements to the north. However, former New Englanders, New Yorkers, and emigrants from the northern tier of the midwestern states made up a sizable minority of the Willamette Valley's populace. This was especially true of the merchants and professionals living in river towns such as Portland, Salem, and Corvallis, who tended to place a higher value on education than did their rural neighbors. The Jackson County town of Ashland and its environs did form a notable exception to the Jeffersonian-Jacksonian Democracy's dominion over southern Oregon. Initially settled by emigrants from mid-Ohio and other Whig strongholds, Ashland's founding generation became the backbone of the Rogue River Valley's new, small Republican Party.[3]

Several prominent southern Oregon politicians proposed detaching their region from the rest of Oregon to create a Territory of Jackson in 1857. Unlike the Oregon Territory, Jackson Territory would be open to slavery. The proposal gained attention but did not move forward. Most southern Oregon settlers, like their neighbors to the north, wanted neither free blacks nor slavery allowed into their new home. Oregonians eventually incorporated those two prohibitions into the new state's constitution, the only one to specifically deny residence to African Americans.[4]

By 1860, the burning question of whether slavery would be permitted into the American West's new western territories was tearing the country apart. Because of the split in the national Democratic Party during that year's portentous presidential campaign, Oregon gave Abraham Lincoln (who had vowed to halt slavery's spread into the West) a very slim plurality over Democrat Stephen Douglas. Of the two opposing Democratic candidates, John Breckenridge and Douglas, Breckenridge was an outright defender of slavery's expansion into the western territories. Voters in Jackson, Josephine, and Douglas Counties provided pro-slavery candidate Breckenridge with victory, giving him nearly half of the region's votes cast, with Lincoln and Douglas dividing the remainder about equally. Breckenridge's running mate, Oregon Senator Joseph Lane, was a popular former territorial governor and a resident of Douglas County. Although Lane's presence on the ticket was a factor in southern Oregon's notably high pro-Breckinridge vote, the results definitely indicate a heavily pro-South electorate.[5]

During the Civil War, southern Oregon became known as a hotbed of Copperhead "disloyalty," rife with alleged plots by would-be secessionists. Sympathizers of the Dixie South included Jacksonville's relentlessly pro-slavery newspaper editor, William G. T'Vault, who condemned President Lincoln's "tyranny," waved the populist flag of virulent White supremacy, and spoke out for creation of a slaveholding "Pacific Republic" on the West Coast. Late in 1861, the Republican Portland *Oregonian* quoted noted prominent early settler Jesse Applegate as stating that the southern part of the state "stinks with an element foul and corrupt, bordering . . . on actual treason." Under the headline "Delusion and Treason," one of the newspaper's correspondents reported that "along Bear Creek in Jackson County" a traveler will find "toryism [pro-secession attitudes] disgustingly common."[6]

Although much of the heated rhetoric was simply back-and-forth journalistic hyperbole between partisan newspaper editors, Oregon's Union government established Camp Baker in the Bear Creek Valley as an army post for volunteer cavalry in 1862, due in part to worry over possible insurrection by local residents.

Although feelings in the region remained quite tense throughout the Civil War, fears of guerilla warfare in southern Oregon proved unfounded. A few assaults and brawls occurred, as did calls to hang a gang of unknown but allegedly

"Secesh" residents for horse thievery. An army detachment quickly snuffed out a threatened rebellion by pro-South miners in the remote Josephine County seat of Waldo. The latter incident was quickly suppressed without actual violence. No actual armed conflict occurred in southern Oregon during the Civil War.[7]

* * *

Because of its geographic isolation, southern Oregon endured a thirty-year "pioneer phase" of relatively slow economic growth. Formidable Siskiyou Pass—the highest point along the overland route between California and the Pacific Northwest—made commercial transport a challenge and virtually impossible in winter. The Rogue River's propensity for turbulent midwinter floods frequently swept away the few existing bridges. Grain crops from the Bear Creek Valley's farms, and lumber made at the few small sawmills, brought returns from only a local market. Although livestock were driven for sale in more distant places, the huge cattle operations in California's Central Valley dwarfed southern Oregon's herds.

Although small in population compared to the Willamette Valley, Jackson County's two early settlements had grown into southern Oregon's largest towns by the 1870s. On the western margin of the Bear Creek Valley, the former mining camp of Jacksonville benefited both as county seat and as gateway to the mining districts. Ashland, at the foot of the Siskiyou Mountains, prospered because of its strategic location on the wagon road to California. Each town had a population of nearly a thousand in 1880. Economic isolation ended in the mid-1880s when the Oregon & California (O&C) Railroad Company completed construction through Jackson County and over the Siskiyou Pass, linking the region with Portland, San Francisco, and the rest of the nation. The tracks bypassed Jacksonville but went through Ashland, where the O&C's successor, the Southern Pacific Railroad, built a large depot and roundhouse to service the engines that soon steamed daily over the pass. About ten miles east of Jacksonville, on Bear Creek near the center of the valley, the railroad platted the new town of Medford in 1883.

SOUTHERN OREGON AND THE POPULIST REVOLT

Thirty years after the Civil War, Rogue River Valley farmers enthusiastically participated in the nation's Populist Revolt, the 1890s episode that brought the most serious third-party challenge ever to the hegemony of the country's two major parties. It erupted from an extended period of grinding downturn in agricultural prices, as well as railroads' manipulation of shipping rates. The protest movement originated with the spread of Farmers' Alliance chapters in the Great Plains during the 1870s–1880s, and then grew into the People's, or

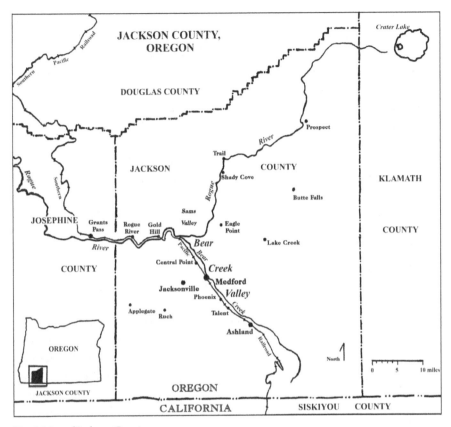

Fig. 1. Map of Jackson County

Populist, Party. The Populists had their greatest success in the central Great Plains, parts of the South, and the far West.

The railroad brought rapid growth to Jackson County after its completion in 1887. The county's population increased over 40 percent between 1880 and 1890. Although urban growth accounted for a significant portion, many new farm families settled in the countryside. During the 1880s, the county established a dozen new electoral precincts due to increased rural population. Rural residents made up about three-quarters of Jackson County's 11,455 people in 1880. The Southern Pacific Railroad's aggressive promotion of the Rogue River valley's agricultural potential lured more farming families to the region. Jackson County newspapers commonly mentioned the arrival of newcomers from Kansas, Nebraska, and other Great Plains states, and editors encouraged more would-be farmers to immigrate. By the mid-1890s, the county's rural folk were cultivating more than 66,000 acres of prime cropland. Grain farming remained the norm, with wheat dominating the annual harvest.[8]

Although a few of Jackson County's rural citizens lived in remote, narrow valleys of the surrounding forested highlands, most resided in or near the Bear Creek Valley. The main valley and adjacent smaller valleys, such as the Applegate Valley and Sams Valley, formed an extensive agricultural hinterland that traded with the merchants of Jacksonville, Ashland, and, increasingly, Medford. A number of other communities, ranging from small towns to tiny hamlets, served the farming population's immediate needs. Among the most important of these were Phoenix, Talent, Eagle Point, Gold Hill, and Woodville (later renamed Rogue River), as well as Central Point, located on Bear Creek a few miles north of Medford. These communities became focal points of Populist organizing efforts during the early 1890s.[9]

The longtime political allegiance of many Jackson County voters caused them to send Democrats to the county courthouse during the 1870s and 1880s, and this allegiance extended to support for Democratic presidential, congressional, and gubernatorial candidates. In contrast, many Oregon counties elsewhere steadily transformed from Democratic to Republican majorities during these years.[10]

Mirroring the country's growing Populist Revolt movement, many southern Oregonian farmers now viewed both the Democratic and Republican parties as enemies. Jackson County's new and lively Populist newspapers persuaded many voters that county government was in the clutches of a corrupt "courthouse ring." During 1891–1892, Jackson County's Farmers' Alliance chapter, the first in southern Oregon, rapidly transformed itself into the new People's Party, challenging the two old parties for control of the courthouse.

Despite widely differing historical interpretations of the Populist Revolt of the 1890s, there is substantial agreement as to its origins and aims. The last quarter of the nineteenth century witnessed tremendous acceleration in the transformation of the United States from an agricultural to an industrial nation. The change brought economic prosperity for some segments of American society and severe economic distress to others, especially to the grain farmers of the Great Plains and cotton farmers of eastern Texas. Farmers found themselves caught in a web of mortgage debt, high railroad rates, and low prices for their harvest. With neither of the two major parties addressing the situation, farmers formed self-help cooperative organizations during the late 1870s and early 1880s that grew into the powerful Farmers' Alliances of the late 1880s. They also forged fragile links with restive industrial wageworkers and urban reformers that took shape as the People's Party. The movement spread rapidly to the western states, including the wheat-farming areas of the Pacific Northwest.[11]

* * *

Southern Oregon, with Jackson County in the lead, became a hotbed of agrarian discontent in the Pacific Northwest. Local farmers' financial distress, caused by poor harvests and low prices, resentment of monopoly by the railroad, and frustration with high taxes and perceived corruption in local government, contributed to the unrest. Bear Creek Valley farmers, like farmers elsewhere in the United States, suffered deeply from the worldwide depression in crop prices. In addition, their anti-monopoly sentiment had a local focus: by 1891, fewer than half a dozen commercial flouring mills operated in Jackson County. Fearing that the mills were forming a trust, farmers labeled them "the mill combination in this little valley." As a consequence, many wheat growers preferred to ship their produce out of the region for processing. Railroad charges, however, put them in an impossible position. During the 1891 harvest, Southern Pacific charged twenty-two cents a bushel for valley grain shipped to San Francisco warehouses. For its part, the SP refused to cooperate with the state railroad commission's 1891 freight rate investigation, which called for a 10 percent reduction in grain shipment rates; the railroad delayed with court action.[12] The issue of alleged corruption and favoritism in county government also took hold amid charges of mismanagement, unfair taxation, and alleged outright graft. Threatened with mortgage foreclosure, valley farmers from Woodville to Eagle Point expressed outrage at entrenched local "cliques," in particular the Democrats' now-hoary "Jacksonville ring."[13]

* * *

In March 1891, among the primary Jackson County organizers of the Farmers' Alliance/People's Party were Phoenix resident Samuel Holt, Talent farmer William Breese, and Holt's Phoenix neighbor, the Reverend Ira Wakefield. In addition, female "lecturers" such as Jessie Beeson and Stella Duclose encouraged women's participation in the movement as well. As in the Great Plains, southern Oregon farm women were highly important in the grassroots development of the Alliance/Populist movement.[14] By the end of that summer, Jackson County contained more than twenty separate sub-alliances, scattered from Evans Creek in the northwest to the farmlands south of Ashland. Alliance secretary Breese presented a list titled "Alliance Demands" to the local press in early 1892. These demands included insistence on a far more aggressive state railroad commission—one composed of "fearless, honest and capable men"—and for state relief from mortgage foreclosure, particularly from the "heartless Shylocks" who dispossessed "wives and children of the unfortunate ... [from] the sacred spot which they called 'home.'" Breese also proposed a ten-month stay on all such debt executions. Local Alliance members demanded tax reduction, an "economy" program by the profligate county government, and an end to corrupt rule by "wire-pullers and rings." Breese admitted the "tremendous influence" of the non-Populist local press, and he invited fair criticism of the demands. However, he threatened editors of the Republican Ashland *Tidings* and Jacksonville's *Democratic Times* with boycott of "any newspaper that opposes [the Alliance] with abuse, misrepresentation or ridicule."[15]

* * *

Birthed by the Farmers' Alliance movement, the new People's Party was officially organized in southern Oregon in late 1891. By December, Holt, Breese, and Wakefield emerged among the main leaders of the local People's Party. The party's initial public statement unfurled the banner of reform. The Reverend Wakefield, writing in a florid style that typified Populist rhetoric elsewhere in the nation, proclaimed that "this is a struggle of the people against the plutocracy." Editors of both the *Democratic Times* and the *Tidings* obviously were troubled by the insurgent challenge. The *Times* published a steady stream of pleas to rural voters during the spring, claiming that "the real People's party is still the democratic party."[16]

Committed longtime agrarian reformers like William Breese and Samuel Holt had both come to southern Oregon in 1881. One of Oregon's delegates to the People's Party 1892 national convention in Omaha, Holt went on to become president of the Oregon State Alliance. Even the *Tidings* admitted that Holt was a "clear, forceful speaker" who effectively made his case to voters. The local two-party press was far less respectful of Ira Wakefield, a New Englander and ardent prohibitionist whom the *Democratic Times* scorned as a "political preacher ... pregnant with theories." In Medford, the Populist *Southern Oregon Mail* carried Wakefield's weekly letters, full of rhetorical trumpet calls to the troops.[17]

The Populists' rhetoric stressed solidarity, including the use of "Brother" and "Brethren" in addressing their fellows. The tone of numerous editorial letters displayed a sense of religious fervor and confidence in the power of unity to effect change. Periodically, large Farmers' Alliance picnics and People's Party rallies took place at different locations in the valley. Brother Stephen Nealon hosted a May 1892 Table Rock Alliance picnic on the north bank of the Rogue River in Sams Valley. It brought a large crowd of self-proclaimed Old Hay Seeds to listen to Populist candidates. The following year a similar "grand picnic," followed by dancing, took place at Beeson's Grove near Talent.[18] In addition to mass rallies, Jackson County Populists attempted to forge self-reliance through cooperative economic ventures, but none of these proved successful. However, local Populists succeeded in establishing a viable "reform press" as an alternative to the old-party newspapers. The Medford *Mail,* founded in

1889, took a generally nonpartisan stand until 1892, when a new publisher/ editor turned it into a Populist organ. Renamed the *Southern Oregon Mail* to broaden its rural appeal, and with a masthead proclaiming, "A Paper Of, By and For the People!," the *Mail* served as an important and upbeat, even exuberant, voice from April through the November 1892 election. During the 1894 and 1896 elections, the normally Democratic *Valley Record* of Ashland took on a marked Populist hue prior to the "fusion ticket" of Democrats and Populists, who ran the same candidate for president, William Jennings Bryan, during the election of 1896.[19]

* * *

Bitterly opposed by the local elites and isolated from the People's Party's main geographic wellsprings in the Great Plains, Jackson County Populist leaders nevertheless built a grassroots organization. They mounted an aggressive challenge to the local political order from 1892 through 1896. Visits of nationally known Populists added further excitement to the forthcoming 1892 elections. Ironically, it was the detested Southern Pacific Railroad that brought former Union Army general James B. Weaver to the Rogue River Valley in May. Weaver stepped off the train at Medford and proceeded to the county fairgrounds, where an eager crowd awaited him. "Wagon load after wagon load" of expectant people had come to hear the "grand and gentlemanly" speaker, soon to become the Populists' nominee in the 1892 presidential race. Less than two weeks later, Populist orator Mary Elizabeth Lease arrived in the valley. Lease, known as the Kansas Cyclone, spoke at Ashland, Medford, Jacksonville, and Gold Hill. The *Mail* crowed that "never before had there been such an uprising" in the county as the crowds that turned out to hear her. Famous for allegedly advising Kansas farmers to "raise less corn and more hell," Lease delighted her Jackson County listeners by debunking the Republicans' blame of agricultural overproduction for farm ills with the quip, "The only over production that Kansas ... ever had, was an over production of fools."[20]

The November 1892 election in Jackson County returned an astounding 50 percent for General Weaver in the three-way presidential race, showing the Populists' solid gains among both farmers and residents of the new town of Medford. A similar voting pattern prevailed in neighboring Josephine and Douglas Counties. Flush with the scent of victory, the *Mail* predicted the local People's Party would "certainly carry everything" in 1894. The editor's confidence proved well-founded. The party's momentum continued to grow during 1893 and 1894, thanks in part to a financial scandal that implicated members of the courthouse "ring," as well as to the deepening national depression—the Panic of 1893. Farm mortgage foreclosures in the Rogue River Valley gained increasing press coverage, and by 1894 talk of an impending nationwide railway strike further heightened farmers' fear.[21]

The 1894 campaign was thus under way amid an atmosphere of local and national crisis. Southern Oregon's People's Party attracted to its ranks some aggressive new members who rapidly came to the fore. Prominent among them was former Democrat John A. Jeffrey, Populist candidate for state representative. Although Jackson County Populists had the first of their many internal squabbles during the campaign (due largely to the actions of Jeffrey and other newcomers), the party swept the June election. Voters opened the doors of the county's allegedly "ring"-infested courthouse to a number of Populist officeholders. They also sent men like Jeffrey to Salem.[22]

One aspect that blurred the local People's Party identity and eventually divided its ranks was the emergence in the mid-1890s of a new kind of Populist candidate. Begun by dedicated reformers such as Holt and Breese, the local party's leadership had changed in composition when the party attracted office-seekers who previously had failed to rise to prominence within the two major parties. Opportunists such as John Jeffrey, stymied by factions within the old parties, now joined the People's Party. Young Kaspar K. Kubli, a University of Oregon graduate and member of a prominent Jacksonville family, announced his conversion from the Democrats to Populist in 1894. Failing to obtain a candidacy, he later left the valley to attend law school. William E. Phipps, a former Democrat who joined the Populists, became prominent in the fusionist or "union" wing of the party. Phipps and John Jeffrey led the fatal split from the dedicated-reformist Holt/Breese wing in 1898.[23]

John Jeffrey became one of Jackson County's more charismatic latecomer Populist politicians. An Arkansan who had arrived in the Rogue River Valley as a boy, Jeffrey attended the state agricultural college in Corvallis and became active in the Democratic Party. Enjoying name recognition throughout the county, Jeffrey switched to the Populists. Elected as state representative in 1894, he then won the county district attorney race in 1896. The *Democratic Times* coined the sobriquet "little Johnny" for the diminutive young attorney. Its editor made fun of the former Democrat as a "sprig of a boy" and a rabble-rouser who continually "bamboozled the people ... with that little speech of his." The Ashland *Tidings* portrayed Jeffrey as a cynical demagogue who played to the rubes, reporting at length on one rural speech wherein Jeffrey lambasted a host of conspiracies, from the Jacksonville Ring and Wall Street to the Rothschilds, the powerful German-Jewish banking family that became the subject of persistent conspiracy theories by American farmers and other debtors.[24]

Jeffrey's campaign rhetoric brings forward the issue of the Populists' anti-Semitism, as well as its ethnic and religious nativism. Jackson County

Populists certainly sprinkled their communications with references to "shy-locks," but so, too, did editors of the local two-party press. Similarly, the Popu-list papers' expressed disdain for Oregon's East Asian immigrants would have been no more extreme than that of the community in general. However, some local Populists, including John Jeffrey, apparently harbored anti-Catholic at-titudes that became a matter of public controversy during the 1896 election. Predominantly rural and Protestant, southern Oregon residents would seem to have had little reason to fear Papist political or educational conspiracies, but a local chapter of the American Protective Association (APA), a national anti-Catholic organization (and thus, in that way, a precursor to the national Ku Klux Klan of the 1920s), formed by 1895.[25]

The anti-APA *Democratic Times* reported in early 1896 that the region included nearly a dozen branches of the American Protective Association and that more were planned. In May, it noted that APA organizers were working the hustings preparatory to the June election and claimed "nearly all members . . . are Republicans and Populists." The *Times* identified a number of county Populist candidates as APA members, among them Ira Wakefield and John Jeffrey. The *Times* customarily provided space for opponents to respond to various editorial statements. However, neither Jeffrey (who was a member of APA-leader Reverend Eli Fisher's congregation) nor any other Populists rebut-ted the charges. Although anti-Catholicism may not have been an overt part of southern Oregon Populists' 1896 campaign, the nativist sentiments of some candidates was probably shared by many Jackson County residents.[26]

Continuing their electoral juggernaut, local Populists geared up for local and state elections as well as the 1896 presidential race. Likened by the *Mail* to "a swarm of bees," numerous rural people arrived in town for the Populists' April convention. The Ashland *Tidings* dourly reported the June local election results as "almost a clean sweep" for the People's Party. Its edi-tor joined other Republican voices throughout the country in denouncing the "Popocrats" after the national Democrats and Populists joined together under "fusion" presidential candidate William Jennings Bryan. Despite Republican entreaties, southern Oregon, like many other rural areas in the West, bucked GOP presidential candidate William McKinley's national tide. Continuing its legacy of contrarian politics, Jackson County gave Bryan over 60 percent of its vote, whereas statewide, McKinley won with more than half the vote. Precinct returns show consistent Populist dominance in the county's hinterland. Rural voters formed the new Populist majority, whether their communities had formerly tended to vote Democratic or Republican, while Jacksonville and Ashland remained bastions of Democrats and the GOP, respectively.[27]

During the 1890s, southern Oregon's People's Party had mounted a stunningly successful insurgency through the ballot box. However, the restive movement had expended itself before the end of the decade. Despite their ringing campaign rhetoric, local Populists' achievements in office, whether at the Salem capitol or the county courthouse, proved quite limited and contradictory. When, in 1894, Jackson County's People's Party first elected members to office, it was filled with promises of clean government and tax relief. By 1898, after four years in office, Jackson County's Populists—now rent by internal divisions and charges of nepotism, and spurned by most rural voters with the return of national economic prosperity—were swept out of the courthouse, never to return. John Jeffrey abandoned the People's Party and started his own fusionist "Union People's party," which soon joined the local Democrats. The *Democratic Times* promptly changed its description of him from "little Johnny" to "the Honorable J. A. Jeffrey." However, Jeffrey, the ambitious Democratic politico who had, perhaps quite cynically, donned Populist "sheep's clothing," eventually departed the scene, moving to Portland, where he practiced law and obtained a local judgeship as a Democrat. Former Democrat (and anti-Catholic future Klansman) Kaspar Kubli, following his graduation from Harvard Law School, moved to Portland. There, he rose to prominence in the ranks of Multnomah County Republicans. Medford attorney (as well as future newspaper owner and KKK supporter) William Phipps remained in the county, becoming a perennially unsuccessful Democratic candidate for local office. Jackson County's Populist-dominated decade was followed by a period of local Republican hegemony that, except for a break in 1912–1916, lasted until the Great Depression.[28]

Although the old-time Populists still fielded candidates for all county offices in 1898, with the long agricultural depression now a fading memory and the war with Spain commanding headlines, both they and the Democrats failed to stave off a Republican sweep. The People's Party polled an average of only 12 percent. Their best showing came in the remote backcountry precincts farthest from the railroad. Medford residents and farmers near the railroad in the main valley abandoned the party. This last slate of candidates consisted of the party's remnant old believers, little-known residents of the county's most remote rural districts. Jackson County's Populist decade was over.

* * *

The public experience of populism in Jackson County entailed certain elements that came together as a potent political force. Among these was the distress farmers felt during a period of intense economic hardship. In addition, their sense of outrage grew when confronted with alleged town-based political "corruption." Local farmers' time of struggle enabled solidarity to overcome individual rural communities' extreme localism by focusing their attention on an identifiable enemy. Local newspapers, using traditional rhetoric of American republicanism, effectively reinforced these feelings. Grassroots activities such as regular meetings and mass rallies deepened the sense of a righteous crusade. In Jackson County, this excitement soon attracted opportunistic demagogues who built support with appeals to nativism and fears of distant conspiracies. These particular elements continued and even intensified in Jackson County after the 1890s, contributing to a pattern of rancorous protest that persisted into the twentieth century.

Fig 2. During the 1890s, Rogue River Valley wheat farmers like these became the backbone of Jackson County's Populist Revolt. (SOHS # 14322)

Fig 3. Jacksonville's county courthouse in the early 1890s, which local Peoples Party voters strove to wrench away from an entrenched, allegedly corrupt "Jacksonville Ring." (SOHS #868)

Fig 4. Main Street, in the new railroad town of Medford, early 1890s. (Author's collection)

Fig 5. The Rogue Valley's orchard-boom elite, the "Colony Club," at the new Medford Hotel in about 1914. (SOHS #10898)

Fig 6. Pear orchard between Jacksonville and Medford, ca. 1920–1925; the view is toward Medford. (SOHS #3227)

Fig 7. Ku Klux Klan members marching in 4th of July parade, Ashland, ca. 1923. (SOHS #6973)

Fig 8. William Phipps, Medford attorney and former Populist who later supported the KKK in his newspaper, the Medford *Clarion*. (SOHS #9317)

3

Into the New Century
Progressive Era Tensions and the Ku Klux Klan

Southern Oregon underwent a great transformation after 1900. Begun by the railroad's link to San Francisco and Portland fifteen years before, the region's integration into national and international markets accelerated after the turn of the century. Much of the area's economic and social change was concentrated within the main Rogue River Valley, especially in and around Medford. Jackson County's population nearly doubled during the first decade of the new century. Political transformation occurred as well, particularly in terms of the number and power of new players. However, much of Jackson County's earlier political pattern, including agrarian discontent, persisted.

1900–1920: BOOM, BUST, DISCORD

Many historians identify the years from 1900 through 1920 as America's Progressive Era. During this period the region's natural resources and agricultural potential saw rapid development. Southern Oregon's dependence on wheat cultivation changed after the mid-1890s with the first large-scale planting of fruit trees. Orchards of apples, peaches, and especially pears replaced former grain fields and pasture in the Rogue River Valley's richest lands. By 1910, with southern Oregon fruit selling well in London, the Southern Pacific promoted Jackson County as one of the West's premier fruit-growing regions.[1]

Speculative (if short-lived) coal mining schemes in the foothills east of Medford during the first decade of the century set the stage for expensive development, beginning in 1907, by outside investors of the Blue Ledge copper mine in the rugged headwaters of the Applegate River. Renewed hope for mineral wealth from the Siskiyou Mountains complemented local promoters' expectations of profit from vast federal and private forestlands of the Cascade Range. Newly established Crater Lake National Park brought more railroad tourists through Jackson County, and construction of an improved auto road from Medford up the Rogue River to Crater Lake's caldera rim—a goal of local boosters—began in 1909. The Rogue River's irrigation and electric-generating potential likewise attracted development. A new power company completed a hydroelectric dam on the river near Table Rock in 1902, promising to furnish light and power "to every town in the valley." This operation soon became part of the California-Oregon Power Company (Copco), a Medford-based but largely Californian-owned corporation that also controlled the irrigation developments of the Rogue River Valley Canal Company.[2]

Medford became the economic and social dynamo of the region during the first decade of the twentieth century, with the town's population growing from fewer than 1,800 people in 1900 to almost 9,000 ten years later. Boasting sixteen fraternal lodges in 1901, and forming its own, very active Commercial Club three years later, Medford and its boosters dominated the region's Good Roads organization, ensuring that highway improvements would continue Medford's dominance. The city grew as southern Oregon's "central place," outpacing all rivals and causing concerns and displeasure among merchants in the two older towns, Jacksonville and Ashland. Further spurring Medford's rise was the pear-orchard boom that began in about 1905. After apple crops had declined because of blight, orchardists turned to slow-ripening varieties of "winter pears" that brought high prices as a luxury-food item on the East Coast and in Europe.[3]

Although many pear orchardists were of modest means, affluent easterners made up a highly visible element of the valley's newcomers. The Potter Palmer family, wealthy hoteliers of Chicago, bought extensive orchard land near Table Rock. Other urban midwesterners, many of them affluent Chicago-area graduates of Ivy League colleges, purchased substantial orchard properties and built large homes in and around Medford. Replacing the bipolar competition of Jacksonville and Ashland, Medford, with its thriving Main Street downtown and a nearby "packinghouse row" along the railroad, drove the new order of things. Adjacent to Medford were larger orchard holdings, many of them owned by the wealthier class of grower, such as Reginald Parsons (who had graduated from the University of California, Berkeley) and the Carpenter brothers, Leonard and Alfred, both Harvard graduates. These three men established a major pear wholesaling operation, Southern Oregon Sales.

The "orchard barons," along with professionals and merchants attracted to Medford during the boom years, formed a new and different social stratum in the region. Symbolizing this change were the Rogue Valley University Club—founded in 1910 with almost fifty charter members—and the exclusive, orchardist-dominated Colony Club. Sunday afternoons during harvest season customarily brought socially prominent Colonist families to dine at the new Medford Hotel, where the lobby telegraph provided the latest fruit prices from New York. One notable émigré from Chicago, Harvard graduate and national amateur golf champion Chandler Egan, came to Medford in

1911. He purchased more than a hundred acres of orchard land and designed golf courses for nearly twenty private country clubs in western cities, including Medford's new Rogue Valley Country Club in the early 1920s. The cosmopolitan character of Medford's new gentry distinguished it from the commercial and social elites of other small cities in the Pacific Northwest.[4]

By 1915, Jackson County exhibited social and economic divisions in a new but familiar geographic pattern. In the Bear Creek Valley, and constituting the bulk of its fertile and densely settled agricultural lands, were most of the county's smaller orchards, pasture-raised-cattle ranches, and dairy farms. Their productivity and value lessened with increased distance from Medford and the fertile areas closest to Bear Creek. This outer-valley area included the county's older towns—Ashland (now the county's second-largest municipality) and rapidly declining Jacksonville, Central Point, Eagle Point, Phoenix, and Talent. With ready access to the railroad, and linked to Medford and to each other by the newly built Pacific Highway, residents of this zone were not isolated. However, small-acreage orchards were the norm here, and many owners found themselves in serious economic trouble by the new century's second decade.[5]

More distant was the county's backcountry, which included the foothills and smaller valleys tributary to the Rogue River Valley. Hamlets such as Ruch, Wimer, Antioch, Butte Falls, and Prospect served its scattered inhabitants. Open-range ranching, small-scale farming, and seasonal work (mining, logging, Forest Service work, county road crews) brought modest incomes. Distance and poor roads meant isolation. Residents only occasionally traveled to Medford. In contrast to the heavily populated Bear Creek Valley, where by far the largest portion of the county's post-1900 arrivals lived, many hinterland families had resided in southern Oregon since the Populist Revolt or before.

The region's initial pear boom ended in about 1912. A feverish speculative boom in farmland, home lots, and commercial property went bust, leading to a sudden major drop in values. Medford boosters, who had formed a group called the 25,000 Club in 1908, with the aim of increasing the population to that number within five years, instead saw their town lose residents after 1910, declining from 8,900 to 5,700 by 1920. Orchardists faced lower pear prices in war-ravaged Europe after 1914. They battled the codling-moth infestation and suffered from drought that shriveled harvests. Special pest-control treatments, large-scale new irrigation projects, and other expensive survival measures began to characterize the valley's fruit industry during the second decade of the twentieth century. Formerly individualistic orchardists formed the Fruit Growers League, the Rogue River Fruit and Produce Association, and other cooperative ventures. Ashland grappled with the economic downturn by seeking to lure more tourists off the Pacific Highway. Home of the region's annual Chautauqua festival since the 1890s, the ambitious city piped mineral-springs water several miles to the heart of town, where it developed Lithia Park, a large new city park at the site of the Chautauqua Grove.[6]

* * *

Progressive Era politics in early twentieth-century Jackson County reflected a new geography of political power. Coming from the hearth of local Republicanism, Ashland's well-established stalwarts dominated the county's courthouse in Jacksonville and its Salem delegation from 1900 through 1910. Inevitably, they became known as the Ashland Ring. Subsequently, Medford politicians, both Republican and Democratic, took the lead as officeholders, resulting in a new epithet, the Medford Gang, by 1912. Although Jacksonville belatedly built a spur railroad to Medford's Southern Pacific, its fortunes continued to fade after 1900. Party labels masked the presence of numerous factions and personal cliques. The valley's growth coincided with rapid spread of less partisan politics elsewhere in the West, and party affiliations of both office-seekers and voters were relatively fluid. Instead, local issues—from prohibition to relocating the county-seat—were up for grabs among competing political elites.[7] Newspapers continued to take strong stands on national issues, but their local crusades now defied neat party-line categorization. After 1907, the Republican morning-daily *Mail* competed with the evening (and superficially Democrat) Medford *Tribune*; the two newspapers soon combined into a single operation. Joining the *Tribune's* editorial staff was young Robert Ruhl, another Harvard graduate. A nominal Republican and self-proclaimed "independent," he became owner/editor of the *Mail Tribune*. Ruhl steered the paper toward a pronounced progressive stand on local and national matters.[8]

Jackson County voters focused on several local issues during the Progressive Era. A strong streak of Anglo-Saxon Protestant nativism served to keep southern Oregon a self-proclaimed "whiteman's country." A rumored clandestine land-buying "invasion" by Japanese farmers awakened much concern in 1908. Public pressure on landholding companies to sell only to White citizens stemmed the alleged yellow peril, and the valley's few Japanese orchard workers apparently were not invited to return the following harvest season. Ashland's Commercial Club would crow that, in 1915, the town's population was "almost wholly American, no negroes or Japanese."[9]

Religious prejudice erupted periodically, as in February 1914, when "A.P.A. supporters" allegedly vandalized the Sisters of the Holy Name convent in Jacksonville while supposedly searching for secret underground tunnels.

The following month, one Ashland resident wrote to the *Tribune* defending local anti-Papists from its charges of bigotry. "There were," the writer stated, "more good . . . people right here in Ashland and Medford" who regularly read the *Menace* (the national anti-Catholic publication) than who subscribed to the "cowardly, pope-ruled" *Tribune*.[10]

Moral issues dominated many elections. Although gambling and prostitution had been permitted in Medford so long as these activities remained well screened from public view, city officials sent streetwalkers packing when they became too numerous and brazen. Battles over prohibition of alcohol punctuated the county's Progressive Era political discourse. Following the county's decision to remain "wet" in 1904, Ashland, home to a powerful contingent of the Women's Christian Temperance Union (WCTU), went dry in 1907. Ashland and most small towns in the main valley voted consistently for prohibition. Hinterland voters, however, largely rejected it. Medford voters barely defeated prohibitionists' local-option measure the following year, even though the city's Protestant ministers had organized a large parade of Sunday-school children down Main Street shortly before election day. Women's suffrage, passed by Oregonians in 1912, gave added strength to anti-alcohol forces, and statewide prohibition came with the next biennial election.[11]

The exciting presidential election of 1912 (between Republican William Howard Taft, Democrat Woodrow Wilson, Progressive Theodore Roosevelt, and Socialist Eugene Debs) brought victory for both national and local Democrats in the Jackson County vote, although Ashland gave Theodore Roosevelt a slim plurality. Ashland found itself without representation on the Jackson County court of commissioners for the first time in many years, and, claimed the *Tribune*, had only its own anti-Medford stubbornness to blame. Socialist Party presidential candidate Eugene Debs made a strong showing in a handful of the old Populist die-hard precincts, such as the Evans Creek and Applegate Valleys. By World War I, however, Republicans again held most of the important local positions.[12]

Local anti-monopoly feelings—voiced most strongly by Jackson County's few Socialist letter-writers—remained strong despite the Medford Commercial Club's endorsement of Southern Pacific Railroad's position in lawsuits. In addition, the county's major private electric utility came in for a symbolic drubbing at the polls in 1908. By 1912, however, the Medford press condemned local "radical socialist agitators" as men who would "destroy the prosperity of the Rogue river valley," and suggested that they might be members of the Industrial Workers of the World. As with prospective Japanese or other non-Caucasian immigrants to the valley, labor radicals were given little opportunity to flourish in Jackson County.[13]

Rural grievances persisted, transformed, and probably deepened during the Progressive Era. Correspondents from remote hamlets, once a regular feature in the main valley newspapers, faded from their pages—replaced by occasional (and often patronizing) local-color stories. Jackson County backcountry residents held a reputation among state officials for distinctly unprogressive behavior, especially as reflected in numerous violations of the prohibition and game laws. Nevertheless, persistent localism divided rural people from each other—with different communities allegedly receiving "more than their share" of county-funded projects or officeholders.[14]

THE INVISIBLE EMPIRE COMES TO JACKSON COUNTY

By the summer of 1921, Robert W. Ruhl, now full owner and editor of the Medford *Mail Tribune*, had become an influential voice in Jackson County. Having arrived at the height of the orchard boom, he had witnessed tremendous economic growth followed by the slump. Now Ruhl looked confidently toward a return of boom times in a July 27 editorial: he stated that, "as the "biggest little city" on the Pacific Coast," Medford had "no idle millionaires . . . no problems, . . . nothing but trout fishing, fruit picking, and a general Twentieth Century Paradise"; he closed the paragraph with, "Welcome, gentlemen. The city of Destiny awaits you!" As a progressive Republican who stressed his paper's independence, Ruhl took an editorial jab at Portland as a "transplanted Back Bay, the mecca of bond clippers and moss-covered conservatives." Two weeks earlier, he had commented on the appearance of the Ku Klux Klan there, and bragged that Medford, in contrast, was a place where "those finer human feelings, which aspire to peace on earth, good will to man, flourish."[15]

The forty-one-year-old Ruhl, who had grown up near Chicago in Rockford, Illinois, was proud of his adopted hometown. After serving on the staff of the Harvard *Crimson* with fellow 1903 class member Franklin Delano Roosevelt, he worked for the New York *Globe* and the Spokane *Spokesman-Review* before coming to Medford. Ruhl's paean to Medford's civic qualities was simply booster hyperbole. He was apparently genuinely unaware that Medford had in fact just become the first Oregon outpost of the Invisible Empire of the Knights of the Ku Klux Klan. Ruhl soon became the spearhead of opposition to the group when its local presence became public. Within a few months, the Klan dominated the politics of Jackson County. State and local elections in 1922 set off, in Ruhl's words, the "bitterest political campaign" in the county's history.[16]

By the early 1920s, southern Oregon residents were anticipating a return of prosperity. The war was over. International markets for winter pears and other crops seemed to be regaining strength. Between the end of the war and the onset of the Great Depression, the county experienced a 64 percent surge in population, most of it concentrated in and around Medford, which grew during this period to more than 11,000 people. Despite the optimism, serious economic and social problems remained. The postwar slump, especially the return of nationwide agricultural depression, slowed the expected recovery. Jacksonville's main bank failed in 1921, which led to a controversial grand jury probe and much blame all around. Prohibition, in force for the past half dozen years in Oregon, had broken into open war between law enforcement agents and moonshiners in the thinly settled fringes of the valley. Because moonshine stills were hard to detect in remote areas, rural residents dominated among those suspected or arrested for producing illegal spirits. Bootleg sales provided needed dollars to hard-strapped small farmers and ranchers during the agricultural depression of the 1920s and early 1930s. The August 27, 1921, issue of the *Mail Tribune* reported the convictions of three farmers, one living near Gold Hill and the other two in the Applegate Valley, for operating illicit stills. State revenue agents concentrated their searches in these and other hinterland vicinities. Newspapers reported a rising number of raids, drunken brawls, and shootings in the context of a "crime wave" in the county.[17] Budgetary controversies—from prospective street-paving costs to the salaries of civil servants—burgeoned in Medford and county government during 1921–1922. However, one political and economic issue became paramount in the orchard lands and in Medford: water supply.

Sometime in 1921 the Ku Klux Klan appeared in Jackson County and began an initially quiet recruitment effort. Actual membership by 1922 is unknown. But together with its nonmember supporters, the local Klan's political influence was substantial. A mid-1922 charter-granting ceremony in Roseburg (seat of Douglas County) drew approximately two thousand masked Klansmen "from throughout southern Oregon."[18]

Charges of secret involvement by Klan members in Jackson County's controversial water politics—conflicts between opposing irrigation districts as well as the City of Medford over water rights—would become just one of the factors in the Ku Klux Klan's rise in Jackson County. Situated in the most arid section of Oregon west of the Cascade Range, Medford's reputation as a wide-awake, prosperous city depended on a secure source of abundant domestic water. Its existing water source at Fish Lake, a reservoir in the Cascade Range, was taxed to the limit by 1921. Unflattering comments in the Portland press about the taste and appearance of Medford's drinking water unsettled the community's self-image. In addition, the city shared water rights to Fish Lake with the Rogue River Valley Canal Company and the Medford Irrigation District, both of which competed for water to serve thirsty orchards outside of town.[19]

Severe drought and water rationing during the summer of 1921 drove angry orchardists and city residents to hold mass meetings to protest water policy. Yet proposals for development of a new city water source at Big Butte Springs, high in the Cascades, created additional divisiveness; major capital investments were required, and water rights there also were in legal dispute. South of the city, the newly established Talent Irrigation District (TID), although not competing with Medford water users, likewise grappled with water-rights problems. During the long, hot summer of 1921, Jackson County seemed to be encountering serious limits to its growth. Various irrigation-district members, who were also alleged Klan members, aggressively pressed their case with threat of lawsuits over disputed water rights.[20]

Historians of the 1920s Ku Klux Klan have revised the once-standard profile of Klan members as largely lower-middle-class men to account for the fact that substantial numbers of wealthier, more socially prominent men joined the Klan. Although many Jackson County members may indeed have fit the description of "petit bourgeois," some of them were among the wealthier urban residents. Prominent orchardist Raymond Reter was one of a "score of reputable business and professional men" who were inducted at the local Klan's first meeting. A contemporary study of the Oregon Klan counted an assistant district attorney and officials of the telephone company, Standard Oil, and the Southern Pacific Railroad on the rolls in Jackson County.[21]

Although their economic backgrounds may have varied widely, common to many local Klansmen were religious nativism, moralistic concerns, and populistic economic resentments. Orchardist and dairyman D. M. Lowe, unsuccessful Klan-backed candidate for county sheriff in 1922, gave a post-election analysis that expressed all three of these sentiments. Lowe complained that he had been "opposed by the *Mail Tribune*, . . . the Medford banks were against me," and, referring to the power company (Copco) and its associated irrigation-canal firm, he charged that "the two largest corporations in the valley" had opposed him, as had "all the ex-saloon keepers . . . all the bootleggers . . . and last but not least, every Roman Catholic . . . fought me to a finish." Lowe warned, "If this sweet-scented bunch imagine[s] for a moment that they can impose any humiliating terms of surrender on the people, . . . they are just kidding themselves."[22]

Nativism had its most overt expression in the pages of the Medford *Clarion*, founded in 1921. Owner and editor William E. Phipps, Medford attorney and a prominent Populist of the late 1890s, had run unsuccessfully for the Oregon legislature in 1920. Although Phipps denied being a member of the Klan, he nevertheless filled his weekly newspaper with pugnacious pro-Klan commentaries. The *Clarion* featured anti-Semitic articles from Henry

Ford's Dearborn *Independent,* anti-Catholic columns by the nationally known Reverend Robert Shuler of Los Angeles, and anti-Papist screeds from the Klan-published *Searchlight* and *Western American.* While Robert Ruhl and the *Mail Tribune* rallied anti-Klan forces, Phipps made the *Clarion* into Jackson County's Ku Klux Klan mouthpiece. The stage was set in 1922 for a rigorous newspaper war between the two publications.[23]

Although he regularly denounced Jewish "conspiracies," Phipps's main target, like that of other Oregon KKK propagandists, was Roman Catholicism. He assured readers that he was not against individual Catholics, but, like other Protestant nativists of the period, he portrayed the Catholic Church as an alien, corrupt power attempting to gain control over the nation's politics through the votes of its misguided adherents. In an editorial titled "The Arrogance of Absolutism," Phipps asked whether his neighbors realized that the "effort of the ages" was being made to "stamp the blight of Roman hierarchy on this great country?" "Look at Spain, at Ireland, at Mexico [three Catholic countries then undergoing serious upheaval and violence at the time]," he wrote, "and ask yourself if you want this." Phipps accused Ruhl, a Unitarian, of publishing a "most flagrant pro-Catholic sheet," dismissed the anti-Klan editor of a Klamath County newspaper as a "K.C." (Knights of Columbus member), and complained of a Catholic-led boycott of the *Clarion.* Phipps's crusade appealed to many local readers, and the paper's circulation increased significantly during 1922–1923.[24]

Phipps and local Klan officials were in the vanguard of the county's fight over Oregon's "compulsory school initiative" during the 1922 election. The measure required all parents to send their children to public schools, eliminating all Catholic and other parochial or private school systems. Medford mayor Charles E. Gates accepted honorary membership in the local Klavern in May. The affable "Pop" Gates, owner of southern Oregon's largest Ford sales agency and an announced "possible candidate" for the Republican gubernatorial nomination, provided a glowing account of the ceremony as "one no Christian man could take exception to." The following week, a large and appreciative Ashland audience heard the pro-school bill speech of the Reverend Reuben H. Sawyer, Klan lecturer from Portland. A sizable contingent of hooded Klansmen marched in Ashland's Fourth of July parade.[25]

Just as women had played an important if subservient role in the local Farmers' Alliance and People's Party movement of the 1890s, so too did the local Klan's female auxiliary. Although rarely mentioned in the local press, photographs from the period demonstrate that the Klan's Ladies of the Invisible Empire (the LOTIES) and the subsequent, more independent Women of the Ku Klux Klan organizations were active in southern Oregon. These women, as they did elsewhere during the 1920s, would have spearheaded economic boycotts of Catholic businesses and applied social pressure to Protestant church members who did not seem sufficiently militant. As historian Kathleen Blee has demonstrated, Klanswomen formed the "poison squad of whispering women" and became crucial actors in the movement, giving the 1920s Klan much of its grassroots political and economic effectiveness in small towns. Ashland's potent WCTU forces likely supplied some of the local Klan's female supporters. With political suffrage attained nationwide, many middle-class Protestant women flocked to the Klan movement not merely as an adjunct to their husbands' organization but as a means to consolidate and further their own political and moral reform agenda. Many Jackson County Klanswomen likely had these same goals.[26]

Southern Oregon earned nationwide notoriety in 1922 when masked men, identified as local Klan members, used vigilante actions to enforce moral regulation. Three separate incidents of "night-riding" involved hooded vigilantes abducting and threatening to lynch individuals, bringing unwanted attention to Jackson County. One of the victims, an African American railroad porter who just had been released from the county jail for Prohibition violations, was kidnapped at dusk and driven south to where the Pacific Highway crossed the crest of Siskiyou Pass. After being hoisted off the ground three times by a rope around his neck and admonished about his bootlegging, the man fled south toward the California border to taunts of a common racial epithet: "Can you run?" the group shouted as they fired "revolver shots about his feet." The night-riding incidents became a national story when *Outlook* magazine exposed the "Ku-Kluxing" of Oregon and christened them the "Southern Oregon Outrages." Former southern Oregon Populist John Jeffrey came down from Portland to serve as the defendants' legal counsel during the grand jury probe. He cast his clients as solid citizens and accused local anti-Klan forces of making them into scapegoats for political purposes. Another one-time Jackson County Populist, Kaspar K. Kubli, had emerged as a prominent pro-Klan voice in Salem. Representing the Portland area in the legislature, he was elected as Speaker of the House.[27]

The county also experienced negative statewide publicity over a bitter Klan-backed recall campaign against sheriff and longtime Eagle Point resident Charles Terrill. Phipps and other moralists accused Terrill of "open . . . collusion with moonshiners." The sheriff further earned the Klan's ire by responding to Oregon Governor Ben Olcott's investigation of the vigilante episodes with a denunciation of the Klan as "a menace to public welfare." Phipps fueled outrage during the recall campaign with charges that Sheriff Terrill drew a salary that smacked of graft, and similarly charged other officials and institutions with corruption and greed.[28]

The *Clarion's* editor stoked social and economic resentments in southern Oregon, reviving the rhetoric of southern Oregon's Populist insurgency. Phipps editorialized in a populist vein during 1922 about the unfair practices of a host of local villains, including fruit associations, commission men, creameries, and consignment houses. His newspaper flayed Wall Street and federal tax inequalities that favored the rich. He also called readers' attention to disparities in wealth in the Rogue River Valley in 1922. Writing that "a decade ago Jackson County . . . was one of the most prosperous sections in the United States," Phipps described the successful boom-time arrivals as men who "had nothing but a superb nerve" but who were "now living on the fat of the land and clothed in purple and fine linen." He identified "this prosperous element" as "the office holders, contractors of public works, commission fruit-and-produce dealers, and lawyers who get frequent digs in county or city treasuries." He alluded to the "occasional merchant who profiteered during and after the war," pointing out that smaller tradesmen, in contrast, had been "barely able to meet expenses and avoid bankruptcy." Speaking to his rural readers, Phipps pointed out that their "numerous good and productive farms and orchards . . . are . . . covered by bonded indebtedness, [and now] have . . . little or no sale value." He concluded with a resounding, "These conditions must be changed!"[29]

Dismissing Robert Ruhl's anti-Klan crusade as the "Wail of the Gang," Phipps claimed that what "the *Tribune* . . . calls hatred and discord is only the deterrent voice of the people." When the *Mail Tribune's* printing plant was broken into (by what Ruhl termed a "band of hooded vandals") and crucial linotype bands were stolen, the *Clarion's* owner sarcastically belittled the incident and went on to dismiss the *Clarion's* opponents as "enemies of our democratic form of government . . . grafters, lawbreakers, and . . . ultramountain [*sic*; the term 'ultramontane' refers to belief in the absolute power of the Papacy] elements."[30] Phipps's gloves-off style of populist journalism earned much praise from readers, and his words resonated with small businessmen and orchardists.[31]

The newspaper war between William Phipps and Robert Ruhl highlighted the social and political fragmentation in Jackson County during the election year of 1922. One widely publicized split occurred in May when several members of Medford's American Legion post resigned, citing the post's failure to condemn the local Ku Klux Klan. Among the prominent men involved in this protest was Medford Democratic attorney Edward E. Kelly, who had come from the Chicago area during the boom. "Colonel" Kelly, veteran of both the Spanish-American War and World War I, was a tall, imposing figure who dominated Medford's Elks Club and other organizations, including the county's Democratic Party. He called the Klan the "gravest menace to internal peace . . . since the Civil War" and demanded that the Legion's state commander come out against religious prejudice. The local Legion's acrimonious fight over the Klan "parted friends, . . . some of whom had fought side by side overseas." Writing in August 1922, Helen Colvig Cook, member of the county's prominent Colvig family, informed her sister-in-law that "the Ku Klux [is] trying to run the primary election, the [anti-Catholic school bill] election, the [county sheriff] recall . . . not to mention the [night-rider vigilante] grand jury investigation." The months of conflict "have torn [Medford] wide open—feeling is very bitter on both sides & friendships of years standing are broken up." [32]

Although Klan backers included local Democrats, a faction of Republican lawyers tapped the discontent of orchardists and small-town residents by running on what the *Tribune* called the "Klan ticket." Republican Charles Thomas ran for the judgeship that would hear the night-riding cases soon after the election, and Thomas's colleague Ralph Cowgill campaigned for state representative. Helen Colvig Cook described Cowgill as "a Kluxer" whom the county's "anti-Koo-Koos" hoped to defeat. In response to the Klan slate, Edward Kelly and other opponents of the Thomas/Cowgill group established the Independent American Voters League in August and put up candidates for local offices. Hoping to attract the votes of women, the league ran Alice Hanley, daughter of well-known pioneer settlers, for state representative. Phipps scoffed at the Voters League as "a Non-partisan league . . . [an] aggregation of antiquated political has-beens" and renamed it the Bootleggers' Protective Association. [33]

During the closing weeks of the 1922 campaign, Charles Thomas and Ralph Cowgill, both directly involved in the county's two newly organized irrigation districts, disrupted a meeting between Voters League candidates and Talent orchardists. This episode highlights the murky connection between the Klan and water politics during the election. Thomas and Cowgill were accompanied by about fifty supporters, whom Voters League spokesman Evan Reames branded "a mob of . . . the Ku Klux Klan." Thomas, who served as counsel for the Talent Irrigation District, hotly disputed Reames's accusations of legal improprieties. He and his men heckled and shouted until the meeting abruptly ended. Reames, attorney for the power company Copco and its irrigation subsidiary, and Thomas were not the only men on opposite sides of irrigation questions in the Klan/Voters League fight. Klan-backed Ralph Cowgill, running for state representative, served as engineer for the Medford Irrigation District, which was currently locked in legal battles with Reames's client. Cowgill formerly had been employed by Reames's client, the Rogue River Valley Canal Company, and personal grudges may have played an important part in the conflict. Attorney William Phipps, too, had a personal stake in the local water situation. He had represented disgruntled Medford property owners during the 1921 drought and had made "water graft" a major issue in his 1922 editorial columns.[34]

Results of the 1922 election in Jackson County showed the power of Ku Klux Klan supporters. The Independent American Voters League lost badly to the Klan ticket in the election. Ashland and most other communities in the main valley supported "Klan candidate" Thomas and his colleagues. A similar geographic alliance of Ashland and small-town/orchardist voters, arrayed against most residents of Medford as well as those in the distant hinterland precinct, very nearly recalled Sheriff Terrill. Other Klan-associated contests, including the gubernatorial race, showed a similar pattern of support. The surprising exception was Jackson County's defeat of the School Bill, which passed handily statewide. A reservoir of goodwill for the Catholic nuns who had treated many Jackson County residents at their Sacred Heart Hospital during the 1918–1919 influenza epidemic was a likely factor in this result. Because the Sisters of Providence also operated Medford's Sacred Heart grade school, residents doubtless worried that, if the school had been forced to close by passage of the School Bill, perhaps the nuns would have closed the city's only modern medical facility.[35]

Threatened by drought and anxious about clouded water rights, many of the valley's orchardists probably saw the alleged Klan candidates as their champions in 1922. Thomas and his fellows painted the Voters League as part of Medford's elitist "gang" (E. E. Kelly, for example, was known for owning Kelly Island, a personal fishing retreat on the Rogue River). Phipps's editorials aroused populist sentiments, which combined with the nativist or moralist leanings of many residents. In addition, both water politics and anti-Medford localism certainly contributed to the Invisible Empire's 1922 electoral power in the small towns and farming districts of the main Bear Creek Valley.

In the hinterland, however, the Klan did not play well; there, other concerns deflected the hooded order. Remote rural voters did not follow the populist piper of the *Clarion* in 1922 because they were unaffected by the valley's irrigation imbroglio, did not share the "joiner"/lodge-member mentality of many small-town residents, and felt strong antipathy for the Klan's law-and-order Prohibition campaign. The Klan's position on curtailing moonshining may have been the main element dividing the county's most rural voters—those of the hinterland—from their fellow farming citizens of the main valley.

Following the 1922 general election, the forthcoming night-rider trials kept the community's attention focused on the Klan for several more months. In March 1923, newly elected judge Charles M. Thomas (who would rule in favor of the Talent Irrigation District's water rights later in the year) presided over the first trial, held in Jacksonville's venerable courthouse.[36]

Oregon's assistant attorney general L. A. Liljeqvist headed the prosecution; the three well-known defendants—a former Medford chief of police, chiropractor-Methodist minister Jouette P. Bray, and young orchardist Howard Hill—had been charged with riot. Newspaper reporters, including a representative of the Hearst press, added to the sensationalist atmosphere, publishing rumors that witnesses had come to the courtroom armed with handguns. The defense attorneys, including John Jeffrey, spent much effort discrediting the morals of the night riders' victims. The jury deliberated for forty minutes before finding the defendants innocent. The courtroom audience, packed with the accused men's supporters, erupted into shouts and applause. Liljeqvist departed immediately for Salem, and within a few days the state dropped the remaining cases. The acquittal prompted Robert Ruhl to shake his head and call on readers to move on to more positive concerns. William Phipps, portraying the trial as the end result of "opulent Jews and the hierarchy of Rome ... attacking an American order," declared the case closed.[37]

Although the Klan faded from the front pages of the Medford press after the trial, it remained influential in southern Oregon for a few more years. In June 1923, nearly three hundred Klansmen gathered in Grants Pass, the seat of Josephine County, marching in support of anti-Catholic candidates in the upcoming school board election.[38] Ashland was one of the Klan's last strongholds in the region: in the fall of 1924, the socially conservative cultural capital of southern Oregon—home to the annual Chautauqua festival and the region's state normal school—witnessed a "tremendous" Klan parade down its main boulevard. An airplane circled the town, bearing an electrically illuminated cross during the evening's Klan-induction event, and afterward, participants enjoyed an "ice cream feed" prepared by the Ladies of the Invisible Empire.[39]

Because he had worked tirelessly against the Klan when many other Oregon editors had either equivocated or stood with the KKK, Robert Ruhl received the thanks of Oregon's outgoing governor Ben Olcott (who had been defeated in 1922 by Klan supporter Walter Pierce) and Medford's Roman Catholic priest. Anti-Klan newspapermen in other parts of the state sought his advice.[40] Increasingly implicated in murderous violence in other states, and tarred with financial scandal in Oregon, the Invisible Empire rapidly lost ground after 1924. William Phipps, after moderating the tone of his editorials, sold the *Clarion* in 1924. Phipps ran unsuccessfully for county commissioner and other offices during the late 1920s and early 1930s.

Jackson County's moralists were in full retreat when Colonel Kelly's son, Edward C. Kelly, wrote to his fiancé describing the American Legion's state convention, held in Medford in 1928, as an openly "intoxicated" affair that showed "the hypocrisy of Volsteadism" [Prohibition] in this little city." Kelly, a young attorney, Roman Catholic, and rising Democratic star in Jackson County, gloated that "the beauty" of the three-day public spree was that the "W.C.T.U., the preachers, the Prohi's, and [the Klan-associated Republican Party county chairman] . . . have uttered no words of protest."[41]

In the mid-1920s, another contentious issue was resolved: the Talent and Medford irrigation districts settled their water-supply problems by purchasing water rights and constructing additional water-storage facilities. The City of Medford also undertook the expensive development of Big Butte Springs, resulting in the boosters' new motto, "A Mountain Spring in Every Home." In 1926, Medford triumphed in its long battle to wrest the county seat from Jacksonville, and within two years the city's commercial elite was busily promoting development of a large airport and modern terminal. The old courthouse in Jacksonville saw its last trial in 1927. Four years prior, in the autumn of 1923, little over a year after the KKK night-rider incidents, the three young DeAutremont brothers, one of them a former member of the radical Industrial Workers of the World, had drifted into Jackson County with plans to rob a train. The brothers' daring but bungled holdup of the Southern Pacific train at the Siskiyou Pass tunnel, during which they murdered four railroad men, again focused national attention on a violent episode in Jackson County. The posse's tracking hounds lost the trail of the DeAutremonts in the rugged Siskiyous; the three men remained at large until identified in 1927, brought back to the county, convicted of murder, and given life sentences in the state penitentiary.[42]

Out in Jackson County's backcountry, agrarian protest lived on. Progressive Party firebrand Robert "Fighting Bob" LaFollette's 1924 populistic third-party presidential campaign did extremely well with southern Oregon's rural voters, contributing to a record-breaking turnout. Easily outpolling the Democratic candidate in the countywide vote, the aging "voice of the common people" from Wisconsin won resoundingly in old Populist strongholds such as Applegate Valley, Butte Creek, Trail, Rogue River (Woodville), and Evans Creek Valley.[43]

4

The Depression and New Voices of Protest
Mssrs. Banks and Fehl

On October 7, 1929, Llewellyn A. Banks arrived at the Main Street offices of the Medford *Daily News* to put the finishing touches on his first editorial column. As new owner of the paper, Banks composed an upbeat salutatory address to greet his readers. He was a prominent orchardist, and the piece reflected his personal hopes: "The most bountiful harvest within the history of Southern Oregon has now become a reality. . . . Many mortgages will be lifted, burdensome debts will be paid, many hearts are being made glad. . . . All share in this era of prosperity."[1] Banks penned this optimistic prediction three weeks prior to the Wall Street stock market crash on Black Tuesday, October 29, 1929.

* * *

Llewellyn Banks was a risk-taker, a distinctive type that characterized the 1920s as the prosperity decade. His entry into the newspaper business at age fifty-eight was the latest in a series of expensive gambles. The Ohio-born Banks, owner of extensive citrus groves in southern California since 1916, became involved in the Rogue Valley's fruit industry in the early 1920s, and he moved to the valley in 1926. Although he maintained his California properties for several years, Banks entered Jackson County's pear-orchard industry with verve. He purchased Suncrest Orchards, near Talent, one of the valley's larger pear tracts. Finding himself in conflict with local fruit-packers' pricing policies, Banks opened his own packinghouse on the railroad south of Medford, and with his wife Edith bought an imposing new Tudor Revival–style home on Medford's West Main Street. The aggressive newcomer soon challenged the leadership of the Fruit Growers League and—promoting a very different kind of fruit marketing than had been the norm for years—entered into battle against the packers' association.

Banks's 1929 purchase of the *News* probably evoked considerable comment among the city's business leaders, some of whom had benefited from his presence. Over the previous year, for example, Banks's expenditures on wide-ranging legal work done by E. E. Kelly's Medford law firm earned admiration from Kelly's son, Edward C. Kelly, who commented in a June letter that, "L. A. Banks arrived from Riverside [California] this week, and has a lot of work for us to do. . . . My bank account is beginning to look pretty good." Banks, whose many property dealings in 1928 brought the Kelly firm "real good fees," regularly hosted the Kelly family at his home. One evening the younger Kelly, given the use of Banks's automobile while his parents played bridge with Llewellyn and Edith Banks, found that driving the "new Cadillac around town . . . sure was a thrill," and he anticipated the chance for a "good trip . . . [in the] aeroplane" that the orchardist was planning to buy later that year.[2]

Competitor Robert Ruhl probably looked on Banks's newspaper proposition with concern. Since its inception in 1924 as a direct successor to William Phipps's *Clarion*, the *News* had struggled to compete with the long-established afternoon daily, the *Mail Tribune*. However, Banks moved the *News* into a larger plant on West Main Street, installing a new typograph and twelve-ton press and hiring a designer for an expensive remodeling of the front office. Banks intended the *News*, with redesigned masthead, to be his sounding board, and his editorial voice to be an alternative to that of Robert Ruhl.[3]

THE NEW ERA FADES

Using the predicted excellent 1929 pear harvest as a metaphor for the region's economy, and borrowing the confident slogan of the country's Republican administration, Banks declared in his October 8 column a "'New Era' for Southern Oregon."[4] Optimism seemed justified. More than three thousand pickers labored in local orchards that season, and the Medford Chamber of Commerce reported a half-million-dollar increase over the city's previous total annual payroll. Having completed its expensive new municipal water system and become the county seat two years before, the city now planned construction of a new county courthouse—to be built entirely with funds generated from federal timber sales in the surrounding mountains. From the steps of the courthouse, one would be able to hear the work-hour whistle of the Owen-Oregon Lumber Company's modern, all-electric sawmill, which had opened in 1927 on Medford's outskirts as the county's largest single employer. Owen-Oregon brought logs down from the forests near Butte Falls, daily halting traffic on the Pacific Highway as the locomotive pulled the long log train to the millpond. To the north, construction was under way on Medford's new municipal airport. The city's mayor, describing southern Oregon's growth between 1925 and 1929 as "steady and sure," foresaw "no cloud upon the horizon of this great empire to give us any alarm for the future." The bright mood prevailed in private correspondence as well. Agnes (Mrs. E. E.) Kelly wrote to her prospective daughter-in-law, young Edward's fiancé in Washington, DC, in 1928 that "[business] is picking up. The [Owen-Oregon] sawmill will no doubt run double-shift beginning Monday. Tourist traffic is increasing too. The merchants are optimistic."[5]

Robert Ruhl's newspaper supported Herbert Hoover in the 1928 election because Ruhl felt that Hoover, a former Oregonian, "understood" the state and would "do big things for the West." However, Democrat E. C. Kelly noted that Ruhl did not take the Republican campaign promises "too seriously." To Kelly's surprise, the Republican candidate's midsummer visit to southern Oregon had provoked only mild interest: "Hoover is here today, fishing on the Rogue River. Strange, but people here aren't much excited about it." Nevertheless, that November the region's voters gave Hoover an overwhelming majority over his Democratic opponent, New Yorker (and anti-Prohibition Roman Catholic) Al Smith.[6]

* * *

Despite the late 1920s optimism of affluent residents like Agnes Kelly, the Wall Street collapse did not involve a sudden reversal of fortune for Jackson County. Economic problems had been building for several years. Southern Pacific Railroad completed its Natron Cut-off route from Klamath Falls north to the Willamette Valley in 1926, avoiding the steep grades over Siskiyou Pass. As a result, much freight traffic bypassed the Rogue River Valley, and the number of trains and railroad employees in Jackson County declined.[7]

In addition to its reliance on railroad service, Jackson County's economic health depended on strong markets for lumber and fruit. Wisconsin-based Owen-Oregon Lumber Company had completed its new, large-capacity mill just as the nation's residential building boom came to an end. Overproduction by West Coast and southern lumber mills caused disastrous price declines even before the Wall Street stock market crash, and stacks of unsold lumber began to accumulate in the company's yard. Owen-Oregon, like most West Coast lumber manufacturers, resorted to severe pay cuts, layoffs, and temporary shutdowns during 1930–1931 in a failing struggle to stay solvent. Blue-collar mill workers in Medford, and the company's logging crews in the backcountry town of Butte Falls, bore the brunt of these economy measures.[8]

Valley orchardists faced a similar crisis. During the early 1920s, manufacturers, agricultural agents, and bankers urged fruit growers and other farmers throughout the West to purchase tractors and other expensive equipment to modernize their operations. With the depressed prices that followed World War I, this became a recipe for disaster. One Medford packer complained in 1931 that "overproduction" was the local fruit industry's biggest problem.

Urging that no more government funds go toward "the reclamation [irrigation development] of more land," he pleaded that federal assistance go to stabilize the existing irrigation districts of Medford and Talent, which had recently defaulted on their bond interest payments. The Fruit Growers League, which in 1930 represented the interests of about half of the valley's four hundred commercial orchardists, hoped that increased advertising and aggressive marketing would improve their situation. New, shakily financed fruit and dairy cooperatives struggled to protect the interests of smaller owners. Because agricultural overproduction of crops was international in scope, such measures would have been ineffective in any case. However, fruit growers grappled not only with the nationwide agricultural price slump of the 1920s. They also faced higher production and shipping costs, as well as the loss of international markets. The US Department of Agriculture, reacting to European demands in 1926, imposed quarantine on valley pears because of the presence of lead-arsenate spray residues. Some of the smaller growers, particularly around Talent, organized to resist the government's new health requirements.[9]

Most growers, who depended on arsenate-of-lead spray to combat infestations of codling moth, were able to meet the new regulations after successful experiments in soaking and washing fruit, but some orchardists suffered serious losses. Among them was Llewellyn Banks, whose forty-one railcars of Glen Rosa–brand pears were seized by federal agents in Chicago. His newspaper warned the region that its entire pear industry was "in jeopardy." Deepening orchardists' distress, the Southern Pacific Railroad instituted a substantial freight-rate increase after 1930. Local orchardists called it a "death blow." In addition, that year's protective Smoot-Hawley Tariff sparked France to a retaliatory embargo on American fruit, closing off an important market for local pears. Ironically, Republican congressman Willis C. Hawley, cosponsor of the tariff measure, was southern Oregon's longtime representative in Washington.[10]

Through 1930, some growers cut expenses by letting their trees go uncultivated and unsprayed, with resulting pests and diseases spreading to neighboring orchards. And with demand sharply curtailed, tons of unharvested fruit dropped to the ground and rotted. Local apple growers found one new outlet for their fruit in 1930, when Medford's city council approved the street-corner sale of apples by indigent families.[11]

Unemployment emerged as a major public issue in Jackson County in 1930–1931. The county's Unemployed Relief Association became active, working with local governments and employers to provide part-time jobs and other assistance. Members of the association cut and sold firewood, gleaned the orchards, and performed other self-help tasks. Most of the county's relief effort involved voluntary programs such as churchwomen canning surplus fruit and repairing winter clothing. To provide dietary diversity to the unemployed, relief officials bartered excess canned fruit from the valley for canned salmon and mutton from southern Oregon's coastal communities. As the Depression deepened, the inadequacy of these projects grew apparent. Jackson County's poor farm was filled to capacity by the end of 1931, and the Unemployed Relief Association was moribund. The main form of relief in 1931–1932 involved work on state-funded road reconstruction. Because of the mild climate and previous availability of seasonal work, indigent people flocked to the Rogue River Valley from outside the area. In response, "Hire Local" became the slogan, and localism flourished. County residents not only resented the use of Californians in the orchards, they also criticized hiring workers from adjacent Oregon counties for work on Jackson County's sections of roads that served the entire region.[12]

Robert Ruhl wrote to a Harvard friend in 1932 about receiving *Tribune* subscription payments in the form of chickens, garden produce, venison, and so on. He briefly considered selling the paper if its situation became untenable. Increasing numbers of small businessmen, homeowners, and farmers suffered mortgage foreclosures. In mid-July of 1931, the Medford *Pacific Record Herald*, a weekly owned and edited by building contractor Earl Fehl, listed three sheriff's sales of such properties for the week. By the end of the year, Fehl's legal-notices page carried twice that number. Although the county's tax valuations decreased more than one million dollars between 1931 and 1932, payments remained a serious burden for many residents. Local governments made highly publicized cuts in salaries and purchases, but taxpayer-revolt groups began to form in the rural districts of the county.[13]

During the hard times of 1930 to 1932, people in the backcountry had recourse to subsistence activities on nearby national forest land. In western Jackson County, scores of unemployed men prospected and sluiced for gold on the streams in the Siskiyou Mountains. As beef cattle and milk prices plummeted, bounty hunting of coyotes and trapping of fur-bearers brought small amounts of cash. Rural people supplemented these legal activities by poaching deer and snagging salmon. Prohibition continued to provide another source of illicit income to some rural residents. The bootlegger war, which had flared on and off between law officers and moonshiners in the remote sections of the county during the 1920s, renewed its intensity during 1930–1931 when a series of raids in the foothills east of Medford caused anger among many rural people.[14]

The obstacles to rural residents' ability to earn a livelihood in southern Oregon during the Depression—new health regulations that affected dairymen and orchardists and heavy-handed law-enforcement campaigns against bootlegging—were part of a broader and longer-term trend that bedeviled many individualistic farmers across the country. The American countryside faced multiple and formidable challenges during the so-called Great Transformation wrought by the triumph of American corporate capitalism, the regulatory state, and modernity in general.[15]

BANKS AND FEHL, VOX POPULI IN SOUTHERN OREGON

Social and economic discontents, never far from the political surface, deepened after 1929. The Depression crystallized existing resentments and renewed the willingness of many inhabitants to protest. Two local newspapermen articulated and amplified citizens' anger through sustained editorial crusades.

Llewellyn Banks and Earl Fehl shared several things in common. Both men had been born in Ohio and had moved to southern Oregon as adults after business ventures elsewhere in the West. Both were inexperienced in the newspaper business when they took up their respective late-in-life journalistic careers. Banks and Fehl worked in tandem to revive the hoary "Oregon style" of early Oregon, with its almost joyous use of personal invective and inflammatory rhetoric. Both men regularly wrote opinion pieces that polarized local political sentiment.

* * *

Llewellyn Banks was medium height, and with graying hair and rimless spectacles he struck Jackson County residents as a "distinguished looking" gentleman. Banks invariably appeared in public impeccably dressed, prompting some Medford residents to claim that his closet contained at least forty tailor-made suits. Banks's West Main Street home was carpeted with Oriental rugs, and his two Cadillacs, one a touring car and the other a coupe, added to the impression of wealth.[16]

Banks was born in 1870, in Catawba Island, Ohio, located in the Western Reserve country, along the southwestern shore of Lake Erie that had been settled by New Englanders and New Yorkers during the early nineteenth century. Banks was proud of his New England ancestry. He recalled his orchardist father as a "rigid disciplinarian" who struggled to provide for his nine children in the face of unscrupulous Cleveland fruit-consignment houses. His father died in 1887 with substantial debts when Banks was seventeen. Banks later claimed to have vowed that, if he "ever grew to manhood," he would establish a "cash market" for fruit "at the source of supply, at the grower's home."[17]

At age eighteen, Banks began work as a salesman for a Cleveland fruit distributor. He traveled throughout the fruit-producing regions of the United States for twenty years, learning many aspects of growing and selling. Moving to Los Angeles in 1909, Banks opened his own office to promote "cash marketing" of southern California citrus fruit as an alternative to the prevailing consignment method. Banks began buying orange and lemon groves in Riverside County in 1916, acquiring approximately a thousand acres of citrus trees and an allegedly palatial home by 1920. He operated five "cash-basis" packing plants. As a result, Banks evidently provoked stiff opposition from the established, consignment-based packing associations. In 1921, Banks came to the Bear Creek Valley, which he had visited briefly in 1910, to investigate the circumstances of a local orchardist who owed the Riverside packer a large sum of money. The grower, mired in other debts, signed his orchard over to Banks in return for some cash profit.

Although still maintaining his Riverside residence throughout the 1920s, Banks purchased more than six hundred acres of pear and apple orchard land in Jackson County, and he traveled regularly between California and Oregon. He found Medford's "packinghouse row," all the establishments of which paid by consignment, to be dominated by the same kind of associations he had fought in Riverside. In 1925, Medford's eighteen largest consignment houses formed the Traffic Association, an organization that, to Banks, represented unfair collusion against his and other growers' interests. He opened his own cash-basis packinghouse near Voorhies Crossing, on the south edge of Medford. The following year, with local packers such as David Rosenberg complaining that the combative newcomer "was raising hell in the Rogue River Valley," Banks moved to Medford with second wife, Edith (his former secretary), and their young daughter Ruth.[18]

Banks's arrival coincided with the valley's lead-arsenate crisis. He attributed his troubles with the Department of Agriculture that year to a conspiracy of the Traffic Association and its battery of Medford attorneys. His stand against the packers and against the spray-residue health regulations during what he called "the battle of 1926" won him backing among many of the valley's smaller orchardists. His cash-for-pears arrangement earned Banks their loyalty; one Central Point orchardist's son later recalled, "He was a good fellow, we always thought; he did everything he could to get the money for everybody."[19] After purchasing the *News* in 1929, Banks further cemented his alliance with small growers when he attacked the "chattel mortgage" arrangements whereby packers, such as the Rosenberg brothers, Harry and David, foreclosed on the property of indebted orchardists, thereby accumulating large acreages throughout the valley.

* * *

Earl Fehl's *Pacific Record Herald* had been repeating essentially the same message to its readers nearly every week throughout the 1920s: local government was in the hands of grafters who conspired against the interests of the taxpayer. Fehl, a perennial candidate who ran unsuccessfully for Medford mayor four times during the decade and had launched fifteen lawsuits against the city in the course of twelve years, was an object of ridicule for much of the period. William Phipps, as owner of the *Clarion*, dubbed his competitor's weekly paper the "Fail Weakly." Robert Ruhl made caustic references to "Fehlism" in his editorials of the 1920s; Ruhl seems to have considered him an unpleasant crank. However, Fehl's opinions—usually stated forcefully and in very personal terms just short of libel—began to be read with more seriousness after 1929.[20]

Earl H. Fehl was a rawboned man with reddish-brown hair. Born in 1885 on a farm in Wyandot County, near Marseilles, Ohio, Fehl had moved with his family to the Pacific Northwest in about 1900. He lived in Tacoma, Washington, for about five years, working as a shipping clerk for a furniture manufacturer. Fehl and his older brother Delbert came to Medford in 1907, and they entered the construction trade during the height of the orchard boom. Earl Fehl became a general contractor (later building Medford's large Holly Theater cinema in 1930), real estate broker, and commercial developer. He married Electa Stailey and moved into a comfortable home on the edge of Medford's exclusive Oakdale Avenue neighborhood. Fehl began publishing his weekly newspaper soon after World War One.[21]

Fehl's straightforward writing style contrasted with the occasional murkiness of Banks's prose. Using a term he had hurled at Medford's elite since the early 1920s, Fehl identified the enemy of the people as "the gang." In an editorial titled "The Gang Rules," Fehl averred that Jackson County was controlled by a cabal of attorneys, bankers, office holders, and merchants. It was not the "Purple Gang, of Detroit, the Al Capone Gang, of Chicago. But we have a 'gang' in Jackson County," he continued, one "that is alert, crafty, and sinister." The gang, Fehl warned, sought those "whom they may devour—not in the open, but thru and by the influence they occupy. . . . That is the 'Gang.'"[22]

The *Pacific Record Herald* was Fehl's political voice, and he used it throughout the 1920s to challenge other Medford factions in every city election when he or one of his associates ran for mayor. In 1922, opponents decried Fehl's "campaign of slander and abuse"; in 1924, they called voters' attention to Fehl's numerous expensive lawsuits against the city, including one wherein he claimed water rights to city's Big Butte Springs water source.[23]

Fehl, making the Medford gang his campaign issue in 1924, claimed to regret that he "had to expose things," but "as the champion of the people's rights," he was "forced to do so." Fehl lost the 1924 mayoral race by a four-to-one margin. In the 1926 campaign, declaring that he would run "agin, agin, and agin" and "keep on running until . . . elected," Fehl accused city officials of nepotism and corruption, and he continually flailed the *Mail Tribune* as the voice of the gang. He lost election that year by a two-to-one margin. In 1928, however, Fehl's dogged campaign to become mayor resulted in his narrowest defeat yet. Formerly competing factions united behind single candidates during these years in order to forestall Fehl's bids for power. What Fehl lacked in the way of Llewellyn Banks's flair and personal magnetism, he made up for in tenacity.[24]

Fehl, a longtime foe of the Medford Water Commission, labeled the commission a tool of the *Mail Tribune* and other representatives of the gang. Robert Ruhl's patrician demeanor earned particular scorn. Unforgiving of political opponents, who were legion, Fehl may have astounded some readers with his unwillingness to silence personal rancor even upon the recent death of one political enemy, Bert Anderson: "Prior to [Anderson's] death . . . his poise was that of the arrogant politician, an unlit cigar firmly held at an angle. Bert was the type of politician that has ruled Medford and Jackson County for many a day." Fehl then asked his readers, "Are there any politicians in Heaven?," answering that "We rather doubt it. . . . Where are the meek and lowly who he aided? . . . Friends, there is a lesson in each death."[25]

NEWSPRINT DEMAGOGUES

Llewellyn Banks began his "Once In A While" column in the *News* as an occasional feature, initially writing it in a lucid manner and moderate tone. Banks concentrated on orchardists' problems and severely criticized the Department of Agriculture for its methods during the 1926 quarantine. During 1930, Banks's columns increased in frequency and political distemper; by 1931, "Once In A While" had become a daily, page-one feature. A number of related themes recurred regularly in Banks's writings after 1930: an antigovernment and anticorporate individualism, a blend of western populism that focused on conspiracy theory, a political stance that could be seen in some respects as fascistic, and a visionary—even apocalyptic—approach to the Depression as America's moment of truth.

During 1930 and 1931, Banks expanded his attacks on the US Department of Agriculture to include the agency's Mediterranean-fruit-fly quarantine of Florida citrus growers, drawing parallels to the "illegal" quarantine of southern Oregon pears a few years before. Banks wrote a scathing indictment of Agriculture Secretary William Jardine's "dastardly policies," and suggested the need for solidarity among all fruit growers against government interference. He also expressed support for Iowa dairymen who were fighting the

Cow War over the forced tuberculin testing of their herds by state health inspectors. Before the 1931 Iowa episode had ended, many dairy cattle had been destroyed, and groups of angry farmers had besieged health officials; the governor declared martial law and sent the National Guard to restore order to Cedar County.[26]

Banks repeatedly trumpeted his cash-basis system of fruit marketing in the *News* and decried what he saw as the mortal threat, to growers, of agricultural cooperatives. His cash-basis system involved the buyer's direct payment to the grower, at a mutually agreed dollars-per-ton amount, immediately upon delivery of the fruit. The grower therefore received a guaranteed (although often relatively low) cash price for his produce, and the buyer took all the risks of further marketing. If fruit prices in major centers such as Chicago or New York proved high, however, the original buyer could reap extremely high profits under this system. The widespread consignment-basis system, in contrast, involved the grower in a delayed and dependent payment system with the buyer. A consignment-based packinghouse would accept a grower's fruit for shipment and marketing in return for an often-substantial percentage of the market price; the grower and consignment buyer together shared the marketing risk. During strong market periods, both benefited. Consignment buyers often served as creditors for small growers, and the former therefore tended to grow in economic power and acreage control relative to the latter during times of agricultural depression.[27]

Banks's main agricultural crusade during 1929–1930 concerned the Hoover administration's Agricultural Marketing Act of 1929, which encouraged the formation of large farmers' marketing cooperatives in an effort to rationalize the marketplace. Banks, who had experienced conflict with the powerful cooperative California Fruit Growers' Exchange, considered the legislation a seductive siren's song. He warned fellow valley orchardists that the spread of large cooperatives in southern Oregon would spell the end of independent marketing and would ultimately drive many growers into bankruptcy. Banks detailed an elaborate conspiracy that linked the Agricultural Marketing Act with the efforts of what he called "World Communism" through the agency of Californian David Lubin, a globally prominent proponent of agricultural cooperatives. Banks further warned of bloodshed if the cooperative movement took control in Oregon. Banks held an anti-Semitic conspiratorial view of agricultural cooperatives that dovetailed with the late-1920s national controversy between Henry Ford and California cooperative promoter Aaron Sapiro, during which Ford's publications charged Sapiro with master-minding a "World Jewish conspiracy" to gain control of all aspects of agricultural marketing. David Lubin was also Jewish.[28]

Blaming Herbert Hoover for the spread of cooperatives, Banks also identified the president as the former "Supreme Dictator of Food Supplies"; he was
referring to Hoover's position as the wartime director of the US Food Administration and head of international famine relief in postwar Europe. Banks cast
Hoover as a would-be dictator, suppressing individual freedom. In midsummer
1931, Banks called for Hoover's impeachment on the grounds of his "criminal"
agricultural policies and his collusion with English bankers. Treasury Secretary Andrew Mellon also came under strong personal attack in the *News* as an
unfeeling plutocrat, and Banks described the Federal Reserve Banking System
as "the most diabolical machine ever originated in the deranged mind of greed
and selfishness." He incorporated popular antigovernment resentments into
his personal political declarations, bitterly criticizing the eviction of homeless
men from Seattle's waterfront "Hooverville" in 1931.[29]

It is certain that, as a young salesman traveling in the West during the
1890s, Llewellyn Banks would have become familiar with the rhetoric of
Populist tracts. His newspaper often featured pro-inflationary syndicated
articles reminiscent of the 1890s demands of the Populists for "free coinage
of silver" (so as to lessen the monetary gold standard's burden on debtors).
Banks capitalized on traditional western resentments with statements reminiscent of the Populist Revolt, decrying that, "the west coast states are living
under a government . . . by a group of eastern industrialists"; he asked, "Has
the time not come WHEN THE VOICE FROM THE WEST MUST BE HEARD IN
OUR HALLS OF CONGRESS?"[30]

In another editorial, titled "Betrayal of the West," Banks castigated eastern bankers as living in luxury with "no . . . concern as to the frightful privations
and the sacrifices of the . . . people living west of the Mississippi." His anti–Wall
Street columns—which expressed sympathy for Nicaraguan rebels under Au-
gusto Sandino then fighting the US Marines—described New York financiers
as holding a "Feast of the Beasts," while "millions of America's unemployed
were destitute of food and raiment." Banks also targeted another Populist bête
noire, the Bank of England; he linked Hoover to English banking interests in a
conspiracy to plunder America's wealth.[31]

The orchardist-publisher not only incorporated the "Shylock banker"
anti-Jewish views of some earlier Populists (as well as the more recent views
of Henry Ford) into his editorials, he also espoused a deeper racial, moralistic,
and religious form of anti-Semitism. Asking "who, among the Caucasians
. . . will rise to challenge the [Jewish] Goliath who proposes to stalk through
'the land of the free'?" Banks labeled the Jews a "menace to our free American
institutions," blamed them for "the slime that appears on our [motion picture]
screens," and stated that "the Jew" belonged to a "race without a faith . . .

[except] in his own cleverness, in his ability to outwit his neighbor." Banks's strongly anti-Semitic editorials actually were few in number, however, and he refrained from overtly criticizing Jackson County's few prominent Jews—as Jews—in his columns.[32]

Like many commentators during the early Depression, Llewellyn Banks called for a "man on horseback" to lead America back to social and economic order. Although he often expressed equal contempt for Bolshevism and Italian fascism, the remedy that Banks proposed for the United States seems to have been essentially fascistic in character. Claiming to abhor dictatorship, Banks nevertheless voiced enthusiasm for retired General of the Army John J. Pershing as a "dictator" who "might bring order out of chaos" in the 1932 election. A few weeks later, he proposed a national third-party ticket headed by Pershing and feisty Marine Corps General Smedley D. Butler to establish "law and order throughout the United States."[33]

Banks's clearest expression of support for an American form of fascism came in late 1932 when he welcomed the formation of the Khaki Shirt movement, a stridently anti-Semitic, paramilitary movement that gained brief fame in the aftermath of that year's Bonus Army debacle. "What is the meaning of this Khaki Shirt movement?," asked Banks, who then replied that it showed that "a slumbering nation is awakening." The movement's formation meant that "the millions of American citizens who have permitted politicians to invade and destroy their country, are now about to assert their citizenship." The (soon-to-be-defunct) Khaki Shirts movement further indicated, stated Banks, that the people are about "to marshal their forces. . . . It is a sign that young America has not lost its manhood and its honor."[34]

Throughout 1931 and early 1932, Banks repeatedly referred to the nation's need for "A NEW ORDER." He saw the beginnings of the new order in Louisiana. As governor—and, by early 1932, as senator—Huey Long began to draw wide attention, Banks joined some other journalists in touting the Louisiana "Kingfish" as a national savior. He described Long as "the prophet" who would lead Americans "out of their trials and tribulations" and into "peace and tranquility." "Senator Huey Long," stated Banks, "lifts up the great depression . . . of the American people; he GIVES THEM HOPE. . . . He is our ideal statesman."[35]

A final aspect of Banks's editorial approach was his visionary, professedly Christian emphasis. Many of Banks's columns, including his first and last, espoused a "Christian patriotism" that he contrasted with the allegedly "Pagan" beliefs of his enemies. In one editorial he pledged himself to God to fight "in the cause of Democracy, in the cause of our free America, in defense of our Flag . . . until Liberty and Justice" were reestablished in the United

States.[36] Sending a "Once In A While" commentary back to Medford while visiting New York City, Banks called forth disturbing visions of an America awaiting a new order: milling about in the streets of the skyscraper-filled city were, he wrote, "the great PLEBIAN MASSES, colored with the hues of violet rays . . . of the groups which rule over them." The masses were "willing to be wicked, but hardly knowing how—worshippers at the feet of the giant Moloch which is about to consume them." He claimed that "the farmers in the Plains languish under . . . the ultra-rich manipulators of government who dwell in MODERN SODOM. . . . The pomp, the splendor, the silence . . . seem to cast a pall over the setting."[37]

Some of the politically prominent local people who later opposed Llewellyn Banks may have read his early editorials with a mixture of bemusement and disdain. Robert Ruhl, who confided to his wife, Mabel, in 1931 that he, too, now held a low opinion of Herbert Hoover, began to express concern over the divisive tone of his competitor's editorials.[38] Although Banks's more obscure literary allusions may have left some readers puzzled, his writings attracted a loyal following. The *News* also had a logistical advantage over Ruhl's evening *Tribune* in rural areas: US Mail carriers delivered the morning paper to rural subscribers by the same afternoon.[39]

* * *

Like Llewellyn Banks, Earl Fehl filled his editorials with references to the United States as a Christian nation. The *Record Herald* regularly carried pieces contributed by local Protestant ministers. It also featured Bruce Barton's widely syndicated column, "The Way of Life." Barton, a New York advertising executive, authored the mid-1920s bestseller, *The Man Nobody Knows*, wherein the author portrayed Jesus Christ as the forerunner of the modern American businessman. However, Fehl concentrated on issues of immediate, local interest to his readers. A supporter of Oregon's Old Age Pension League (a forerunner of the Townsend Plan movement that urged replacement of the state's outmoded "poor farm" system with pension payments), Fehl lent credence in his paper to one of the league's 1930 rumors: state officials planned to gather up all aged paupers and force them onto two huge "poor farms."[40]

With the Iowa Cow War in the headlines, Fehl voiced the local fears of small dairy farmers when he censured Medford's new milk ordinance (aimed at combating tuberculosis). Stating that although he believed in "sanitary milk . . . pure milk," he refused to lend "our support to such a damnable piece of legislation . . . nor can we countenance the operation of shame." Fehl wrote of once-prosperous small dairies now impoverished or abandoned as a result of Medford's pasteurization and inspection requirements.[41]

Fehl, still a building contractor, claimed to speak on behalf of the local unemployed when he suggested that the city "GIVE—not-sell—to bona fide citizens, a CITY LOT," provided that recipients erected an approved dwelling within six months. Citing rampant corruption, Fehl often criticized Prohibition, and its enforcement agents in particular. Earl Fehl possessed a canny knowledge of what resentments were deepest and most current among his readers. The *Record Herald* printed a number of letters from rural subscribers who echoed Fehl's editorial opinions after 1929. The paper wisely provided relatively thorough news coverage of Jackson County's rural districts: who visited Medford recently, who attended the school board meeting, who went huckleberry picking in the mountains, and similar items. Once the mainstay of Medford's other papers, such detailed information had not appeared in their pages for years. As an inexpensive weekly (one dollar for a two-year subscription) that catered to rural tastes, the *Record Herald*, like Banks's *News*, grew popular in the county's outlying sections.[42]

THE 1930 ELECTION AND ITS AFTERMATH

At first Llewellyn Banks and Earl Fehl were simply complimenting each other in their editorials, but the two men forged an open political alliance in 1930. With one publishing a daily, and the other a weekly, they were not competing for subscribers. They praised each other as crusaders against the "gang," and urged readers to support the two newspapers' "fearless" policies.

In Oregon and Jackson County, 1930 was an important election year. Among other races (including governor), popular two-term US Senator Charles L. McNary was up for reelection, and the Medford mayoral office would also be contested. Fehl filed for his fifth try at the mayor's seat. Banks entered the senatorial race in early July, running as an Independent against McNary. Fehl's campaign concentrated on the Medford gang, denouncing the local bar association, the *Mail Tribune*, and the current city administration as a band of plutocratic thieves.

After a Medford "nomination rally" at which five hundred farmers and townspeople allegedly gathered to show support, candidate Banks toured the state by train and in his Cadillac. He met with civic clubs and farmers' groups. Described by those who heard him as a dignified but almost hypnotic speaker, Banks seemed like senatorial material to some voters. Although he called for the repeal of the Eighteenth Amendment and "restoration of constitutional government" by disbanding Prohibition-enforcement agencies, Banks's main themes were the Agricultural Marketing Act and McNary for supporting the bill. However, Senator McNary was a progressive on agricultural issues. He remained a messiah-like figure to many farmers for his persistent sponsorship during the 1920s of the McNary-Haugen bills, which proposed "farmers' parity" by means of government price controls and government purchase of farm products. Outside of southern Oregon, Banks made little headway against the Salem Republican. After an initial publicity splash, Banks's campaign became farcical during the closing days. Having failed to provide the secretary of state with the needed information to have his campaign statement appear in the Oregon *Voter's Pamphlet*, Banks accused Salem politicians of conspiring against him. When the Medford publisher claimed that McNary had bolted from the Republican Party, the senator's spokesman curtly replied that the charge was "too ridiculous to discuss." The *Oregonian* and other major newspapers in the state had few kind words to say about Banks. A final bit of campaign ignominy occurred during Banks's late October visit to Roseburg, where a McNary supporter taunted him for still having California license plates on his automobile. Banks became visibly angered, and bystanders intervened before the two men could come to blows. Robert Ruhl wrote privately that Banks's financial situation, both in the pear market and at the *News*, must have placed the candidate "in hot water."[43]

Election day proved disappointing for Banks. McNary won by a landslide, defeating his Democratic opponent by greater than two-to-one. Statewide, Independent candidate Banks received 17,500 votes, a little more than 7 percent of the total. In southern Oregon, however, Banks did remarkably well. He garnered over 12 percent of the Josephine County vote, and, in Jackson County, Banks polled almost 40 percent, coming in second. The *Tribune* allowed that it was a "flatteringly complimentary" vote. Countywide precinct returns were not reported in the press, but the Medford results showed Banks's strongest support in the working-class area around the Owen-Oregon sawmill and other blue-collar neighborhoods. Earl Fehl reported that, outside of the city, Banks's rural support was considerable.[44]

Earl Fehl very nearly won the race for mayor, losing to his "gang" opponent, E. M. Wilson, by a mere fourteen votes out of a total 3,240 cast. Fehl's strongest showing came from the same working-class and lower-middle-class precincts that supported Banks. And as with the Banks-McNary contest, the city's "silk stocking" Oakdale and East Side neighborhoods gave Fehl his lowest returns. Fehl demanded a recount. He and his supporters had helped to organize the Better Government League shortly before election day, and the league supported the November recount. Asking readers to contribute to the organization, the *Record Herald* described it as an organization "the object of which is to promote the interests of better government for all classes of citizens. . . . The need is urgent. Will you help?" Some Jackson County citizens soon proved willing to do so.[45]

The 1930 campaign had important consequences. The speeches and writings of Banks and Fehl defined political issues that an increasing number of county residents, beset by the Depression, understood and appreciated. The local election results confirmed that both men had a solid base of political support. Although neither Banks nor Fehl gained office in 1930, their campaigns forged links with potential volunteers, financial contributors, and voters. The Better Government League took shape briefly as a purportedly populist movement to wrest control of local government back from the "gang." Although it faded as a formal organization soon after the 1930 recount failed to alter the mayoral race's outcome, the league concept revived, under a similar name, two years later.

After the 1930 election, Banks wrote fewer columns about the great national questions. Instead, he joined Earl Fehl in aiming his editorial fire at local issues. Calling attention to farmers' protest movements elsewhere in the nation, particularly in Iowa and Wisconsin, Banks urged Jackson County orchardists to demand "CASH for Pears" or withhold their fruit from market. He urged farmers to resist mortgage foreclosures, by force if necessary, and he called for a taxpayers' revolt against county government. By 1932, he warned of a county bar association conspiracy and targeted the California-Oregon Power Company for a similar portrayal.[46]

Earl Fehl maintained his longtime local focus. A few days after the 1930 election, a tragedy in the brushy foothills near the rural town of Eagle Point provided him with material for many inflammatory editorials over the next two years. On November 14, a team of Prohibition agents and sheriff's deputies surprised four young men at a moonshine still on Reese Creek. One of the men, Everett Dahack, was shot dead during the raid, allegedly without having attempted to flee or resist. A coroner's inquest failed to identify who fired the fatal bullet, and the investigation was dropped, although the shooting was later attributed to officer Joe Cave. One of the deputies accompanying Cave, Louis Jennings, was the son of county sheriff Ralph Jennings. The Dahacks were longtime mountain ranchers in the vicinity of Eagle Point, and Everett Dahack's death aroused considerable bitterness in the county's eastern backcountry. Personal anger at county officials joined existing anti-Prohibition sentiments, creating a perception that the corrupt "cossacks" of the sheriff's office threatened citizens' property and lives. Charging county authorities with conspiracy to "cover up cold-blooded murder," Fehl took up the Dahack shooting and made it into a local cause célèbre.[47]

Early in 1932, Fehl's Dahack-case accusations resulted in a libel suit brought by Officer Cave. Fehl simultaneously faced serious financial problems because of past real estate investments. Banks had paralleled Fehl's rural crusade with a similar effort on behalf of F. A. Bates, an aged gold miner living on a remote section of Foots Creek, near the town of Gold Hill. Banks published the man's account of being harassed by claim-jumpers who threatened to blow up his sluice boxes. He printed the names of the men allegedly involved in the episode, including D. H. Ferry, manager of the Rogue River Gold Company's nearby mining-dredge operation. Outraged at Banks's printing of the accusation, Ferry and others filed libel suits.[48]

The Depression became a trap from which both Earl Fehl and Llewellyn Banks struggled to free themselves. Banks was beset with additional problems: tax delinquency, unpaid debts to the paper's former owner, and a suit brought by union employees for back wages. The $45,000 purchase price for the *News* in mid-1929 now hobbled Banks financially. In hopes of attracting potential buyers, he inflated the paper's circulation figures, and he allegedly threatened to "write up gossip" about Medford merchants if they did not advertise in the *News.* Calling the United Press news syndicate an example of "Wall Street Propaganda," Banks announced that he would no longer carry the news agency's national stories. Unpaid bills had caused United Press to pressure Banks for payment.[49]

Banks warned Fehl that his "enemies are laying a trap . . . with a full expectation of eliminating you for years to come." Banks counseled Fehl to stand firm while the orchardist threw down the gauntlet to their opponents. "I am in closer touch with what is transpiring than ever before," he wrote. "You will recall, Earl, my statement . . . that L. A. Banks will never bargain with . . . the former gang which has controlled Medford's affairs for many years." Banks continued: "Either I will whip them to a standstill or will take a licking of the first magnitude." He stated that he would "invoke the ballot box for an adjustment of differences which can never be settled amicably. I paid the price for admission in this battle to a finish."[50]

The Great Depression reached its low point in southern Oregon during 1932. The Jackson County Bank, the county's second-largest financial institution, failed in March. At least sixty thousand heads of households were out of work that year in Oregon, and more jobless men kept arriving in the Rogue River Valley during the summer. Some of them belonged to the self-described Sunset Division of the Bonus Expeditionary Force (BEF), composed of more than fifty unemployed World War I veterans on their way from California to join the main BEF force in Washington, DC. The men and their families camped in downtown Ashland's Lithia Park for several days before moving on to Medford. Banks and Fehl praised the Bonus Army contingent, while some local American Legionnaires denounced it as a "racket." The only tangible sign of confidence in the region was the new $270,000 Jackson County Courthouse, nearing completion at the intersection of Medford's West Main and Oakdale Streets. Funded largely by late-1920s federal timber-sale revenues, the large concrete structure, faced with Indiana limestone, had an imposing front entrance reached by granite steps. Shortly after the courthouse's formal dedication in August, its steps served as site of the county's largest single sheriff's sale: the bankrupt Owen-Oregon sawmill sold to the Chicago investment bankers who had financed the modern mill's 1926 construction. A few months later, the courthouse steps became the speaker's rostrum for rallies of the insurgent Good Government Congress.[51]

5

1932

Battle for the Courthouse

One prominent historian of the 1930s wrote that, as the United States headed into its first presidential election of the Great Depression, the nation's mood seemed to be more one of stunned bewilderment than of anger at the effects of economic collapse. However, in some areas of the country—including heretofore placid farming regions such as the Corn Belt of western Iowa—political turbulence, with an explicit threat of violence, began to build that year. Jackson County, Oregon, became another such area in 1932.[1]

INSURGENTS ADVANCE: THE 1932 ELECTION FIGHT

In 1932, the spring season brought a primary election campaign to Jackson County. With grassy foothills turning green and orchard blooms coloring the valley's floor, April and May were the time of year that often seemed to fulfill the most outlandish promises of the old Commercial Club brochures. However, as readers of the *Mail Tribune* became aware that spring, restlessness among rural people was not confined to faraway regions. Earl Fehl and his fellow insurgent candidates were driving the back roads of the county, politicking and persuading listeners gathered at schoolhouses and Grange halls.

Llewellyn Banks and Earl Fehl, increasingly besieged by creditors and libel suits, attempted to appropriate Jackson County's badly fragmented Republican Party in a move for political power. Fehl, with full public backing from the *Daily News*, entered the Republican primary race for county judge. He shared the field with four other contestants, including incumbent judge Charles Lamkin of Ashland. The judgeship functioned as head of the county court (now known as the board of county commissioners), and it possessed both executive and judicial duties that made the position the most powerful political office in Jackson County. Running for the Republican district attorney nomination was one of Llewellyn Banks's legal associates, Thomas J. Enright, a young attorney with a law degree from Georgetown University and a newcomer to the county. Although he joined Fehl on stump-speech tours of rural districts throughout May, Enright lacked name familiarity, particularly in comparison to his opponent, Ashland's former city attorney. For the Republican sheriff nomination, Banks and Fehl put up a young Medford service-station owner from the county's eastern backcountry, Phil Lowd. Lowd faced stiff competition from eight other candidates. Ensuring a connection to the other party, Banks and Fehl also supported Gordon Schermerhorn, an independent building contractor in Medford, for the Democratic nomination against incumbent sheriff Ralph Jennings.[2]

Fehl presented himself as a leader who would end "gang rule" and revive "good government." Hammering constantly at local Prohibition corruption and the fatal shooting by law-enforcement agents of young moonshiner Everett Dahack, Fehl spoke before large meetings in the county's outlying districts. A resident of the remote Elk Creek Valley later recalled Fehl's evening speech before a "big crowd" at the schoolhouse: "Everybody on the creek was there to hear him.... He stood up front, reading off his notes and pounding on the desk."[3]

Speaking at the rural Shady Cove school, candidate Fehl alleged egregious instances of graft with the county's Prohibition fund, and he warned, "Watch your step, folks, or they will have you all up in [the penitentiary at] Salem if you can't account for every ten minutes of your life." To a Central Point audience, Fehl made similar points, condemning incumbent district attorney George Codding for malfeasance regarding Prohibition enforcement and related matters. According to Fehl, Codding had sat "in the Liberty Building with . . . a couple of stenographers and an expensive mahogany desk" and coldly covered up the murder of Everett Dahack.[4] (At this time, the district attorney's offices were located in downtown Medford's Liberty Building until completion of the courthouse. The four-story office building on Main Street also served as regional headquarters of Standard Oil, and it housed many of Medford's prominent attorneys, earning it opprobrium from Banks and Fehl as headquarters of the "gang.")

The News, under the headline "Farmers for Fehl," reported that "opinion as expressed on street corners and by ranchers who make it in to town about once a week gives Fehl the Republican nomination." Earl Fehl won the county-judge primary with a solid majority. Although losing their respective contests, political unknowns Enright and Lowd did quite well. Lowd came in a close second in the sheriff race's crowded free-for-all. The Mail Tribune noted with surprise that Enright had "polled a strong vote in the country," where precinct returns show the same rural support for other Banks-Fehl insurgent candidates. For sheriff in the Democratic primary, Banks ally Gordon Schermerhorn edged out longtime incumbent Ralph Jennings. Excluding Ashland, which voted overwhelmingly for its hometown candidates in the 1932 primary, the insurgents' strongest support lay in the main valley's small-town/orchard zone and out in the hinterland. In some rural precincts, Fehl actually received an absolute majority in the field of five candidates. In Medford's lower-income neighborhoods, Fehl won the same strong backing that had almost given him the 1930 mayoral race. His opposition was strongest in Medford's and Ashland's more affluent precincts. Jackson County voters were splitting along both sectional and class lines, a combination that created a potential majority arrayed against the urban establishment.[5]

Alarmed by the results of the May primary, Robert Ruhl counseled voters to beware of demagogues who would divide the community. In return, the *News* and the *Record Herald* heated up their attacks on Ruhl and other members of the Medford gang. Banks focused his column on the "Codding-Tribune Syndicate" that he claimed was trying to silence the *News* by biasing a grand jury investigation of Banks's finances. Banks claimed that Ruhl would benefit from the silencing of its competitor, and thereby was heavily involved in the plot. During the summer, the lively weekly Jacksonville *Miner* and the staid Ashland *Tidings* took an "anti-Banks-Fehl" stand. Portland and Salem newspapers joined in bringing southern Oregon's developing situation to statewide attention.[6]

The summer of 1932 was hot and dry in the Rogue River Valley. During an August heat wave, drought forced the cutoff of irrigation water to many orchards, and volunteers began circulating petitions to recall state circuit court judge Harold D. Norton, a Josephine County Democrat who had defeated incumbent Charles Thomas for the judicial position in 1930. Norton moved to Medford's Oakdale Avenue, where neighbor Earl Fehl built the judge a large new home. Norton would be presiding at the Banks and Fehl libel trials. Despite the pretrial motions by Banks and Fehl to have the case dismissed, Norton refused to do so. Petitions demanding that Norton be recalled appeared immediately afterward. Both Banks and Fehl denied instigating the recall move, but they emphatically supported it in their editorials. The effort to oust Norton was the county's first recall campaign since the Klan's 1922 effort to recall county sheriff Charles Terrill. The county bar association, Democratic warhorse E. E. Kelly (formerly Fehl's and Banks's attorney), and other prominent political leaders denounced the recall. Robert Ruhl, who had supported Norton's Republican opponent in the 1930 election, was out of state when word of the recall attempt became public. He had left the *Tribune's* day-to-day editorial writing in the hands of an assistant editor, with occasional help from fellow Harvard alumnus, prominent orchardist Leonard Carpenter. When told of the recall, Ruhl fired back an indignant column for the paper's Sunday edition, stating that only by "squashing the recall" could Jackson County "avoid being heralded throughout the state as a hotbed of dissension and strife."[7]

Although Ruhl feared Jackson County would become the state's disgruntled "recall capital," the petitioners continued to gather signatures into the fall, creating discord between neighbors in some communities. Robert Ruhl lived in a much different world from most of the county's rural residents, owning a comfortable home close to the Rogue Valley Country Club, where the publisher frequently played golf. Ruhl and his wife, Mabel, often traveled for pleasure, touring different parts of the United States each summer by automobile or train. The editor visited with college classmates or other acquaintances and sent regular travelogue pieces back to the *Tribune*. However, the Depression strapped Ruhl's finances. By the summer of 1932, he complained of being "short of cash to the point of tears."[8]

Initially, Ruhl was reluctant to engage in all-out battle against the Banks-Fehl political movement, a fact that would later earn him gentle scolding from friends.[9] His hesitancy may have been due in part to the prospect of losing subscribers. Many rural readers, feeling that the *Tribune* "didn't tell the truth," cancelled their subscriptions in 1932.[10] The *Tribune's* circulation manager, Gerald Latham, drove through the rural Applegate Valley and upper Rogue River areas to contact former and potential subscribers but met hostile receptions from several ranchers: upon learning that he represented the *Tribune*, they cursed Latham and ordered him off their property.[11] Although D. H. Ferry, the anti-Banks dredge manager from the town of Rogue River, volunteered to distribute free copies of the *Tribune* among "some of the country people" in his district, the paper suffered from the informal boycott.[12]

From the presidential race to the local contests, the 1932 general election offered Jackson County voters clear choices. Anti-Hoover and anti-Prohibition sentiments were especially strong in southern Oregon. Robert Ruhl, gamely sticking by the Republican candidate, assured readers that the worst of the Depression was over. Ruhl's editorial praise of Hoover was quite restrained, and the editor would soon become a strong and consistent supporter of Franklin Roosevelt's New Deal. Ruhl saved his strongest rhetoric for the three most important local contests: county judge, district attorney, and sheriff. Ruhl appealed for rationality, for harmony, attempting to dissuade gullible newcomers from voting for Fehl, explaining Fehl's political efforts as the result of "thwarted ego." Ruhl hinted that the spate of last-minute election filings by "independents" for numerous other county positions—from school superintendent to county clerk—were part of a well-orchestrated political campaign by Banks-Fehl forces.[13]

Earl Fehl continued his forceful stump speeches throughout the county, including one before a large rally at the Medford armory. His *Record Herald* reported that "a large number of ladies were present" at the armory, and that they frequently applauded Fehl.[14] When speaking, he waved pages of county budget documents, which he claimed proved the corruption of certain members of the "gang." Fehl also promised to "clean up" the county's relief fund situation. By the closing days of the campaign, amidst "wild charges ... especially in the rural districts," Ruhl admitted that Fehl appeared certain to win. Nevertheless, the *Tribune* parodied the *News*-backed ticket as "The Three Musketeers": Earl Fehl for county judge and new, hand-picked Banks-Fehl candidates M. O. Wilkins (a Banks attorney) for district attorney and Lowell Zundell (a Medford automobile salesman and longtime Banks supporter) for sheriff.[15]

Jackson County's 1932 primary and general elections took on a particularly byzantine quality as a free-for-all by office-seekers. Wilkins, not wanting to alienate his colleagues in the bar association, confused the district attorney's race with his temporizing on the Norton recall. Banks promptly disowned him publicly until the candidate meekly re-pledged himself to the ongoing recall effort shortly before election day. The *Tribune* supported Fehl's opponent, latecomer county judge candidate "Pop" Gates, the former Medford mayor whom Ruhl had criticized for his opportunistic pro-Klan stand a decade before. Ford dealer Gates enjoyed wide familiarity that might tip the balance against Fehl, and a coalition of the county's anti-Banks-Fehl residents had persuaded him to run. Dividing the establishment's base of support, however, was the entry of another former Medford mayor, A. W. Pipes, into the race. And William Phipps, attorney and early-1920s Klan supporter, was another contestant for county judge, running as a Democrat. The aging Phipps, ever on the alert and sensing possible advantage from the crowded field, was making his last try for elective office.

Zundell had entered the crowded sheriff's race to draw votes away from incumbent Sheriff Ralph Jennings, now a write-in candidate with the backing of the county's embattled "dry" (Prohibitionist) forces. Although Jennings lost the Democratic primary to the *News*-backed Gordon Schermerhorn, he refused to surrender his office without a fight.

* * *

On Tuesday afternoon, November 8, the *Mail Tribune* reported that a record number of people, particularly voters in the "country districts," were coming to the county's polling places. Their votes contributed to the county victory for Franklin D. Roosevelt—who received over 55 percent of the votes to Hoover's 40 percent. Two important state initiatives on the ballot were repeal of Oregon's Prohibition amendment and a referendum on the Zorn-MacPherson Bill, a drastic statewide austerity measure for higher education, which, among other actions, would have turned Ashland's four-year Southern Oregon Normal School into a two-year junior college. The county voted overwhelmingly in favor of Prohibition repeal, and it defeated the Zorn bill by a huge margin.[16]

Although M. O. Wilkins, Banks's undependable ally, lost to incumbent district attorney Codding, Zundell made a respectable showing in the race for sheriff. Most importantly, Earl Fehl and Gordon Schermerhorn, who allied himself with Fehl, won office as county judge and county sheriff, respectively. Except in the affluent neighborhoods of East Medford and Oakdale that had always opposed him, Fehl did well throughout the county. Hinterland communities such as Applegate, Butte Falls, Eagle Point, Evans Creek, Sams Valley, and Trail gave Fehl huge margins of victory. He received similar support in the small-town/orchard zone communities of Central Point, Gold Hill, Phoenix, and Talent. Even normally conservative Ashland gave Fehl a majority. Had they not divided the anti-Fehl vote, Phipps's and Pipes's combined total might have given the county judge office to Gates. Schermerhorn barely led the write-in vote for Jennings, whose support came from Medford, Ashland, and his hometown of Jacksonville. Sheriff Jennings immediately called for a recount. To Llewellyn Banks and Earl Fehl, on the other hand, it seemed clear that the county had delivered a mandate to end "gang rule" and return political control to the people.[17]

TO THE TRENCHES: COURTHOUSE STALEMATE

Robert Ruhl saw one silver lining in the stormy election results. It appeared that District Attorney Codding had been vindicated and the Dahack case, as a divisive issue, had been laid to rest. Ruhl, accepting the inevitable entry of Earl Fehl into the halls of the new courthouse, again called for harmony. "With the battle of the ballots over," Ruhl urged citizens to unite toward achieving the "bright destiny, which our high type of citizenship and the extent of our resources justify."[18]

Other editors were less optimistic. In neighboring Josephine County, the Grants Pass *Daily Courier* noted that "Medford . . . of late has fallen from her high estate. . . . Now the place has achieved statewide reputation for being all muscle-bound by warring factions." Comparing southern Oregon to a "Balkan powder keg," the *Oregonian* voiced hope "that Jackson County doesn't have its Sarajevo." The Ashland *Tidings* simply wished the "internal strife which is making Jackson County the butt of many jokes throughout the state, to cease." Word of southern Oregon's turmoil reached a British Columbia resident who wrote a bemused, sarcastic letter to a Jackson County friend, remarking, "From what we read the whole valley is ruled by gangsters and outlaws" and that "the Cossacks ride about shooting people down just for fun."[19]

The county's political situation may have seemed ludicrous to outsiders, but the winter of 1932–1933 brought few smiles to the principals involved. Longtime holders of political power would relinquish control of county administration and law enforcement to the Banks-Fehl insurgents on January 1. The sheriff's election recount, although Schermerhorn's attorney used every possible obstacle, offered the establishment a ray of hope. Banks and Fehl, caught in the closing ring of financial disaster, could be held back from obtaining a dangerous amount of power if the recount gave victory to Jennings. The probable miscount of the write-in ballots from rural precincts made this outcome appear very possible. However, Schermerhorn's delaying tactics assured that the recount would not take place until late February 1933.

Because of the Dahack case's libel judgment in 1932, which dispossessed Fehl of his printing plant, the *Record Herald* was now published from Banks's *Daily News* operation on Main Street. Banks's financial troubles during 1932 were such that some of the *News* staff went nine months without wages. Banks occasionally arranged for businesses that advertised in the *News* to pay his employees in the form of clothing and groceries. Exasperated ex-employees sued Banks for back wages, eventually receiving 50 percent of what was due them in an out-of-court settlement. Banks succeeded in postponing a looming receivership decision on the *News* until March 1933, at which time the court—assuming that Judge Norton was removed from office by that time—might be far more favorably disposed.

Banks was surrounded by journalistic opposition. Not only the *Mail Tribune*, with its judicious pronouncements by Ruhl, but the daily Ashland *Tidings*, the Central Point *American* (a weekly edited by a former *News* employee who had quit over Banks's failure to pay him), and the Jacksonville *Miner* aimed steady criticism at the impending "Banks regime." The weekly *Miner* was edited in gadfly style by thirty-year-old Leonard Hall, a scrappy newcomer who jumped right into the feud. Hall, who had acquired newspaper experience in Los Angeles, parodied Banks mercilessly with his front-page "Once Too Often" column and political cartoons. His irreverence outraged some Jacksonville and nearby Applegate Valley residents, who boycotted the *Miner*. After the young editor was assaulted by an elderly Banks supporter on the streets of Jacksonville and received anonymous threats, Hall received permission to carry a handgun.[20]

The threat of violence grew palpable after the election. Banks, making reference to "the hangman's noose," proposed use of a citizens' "vigilance committee" to remove District Attorney Codding and circuit court judge Norton from office. Local posts of the American Legion organized to provide nighttime guards at the homes of these and other county officials. The son of county commissioner Ralph Billings later recalled coming home from his college studies at Corvallis, Oregon, during the 1932 Christmas break, unaware of how tense feelings had become. He arrived at his Ashland home to find armed men stationed in the yard. Robert Ruhl, receiving threats that the *Tribune's* press would be sabotaged, maintained "an armed guard at the plant day and night during the height of the turmoil." The Ruhls, concerned for the safety of their youngest daughter, Alicia, a student at Medford's Catholic academy, instructed the nuns that she was to be kept after school and driven home only by her parents.[21]

Llewellyn Banks claimed that his newspaper had been marked for "destruction and extermination." With Fehl's weekly coming off the same press, the *News's* plant entered a state of siege in late 1932. Located within sight of the *Tribune's* offices, Banks's building also had a full-time force of armed guards. Led by members of the self-styled Greensprings Mountain Boys, from the foothills southeast of Ashland, the guards consisted largely of unemployed young men from Medford and outlying communities. They operated in paramilitary fashion, with a chain of command and orders to "shoot anybody that came through the door" during a break-in. Medford residents nervously joked that "every time a car backfired at night, they crawled under the bed." After Banks began to fear for his personal safety, the Greensprings group functioned as his personal bodyguard. Few of the men received any pay for the duty, but Fehl promised that they would find ample food at the county relief commissary after he was sworn in as judge.[22]

During the closing days of 1932, outgoing county officials struggled to maintain control of the government. Sheriff Jennings's recount suit was slowed when Gordon Schermerhorn, in an attempt to avoid being served legal papers that would postpone his assumption of office, went into hiding. Schermerhorn did not appear in public until after being secretly sworn in as sheriff in the early morning hours of January 1. Hoping to counter Fehl as county judge, the county court's two lame-duck commissioners persuaded the elderly holdover commissioner to resign and immediately replaced him on New Year's Eve with younger Emmett Nealon, who, as the son of the old Populist representative Stephen Nealon, could claim some hinterland allegiance. However, Nealon's potential rural support may well have been counterbalanced by the fact that his sister Eva was a young reporter for the *Tribune*. Fehl and Banks cried foul, and, upon assuming office of the following day, Fehl swore out a warrant for the arrest of the two outgoing commissioners on charges of "mutilation of county records," which new Sheriff Schermerhorn dutifully served.[23]

For the first week of January, as the Oregon attorney general's office investigated the resulting legal tangle, two separate "county commissions" met at the courthouse: one in the formal court chambers and the other in Judge Fehl's new office down the hall. Hundreds of Fehl's supporters, most of them "from the rural sections" noted the *Tidings*, milled in the corridors and on the courthouse lawn. When the state attorney general ruled in favor of Nealon's midnight appointment, Fehl-backer Lowell Zundell threatened to lead three thousand citizens in a protest march on the courthouse. One night, a number of Fehl supporters arrived outside Nealon's Central Point home, demanding his resignation. Medford's American Legion post decried the "mob spirit" of Fehl's adherents and pledged to assist law officers in quelling any disturbance. Fehl, assuming a mantle of statesmanship, issued a widely publicized policy statement, emphasizing the need for "law and order" and rule by duly elected representatives of the people. Fehl indicated he would grudgingly accept the state's legal decision. Just as important, Judge Fehl's policy reorganized unemployment relief fund disbursements and tax delinquency collection under his direct control.[24]

During the 1932 campaign, Judge Fehl allegedly had promised some unemployed rural voters county jobs, "at no less than fifty cents an hour." He assured others of increased largesse from the county relief commissary. In office, Fehl delivered on many of these promises. Some supporters found jobs at the county jail, at the commissary, on road crews, and elsewhere. Others congregated at the relief commissary and became, to the disgust of opponents, "frequent and heavy feeders at this public trough." At a large meeting of supporters in early January, Fehl issued an executive order, opening the commissary to all present. When commissioners Billings and Nealon objected, Fehl warned publicly that "a couple of commissioners . . . are going . . . to keep the old Gang in power from the head man down." Some people in the crowd reportedly shouted "hang them . . . throw them in the river" in reference to Nealon, Norton, and other officials. The "gun guards of the Medford *Daily News*" allegedly enjoyed "wide open" privileges at the commissary, prompting an anti-Banks-Fehl petition to Governor Meier that demanded investigation of the abuses of the relief situation in Jackson County.[25]

Facing more than thirty lawsuits, from libel to collection of debts, Llewellyn Banks saw in the Banks-Fehl supporters at the courthouse a political movement in the making. Arrayed against Banks was a battery of prominent local lawyers, including his former attorneys E. E. Kelly and Gus Newbury, who either now represented his opponents or who themselves took action to obtain payment for past legal services. Banks exclaimed that during a hearing in early 1933 nine attorneys sat at his adversaries' table: "Nine attorneys! I alone was trying to defend myself." By January 1933, although the *News* was close to bankruptcy, Banks printed every day. One affluent supporter, a lumber mill owner in Ashland, offered to send Banks each day, by special evening courier, clippings of "fresh" syndicated news articles from the afternoon issue of the *Tidings*, which Banks could then incorporate into the pages of his morning paper. When creditors confiscated Banks's rolls of newsprint, the publisher obtained another supply from Earl Fehl's wife, Electa (to whom Fehl previously had signed over ownership of many *Record Herald* assets), and transferred its ownership to several loyal employees. Banks's employees distributed copies of the *News* free to people at the courthouse, some carrying the paper to other readers throughout the county.[26] The political stand-off could not endure much longer. The sheriff's recount still loomed, and the anti-Banks-Fehl forces had begun to organize throughout the county.

MOVE AND COUNTERMOVE: BIRTH OF THE GOOD GOVERNMENT CONGRESS

Aside from the *Tribune's* regular anti-extremist pleas, organized opposition to the Banks-Fehl insurgency did not take shape until after the election. Groups had differing priorities. Sheriff Jennings's "dry" backers, calling themselves the League of 7,000, formed in late October 1932 to push his write-in bid. But the league's main purpose seems to have been to rally the county's last-ditch Prohibitionist supporters, particularly in Ashland and Medford. Although the vote of well under four thousand for Jennings belied the group's hopeful name, league organizers kept up the pressure for a recount.[27]

By January, the county's commercial/professional elite mounted a counterattack on the "radical" forces of Banks and Fehl. Led by lawyers such as E. E. Kelly and Porter J. Neff, Medford's establishment sought support among less prominent residents of towns and countryside throughout Jackson County. Some rural residents, such as a rancher and part-time county road supervisor from near Eagle Point, who was reluctant "to go down to Medford" because of unruly crowds, shared the anti-Banks-Fehl attitudes of establishment figures. One Medford citizen, who cited his National Guard service in violence-wracked Butte, Montana, shortly before World War I, worried in early 1933 that "the lives of several honorable men and even of the judge [i.e., Norton] of our court are in danger, needing only a 'spark' to start the fireworks."[28]

* * *

These forces of order had coalesced by mid-January 1933, when the American Legion and the county bar association sponsored a "mass meeting" at the Medford Armory. The valley's sole radio station, KMED (with the *Mail Tribune* a substantial owner), informed citizens of the January 19 evening event, which attracted a crowd of between 1,200 and 1,500 people. Attorney Kelly, one of several speakers, warned that Banks's "propaganda" would soon cause "some poor fool [to go] haywire and become violent." Kelly reviewed the tangled threads of Banks's legal problems, explaining the publisher's attacks as cynical and driven by financial desperation. The meeting's participants, "by an almost unanimous vote," endorsed county officers such as George Codding and expressed confidence in their integrity. The armory meeting led to creation of the Committee of One Hundred, an ad hoc anti-Banks-Fehl association of prominent businessmen and professionals from throughout Jackson County.[29]

Banks and Fehl formed the Good Government Congress in January to counter their rapidly organizing opponents. The idea for the Good Government Congress (which soon became commonly known as the GGC) had been first publicly discussed following Banks's and Fehl's January 12 courthouse rally, which had demanded the resignations of Nealon and Norton. A few days previously, in a column titled "The Declaration of Independence," Banks had called for citizens to "institute a new government ... founded on the principles of our great Democracy." Banks supporters met at the publisher's home that evening, where he outlined his thoughts for a formal organization. Among his listeners were C. Jean Connor and Donald Tryor, unemployed men who soon obtained positions on the News's guard force. After sleeping that night in the sandpile at Ashland's railroad yard, they continued out into the farming areas south of town to contact other prospective organizers. Similar efforts were undertaken by supporters in other areas of the county. The News, in a feature titled "How To Do It," provided detailed instructions for organizing community Good Government Clubs. The clubs soon spread as rapidly through the hinterland as had the Alliances and People's Party clubs forty years earlier. In his column, Banks cautioned organizers to "remember that enemies of the Good Government Congress are not asleep," that "wolves in sheep's clothing" would endeavor to "work themselves in as loyal supporters."[30]

The GGC organizers' first meeting, attended by about fifty people, took place at the courthouse auditorium the evening before the anti-Banks-Fehl rally at the armory. A second organizational meeting followed on January 23 at the auditorium, where Banks claimed that a cadre of nearly three hundred charter members "from every section of the county" jammed the auditorium. Although Judge Fehl provided the facility for these meetings, he kept his distance. Llewellyn Banks, in contrast, was deeply involved in both of them. Although some persons objected to his designation as an "honorary president" with ultimate decision-making power, the meetings followed the publisher's will on most substantive matters. The Good Government Congress announced unrestricted membership for any Jackson County voter who would pay the fifty-cent monthly dues and uphold the congress's "principles of democratic government." The organization soon claimed to have more than six thousand members and twenty chapters throughout the county.[31]

The first general assembly of the Good Government Congress met at the Medford Armory on February 4, a Saturday morning. The Ashland *Tidings* estimated the crowd at about 1,500. Other anti-GGC sources put the number attending above two thousand. GGC executive president Henrietta Martin introduced Llewellyn Banks as the man of the hour. Banks held the audience with his visions of a Jackson County "rehabilitated" through renewed mining, establishment of a huge cannery, and state-run banks providing credit for hard-strapped farms and businesses.[32]

Following Banks to the podium, Fehl (excerpts of his speech were transcribed by a district attorney's stenographer in attendance) returned to his old theme of overturning "gang rule," receiving loud and repeated applause. "Good Government," Fehl observed, "means representative government. . . . The word 'Congress' means representation of all the people." He told his listeners that he had spent "five hard weeks trying [as county judge]... to bring about a reformation of your government." His effort, Fehl stated, had come to "nothing. *Absolutely nothing!*" and that situation would not change "until you people rise up and demand a government that is representative of the people."[33]

Fehl went on to praise Banks as the "one man [who] came to my rescue" when the *Pacific Herald*'s plant was seized by circuit court order. He promised to "work for . . . nothing, to clean this place up." The Good Government Congress later issued, on county court stationery, its resolution of confidence in "faithful and untiring" Judge Fehl and in "Mr. Llewellyn A. Banks, courageous champion of freedom of the press and able exponent and defender of the principles of democracy." The assembly concluded with passage of several resolutions: demands for appointment of a special prosecutor, investigation of alleged fraud connected with the county's "liquor fund," indictment and prosecution of the "murderer" of Everett Dahack, and the removal from office of District Attorney George Codding, who had won reelection in November 1932.[34]

On the afternoon of the February 4 GGC general assembly meeting, what the *Tidings* described as a "calm crowd of 1,000" GGC members and supporters congregated on the plaza outside Ashland's city hall. They massed in support of Banks, who was then inside the Medford civic courtroom facing charges of libel. The Good Government Congress held weekly Monday meetings in Medford thereafter, most of them at the courthouse auditorium. Chapter meetings were held at rural meeting places such as the Lake Creek school and the Rogue Elk Hotel, a fishing resort on the upper Rogue River.[35]

After anti-GGC citizens obtained an injunction against such meetings inside the courthouse, the Good Government Congress would hold much bigger rallies on the courthouse steps. Such was the case on the second Saturday morning general assembly on February 18, scheduled, like the first, for a time when many hinterland residents were in Medford to buy groceries at the city's popular downtown supermarket, the Grocerteria. District Attorney George Codding, who had been promised an "escort of honor" and a cordial hearing by GGC president Henrietta Martin, declined to attend. At the assembly, another large audience heard Earl Fehl make sarcastic reference to "Mr. Robert Ruhl" and declare that southern Oregon's "greatest curse [was] a newspaper that refuses to tell the truth." He also condemned the "eleven or twelve men . . . down on a street corner" who had caused the closure of the courthouse to the congress. In his "Once In A While" column, Banks congratulated the organization on its valiant efforts and predicted that the "Good Government Congress will extend to all part of the State."[36]

Among the crowds that listened approvingly to Banks and Fehl were some individuals who would soon commit felonies with the intention of consolidating the power of the Good Government Congress. Many other GGC supporters would vigorously applaud these actions. Before proceeding to the events of February and March, it is important to examine the composition of the Good Government Congress membership, the people that the GGC's opponents disparaged as ignorant "hillbillies." Their backgrounds were more diverse and, for some, their motivations more shrewd than that smug dismissal would imply.

Fig 9. Medford's Main Street, early 1930s (view from same photo point as Fig. 4). (SOHS #8938)

Fig 10. Llewellyn Banks, wife Edith, and daughter Ruth on a tour of Yosemite National Park, ca. 1930. (Photo courtesy of Ruth Banks)

Fig 11. Llewellyn A. Banks, ca. 1930. (Photo courtesy Ruth Banks).

Fig 12. South (front) and east elevations of the L. A. Banks home, West Main Street, Medford. (Author's collection)

Fig 13. Parlor and library of the commodious Banks home. (Photo courtesy of Ruth Banks)

Fig 14. Earl Fehl, around the time of the 1932 election, in which he handily won the contest for Jackson County Judge. (Author's collection)

Fig 15. Robert Ruhl, Harvard alumnus and owner/editor of the Medford *Mail Tribune*; ca. 1930. (SOHS #14349)

Fig 16. Jackson County's new courthouse, Medford. (SOHS #7247)

Fig 17. The courthouse auditorium, where Judge Fehl convened raucous Good Government Congress meetings. (Author's collection)

Fig 18. The March 6, 1933, GGC rally outside the courthouse. Banks, Fehl, and other speakers are grouped at the top of the stairs at the building's front entrance. (This image as well as Figs. 19, 20, 21, and 27 are from the California-Oregon Power Company 16mm newsreel film, held by the Southern Oregon Historical Society)

Fig. 19. Crowd of GGC supporters on the courthouse lawn, March 6 (the Medford Hotel is visible in the distance). (SOHS)

Fig. 20. Fehl (holding documents) speaking at March 6 rally. (SOHS)

Fig. 21. Crowd cheering and waving hats for L. A. Banks (in dark suit, standing immediately to the left of the dark hat; Fehl is second-to-right of the hat). (SOHS)

6

"A Bunch of Bolsheviks and Hillbillies"?

Many people who joined the Good Government Congress carried a GGC membership card with the holder's name, address, and the organization's motto: "Justice Our Aim, Truth Our Weapon, Public Exposure Our Penalty." The congress's preamble, printed on the reverse side of the card, stated the reasons for the organization's existence: "We, the citizens, property owners, and taxpayers of Jackson County, Oregon, are faced with economic conditions which under the existing order of things have passed beyond individual control." The statement continued with a list of the crises facing the United States and southern Oregon:

> With all industries operating at a loss or . . . closed; with the product of our soil being sold at unprecedented losses . . . ; with tax levies ever on the increase and beyond the earning power of our . . . properties to pay; with half our population destitute and out of employment; with . . . eviction from our homes being imposed under the law; with foreclosures for delinquent taxes effecting [sic] a large section of our people.

It concluded with a rallying cry that, "with conditions unprecedent[ed] and of abnormal nature," it was necessary to "form ourselves into an organization for the protection of our lives, our homes and our properties."[1]

Placing the organization squarely within the historical mainstream of American politics, the preamble stressed members' faith in "the fundamental principles of Democracy" and their subscription "to the spirit and phraseology" of the Declaration of Independence. It concluded with an oath of allegiance to the Constitution and to "ALL JUST LAWS" governing society.

The GGC presented itself as a patriotic upholder of "the people's rights" in the Jeffersonian-Jacksonian tradition. The very term "good government," used in The Federalist Papers, evoked the key political goal of the earliest days of the Republic. Similarly named civic-improvement leagues of western cities during the preceding Progressive Era doubtless inspired the GGC, while the phrase "good government congress" also resonated with the sound of even older American struggles for representative government.[2]

MEN AND WOMEN OF THE GOOD GOVERNMENT CONGRESS

Llewellyn Banks compared the farmers who joined the Good Government Congress to the Concord minutemen of his Massachusetts forebears. Jackson County's threatened establishment leaders scoffed at this analogy. They dismissed GGC members as ignorant rabble. Medford's Post No. 15 of the American Legion characterized the organization as "largely made up of extreme radicals and weak minded people." Another military veteran, who claimed to have "carefully observed each [GGC] meeting for a month," was more charitable. He described the membership as drawn from "mostly among the small rural farmers and the laboring class," virtually all of whom were "white, American citizens of good and sincere intent" but who were "swayed constantly to fever heat."[3]

California-Oregon Power Company's attorney Evan Reames denounced Banks's *News* as "Russian propaganda." Handwritten notes by District Attorney George Codding's staff labeled a number of individual GGC members and supporters with terms such as "agitator," "radical," "anarchist," and "Bolshie." Codding's Ashland informant described one pro-GGC farmer south of town as a "Bolshevik of that group in the Neil Creek district . . . temperamentally stubborn and congenitally dull, associations rural." Red-baiting was a game both sides could play. GGC president Henrietta Martin denounced Leonard Hall's anti-GGC weekly newspaper, the *Miner*, as a "pink sheet" and proudly stated that the only people excluded from the movement were "Communists or [those with] Communistic ideas." Claiming that bar association members had met with men "known to be allied with the Communistic movement," Banks warned that the county's "'special privilege' class, exposed and defeated at every turn in the road, is now appealing to the Communists, to the radicals," to defeat the Good Government Congress.[4]

The "red" accusations of both sides ring hollow upon considering the county's past political history, including the elite's evident success in preventing significant IWW/Wobblie contamination of the local work force during the previous two decades. In terms of GGC members' political beliefs, the epithet "radical" carries weight only if one considers the county's old Populist, Socialist, or Progressive Party voters as meeting that definition.

The more objective *Oregonian* pointed out that the Jackson County movement was composed of "crusaders not communists." It described GGC members as people "of modest means . . . for the most part sincere men and women who have lived in Jackson County for many years—out on the fringes of the rural sections." The local elite likewise emphasized the movement's agrarian background, but sometimes doing so with sarcasm and contempt similar to that expressed by town elites toward the "hayseed" Populists in the 1890s. This was far from unusual. Indeed, as one historian of rural America has recently pointed out, during the 1920s–1930s, farmers were still widely perceived by townsfolk as "uneducated . . . backward, and in need of civilizing."[5]

Anti-GGC observers often employed the term "hillbillies," as in the following report on three GGC members by a district attorney's office investigator: "All were Hill Billies; man short, very long beard, large black felt hat; one old woman, thin; the other fat and middle aged." Robert Ruhl privately referred to swaggering young "Good Governments, [with] their calfskin vests and sawed off shotguns." County commissioner Ralph Billings's son characterized the Banks-Fehl supporters as "moonshiners from Evans Creek, Trail, Butte Falls, and so forth . . . from way off the main runway. . . . When they came to town, they were a pretty rough looking bunch." The little logging town of Butte Falls accounted for sixty-eight signers of an anti-Nealon recall petition.[6]

To George Codding and his assistants, Evans Creek Valley, near the Josephine County line, was one of the most notorious GGC hotbeds. The town of Rogue River, at the mouth of Evans Creek, lay on the railroad and the Pacific Highway. It therefore attracted numerous transients who added their support to the pro-GGC sentiments of longtime Evans Creek Valley residents. The little town's Bonney's Grill served as a meeting place for men such as one Henderson, who "preach[ed] sedition and syndicalism," and Antonsen "a rabid GGC [who] lives 'way back in the sticks up Evans Creek." One of Banks's more affluent backers, from Ashland, agreed that the bulk of GGC supporters were "not Medford people, neither are they Ashland people." He wrote to Banks that "they are the rank and file of the common country folk of the out-country. . . .They are all good citizens." But, he pointed out, "they have suffered an Inferiority Complex so long at the hands of the Medford Gang and of the Ashland Gang, because remember there is an Ashland Gang too."[7]

The picture of "typical GGC members" that emerges from such descriptions is reminiscent of characterizations of stereotypical "hillfolk" of the Ozarks or southern Appalachians. Lending credence to this group portrait are the memoirs of regional writer Wallace Ohrt, who lived on the upper Rogue River, near Trail, during the Depression. He recalled finding the ways of some of his neighbors "shockingly primitive":

Not infrequently, girls married at thirteen or fourteen and were toothless grandmothers at thirty. From the road we sometimes saw babies and toddlers running naked through the woods. The boys picked their noses, seldom wore underwear. . . . Moonshining was so common that it [was] estimated that some five hundred stills may have operated . . . between Medford and Prospect.[8]

All this picturesque local color about Jackson County's hinterland, however, may reveal more about the city-bred attitudes of the commentators, writing or growing up during a period when America's popular, urbanized culture held strong assumptions of what "mountain people" were like. Accounts such as Ohrt's, written later in life and published in the 1970s, reflect some of the reality of that time and place—in his case, particularly those few but vivid youthful impressions that remain forever in one's memory. Nevertheless, they neglect to mention the probability that most southern Oregon hinterland youth in the 1920s and 1930s attended high school, did not marry until about the same age as their city cousins, and were rarely toothless by the age of thirty. The rustic stereotype of the GGC created by the elite likewise contains some truth, but it also distorts. Support for the GGC was more diverse than such remarks would indicate. And, in the hinterland, some residents refused to support the movement and even spoke out against it. Prominent among these was Emmett Nealon. His family's Populist background, plus its tradition of daughters who worked as rural schoolteachers during the early twentieth century, may have given him some influence with older and long-established residents in the northern part of the county.[9]

Llewellyn Banks claimed a GGC membership of more than six thousand (Jackson County's population in 1932–1933, including persons of all ages, was a little over 30,000). Some anti-GGC accounts of "mass meetings" attempted to minimize the organization's numbers by describing "only a few" or "a handful" of supporters in attendance, but photographs and testimony from numerous eyewitnesses (including persons with anti-GGC associations) indicate that such events were very well-attended. Banks's six thousand figure may have been inflated, but the 1932 vote for county judge—which was as clear a public poll of GGC support as any—gave Earl Fehl more than 5,600 votes to the 4,300 votes for his nearest opponent, establishment-backed candidate, former Medford mayor "Pop" Gates.

No official Good Government Congress membership list exists, nor is it known whether there ever was such a list. Instead, a list of three hundred GGC "members" was collected from archival evidence. This list, which includes leaders, acknowledged members, open sympathizers, and confidential supporters, draws from correspondence, newspaper accounts, trial transcripts, and district attorney jury-selection rosters and other investigatory files. The list provides a sample of GGC adherents, both men and women, that permits analysis of the organization's membership in regard to geographic residence, occupation/class, and gender.[10]

In terms of residential zone, of the 280 persons whose addresses could be ascertained, approximately 43 percent lived in the hinterland. Another 31 percent resided in the small-town/rural-orchard intermediate zone of the main valley (exclusive of Ashland city). Nearly one quarter (23 percent) lived in Medford and, of those whose street addresses are known, virtually none of them had homes within the city's affluent neighborhoods. Ashland's city residents account for 4 percent of the total, but a sizable portion of the intermediate-zone total lived in rural settings close to that town.

Occupational status was determined for 146 persons. Of these, by far the largest portion—32 percent—were in the undifferentiated "farmer/rancher" category (and most of these people lived in the hinterland zone). Orchardists (all of them living in the main Bear Creek Valley's intermediate zone) account-ed for 11 percent of the total. Other occupational groups represented included small-business owners (barber, service station owner, auto-court owner, etc., all of whom lived in Medford or the intermediate zone) at 6 percent; presum-ably self-employed artisans (carpenter, blacksmith, mason, etc.) at almost the same percentage; wage-paid service/industrial workers (taxi driver, mail car-rier, nurse, telephone operator, laundress, feed store employee, millhands, and so on) at 12 percent; housewives at 17 percent; and outdoor workers (labor-ers, miners, loggers, and orchard employees) at 15 percent. Professionals and large-business owners (including one physician, one attorney, one banker, and one lumberman) tallied at 7 percent; the remaining seven out of these eleven individuals were identified as "ministers" or "preachers," and their religious duties may have been only of a part-time nature.

The occupational spread shows a clear predominance of rural-oriented workers (over half of the total), whether as landowners or as seasonal employees. However, more urban-oriented endeavors—small businesses, skilled artisan crafts, and service/industrial work—account for nearly one-quarter of the total. The higher-status category of large-business owners and professionals (domi-nated by ministers) is by far the smallest group. Housewives make up almost a fifth of the GGC members whose occupational status could be determined. This figure is almost certainly low for the overall membership, given that the unlisted wives of many men on the sample list probably actively supported the move-ment. Photographs, newspaper accounts, and other evidence of GGC activities demonstrate that women made up a sizeable portion of attendees. Indeed, women held positions of prominence in the Good Government Congress's leadership. Henrietta Martin, wife of Medford's US Weather Bureau director (a position that, thanks to the agency's "fruit frost forecast" duties, had strong ties to local orchardists), is the most obvious example. Martin apparently was a housewife, as news accounts provide almost nothing in the way of personal background for her aside from her husband's occupation. Additionally, the elderly, longtime county residents interviewed as part of the research for this book—most of whom were adolescents or very young adults during 1932 and 1933—recalled no personal details about Henrietta Martin, although most of them clearly remembered hearing of her notorious horsewhipping of Leonard Hall. Detailed biographical material on Martin evidently has passed out of reach with the deaths of the principals in the GGC episode. Martin actively planned and led GGC meetings, spoke forcefully and articulately before large audiences, and remained an aggressive political player even after the tumult of March 1933.

Other prominent female GGC members included Central Point orchardist Ariel Pomeroy and Gold Hill resident Adah Deakin, both of whom regularly spoke at GGC meetings and wrote numerous public letters on behalf of the movement and Llewellyn Banks. The district attorney's Rogue River/ Gold Hill–area informant stressed the GGC's popularity among women there, citing as example one particularly active female resident who served as secretary of the Good Government Club in the remote hamlet of Wimer who "went all around . . . Evans Creek soliciting subscriptions on behalf of Earl Fehl." This anti-Banks-Fehl informant urged fellow GGC opponent Robert Ruhl to help find "some strong woman" who could present the anti-GGC case to female audiences. Another informant revealed (with self-admitted astonishment) the fact that one seemingly respectable member of the Medford Business Women's Club was actually a GGC sympathizer who "expressed her views openly."[11]

Although given particular attention by anti-GGC observers, the importance of women in both the leadership and the rank and file of the GGC was not an anomaly. Rather, it reflected the steady emergence of American women, particularly middle- and lower-economic-class women, as full participants in diverse movements across the entire spectrum of national politics during the 1920s and 1930s. In addition, as pointed out in chapter 2, local rural women had a heritage of political activity dating from the Grange and Alliance movements of the late nineteenth century.[12]

THE GOALS OF GGC MEMBERS

The motivations of Good Government Congress members varied. Some of them, such as S. P. MacDonald, a part-time night watchman at a Medford fruit-packing plant, joined out of short-term self-interest. MacDonald claimed he had been promised a county job by Earl Fehl in return for his support. R. C. Cummings of Rogue River had joined soon after Walter Jones, that town's mayor and Fehl's appointee as road supervisor, gave him a job on the road crew. At the other end of the economic scale, a few elderly and once-politically-prominent Medford residents, such as 1907–1908 mayor J. F. "Doc" Reddy and pioneer banker William Gore, may have supported Banks out of antipathy for the current Medford elite or simply out of resentment at the passing of their power to new hands. Evidently, neither they nor wealthy Ashland doctor Francis G. Swedenburg, Banks's physician and his partner in at least one mining venture, were GGC members, but they voiced open support for Banks and his crusade. Another Ashland resident, Arthur L. Coggins, whose lumber mill was one of the town's largest employers, was one of Banks's many creditors. Coggins, a leader of the antiestablishment Jackson County Taxpayers League, admitted that, out of self-interest, he wished for Banks to stay "alive . . . financially," but he also sympathized with the aims of the GGC movement, stating that its rural members "grasped at the opportunity thru [Banks] to fight the . . . County Gang which has controlled them for a generation."[13]

The Portland *Oregonian* sent a staff reporter down to Medford to cover the fast-breaking story in early March. The reporter, who apparently interviewed a number of GGC supporters, stressed the organization as a "Depression-born" movement and portrayed it with the hues of agrarian revolt. He wrote of the "hundreds of citizens drawn primarily from the rural sections . . . leaving their fields and orchards to march in huge demonstrations . . . in front of the courthouse." Returning "back home after a week spent . . . 'at the front' in the most intense community war experienced in this state in recent years," the reporter rhetorically went on to ask *Oregonian* readers,

> What is the matter with Jackson County? . . . Why should a progressive city with progressive citizens and a rich producing back country be torn by intense civil strife? . . . Why should men be seen on the city streets with guns strapped to their hips? . . . Reduced to simplicity, the answer is "hard times."[14]

In broad terms, people on the far periphery of local power dominated the membership of the Good Government Congress—rural residents and working-class townsfolk, people who had seen the political center of gravity shift steadily to the Medford urban core, with its cosmopolitan elite and outposts of corporate capitalism. Members and sympathizers of the GGC had different motives than did Banks and Fehl, for whom it was an avenue to financial survival and personal political control. For some grassroots members, the organization represented an opportunity to reassert waning rural power. For others, it probably was seen as a way to pull the bosses down to size. For many, although they may not have stated it in such terms, the movement symbolized a crusade for republican "virtue" against the traditional villain of "corruption"—an evil, in this case, made literal by the allegedly corrupt "gang." Jennie Thatcher, a GGC supporter from Talent, probably spoke for many less-articulate members when she stated,

> I think the day is close at hand when we will have to say adieu to our old ideas . . . and political views, and get the rubbish from the machinery of our train, put there by the platform, pulpit, and press . . . by those who hold selfish motives, greed, graft, etc. paramount to truth. . . . Let us hope the "gangsters' day" is at an end.[15]

Like many movements in their early stage, the Good Government Congress at first attracted people of divergent philosophies who saw in it the means to further their own individual political aims. O. H. Goss and Miles Randall, representatives of the county's Unemployed Council and considered "radicals" by the Medford elite, had been attracted to the GGC immediately upon its formation in mid-January. When they challenged the "dictatorial" control of Banks, they found themselves unwelcome and branded as "Communists" by the GGC. Goss later joined the establishment's anti-GGC forces, pointing out Fehl's alleged cynical abuses at the county relief commissary. And other early supporters of the GGC, more conservative politically than Goss, soon abandoned it as too "radical."[16]

RELIGION, NATIVISM, AND THE KLAN CONNECTION
By early February 1933, with the initial schisms and apostasies over, personal support for the GGC and for Banks and Fehl apparently had become nearly identical in the minds of members. The movement coalesced around the two men as saviors and as martyrs. Indeed, over the course of its short existence as a viable organization, the GGC increasingly added the rhetoric of "patriotic Christianity" to its preamble's original republican rhetoric. The persistent biblical allusions in Banks's and Fehl's newspaper editorials laid the foundation for this growing symbolic element. Several local Protestant ministers (none of whom seem to have served congregations at established mainline churches) were prominent in the organization. The Reverend Edwin Malkemus opened several GGC assemblies with prayer. One of Banks's supporters wrote to him that there would have been "no depression or crime wave" if America had "followed the teachings of Jesus Christ," and that it was a "sick nation" that only "a miracle of Christ" could cure.[17]

D. H. Ferry, the anti-Banks informant in the Rogue River/Gold Hill area, noted Banks's popularity there among the "old folks, especially religious women," and he urged Ruhl to aim a countervailing editorial appeal at "the churchy people." According to witnesses at one of the GGC courthouse auditorium meetings, Banks's personal magnetism apparently combined with religious fervor in a curious action that brought an approving roar from the crowd: after speaking to the assembly, the publisher halted, took his fountain pen and a kitchen match from his coat pocket, and made them into a cross for all to see, "which brought a great many people to their feet shouting, and the rest all followed with some kind of noise." O. H. Goss, a GGC critic, forcefully described later GGC meetings as "a constant barrage of prayer, flag waving and pompous phrases . . . seething with a witches brew of hatred and prejudice." Thomas L. Breechen, an Ashland resident and leading officer of the organization, spoke at length before several large GGC meetings on "the foreign population"; his remarks included a repertoire of jokes about "Irish, Swedish, and Jewish people" and other ethnic groups.[18]

Considering Banks's well-known anti-Semitic views, Breechen's choice of speaking topics, and especially Jackson County's heritage of religious and ethnic prejudice, the apparent existence of a strong nativist sub-element in the Good Government Congress movement is not surprising. Particularly interesting, however, is the alleged association of several men with Llewellyn Banks and the GGC who had been prominent in the county's Ku Klux Klan movement of the 1920s. Among them was D. M. Lowe, the 1922 Klan sheriff candidate (who would continue to manage his dairy farm in Ashland's rural Valley View district well into the 1950s). Jacksonville orchardists E. A. Fleming and Howard Hill, each of whom had close political connections with Banks and the GGC, had been active in the Klan. Hill and the Reverend Jouette P. Bray of Medford, another Banks supporter, were two of the defendants charged in the notorious 1922 night-riding incidents. Attorney William Phipps, the Klan's mouthpiece in 1922, was not an acknowledged GGC supporter. However, he became one of the very few Medford attorneys whom Banks would later trust with his legal defense; as a former anti-gang crusader himself, Phipps may well have openly sympathized with the *Tribune*-bashing rhetoric of the Good Government Congress.[19]

Confusing the apparent KKK/GGC association is the fact that two prominent anti-GGC leaders, George Codding and "Pop" Gates, had also been publicly tied to the Klan during the early 1920s. In hindsight, their brief Klan affiliations probably owed far more to political opportunism than to personal commitment. Based on their activities during the 1920s, the few identifiable KKK/GGC individuals may have been exhibiting the orchardist-dominated intermediate-zone's populistic Klan tenor more than its moralistic or even its nativist tendencies. Fleming, a small orchardist and unsuccessful 1924 candidate for Jacksonville mayor before becoming a GGC stalwart, certainly showed evidence of this trait. And dairy farmer Lowe had made anti-elitism the leitmotif of his 1922 sheriff election campaign.[20]

The appearance of Ku Klux Klan supporters who lived in the county's small-town/orchard zone as members of the Good Government Congress does not deny the very distinct differences between the public goals of the two organizations. Yet the indirect KKK-GGC association lends additional weight to the essentially populist objectives of many Jackson County Klansmen in the 1920s. Given the hindsight on the Klan episode that the GGC episode provides, the local Klan's moralism—as exemplified by its temperance stand—does not appear to have been nearly as important an attraction as was its anti-elitism and nativism. In 1922, the valley's two rural zones had divided politically on the Klan's issue of Prohibition enforcement. Intermediate-zone residents who supported the Klan on local political matters (including the sub-rosa issue of water rights) had embraced strict Prohibition enforcement as well, while backcountry residents (most of whom lived well above the valley areas affected by large-scale irrigation projects) had probably voted against Klan candidates, at least in part, because of this very issue.

By 1932, the noble experiment of Prohibition was in shambles. Only hard-core Jackson County "drys" wished it to continue, and the 1932 national election ended the debate forever. Earl Fehl's anti-Prohibition campaign of 1930–1932 aimed at official corruption and the alleged murder of innocent rural citizens no doubt incensed even many once-dry voters of the intermediate zone. By 1933, with both the Klan and Prohibition dead, liquor no longer divided the county's rural people between those of the small-town/orchard zone and those of the more remote backcountry. Now faced with the Depression and a "corrupt gang," many of them united under the Good Government Congress in a countywide manner not seen since the early days of the People's Party.

PROFILES: TEN GOOD GOVERNMENT CONGRESS LOYALISTS

Each of the ten individuals discussed here was an active member or open supporter of the Good Government Congress. All but one of them maintained strong allegiance to the organization and its leaders following the county's political crisis of early 1933. These very brief personal profiles of GGC loyalists add substance to the aggregate portrait of the GGC.

L. M. Sweet lived in the area of Sams Valley where the orchard land fades into the ranches of the hinterland. A contract rural carrier for the US Mail in 1932–1933, he had lived in Sams Valley since before World War I. Sweet personified the continuous thread of anti-elitist, populist sentiments of the county's rural residents from the Klan period through the Depression. In 1922,

Sweet may well have been a member of the Ku Klux Klan; he certainly was an open and vociferous supporter of the "Klan ticket" of Walter Pierce, Charles Thomas, and Ralph Cowgill. In 1922, calling himself a "believer in whiteman methods," Sweet scorned the anti-Klan Independent American Voters League. He called the league's leaders "great magicians sitting upon the throne" who waved "their magic wands . . . bidding the poor illiterates come bow down at their feet and swear allegiance to the Gods that be." He further alluded to the anti-Klan *Tribune* as "a filthy bird that besmears a lovely nest."[21]

Ten years later, Sweet was a Banks-Fehl loyalist, distributing free copies of the *News* and *Record Herald* and circulating GGC petitions during his mail deliveries. Although this activity brought him rebuke from the local postmaster, he continued nevertheless. Sweet organized the Sams Valley GGC chapter and was in the forefront of calling for resignation of county commissioner R. E. Nealon, the former Sams Valley resident and "illegal" appointee of the "gang."[22]

Walter J. Jones moved to the town of Rogue River in 1923. Born in Crescent City, California, Jones had worked for the Forest Service for sixteen years in northwestern California, the Alaska Panhandle, and southern Oregon. During the 1920s he engaged in the orchard business near Rogue River, marketing his crop through Llewellyn Banks's fruit-packing plant. A town councilman in the mid-1920s, Jones became a Banks-Fehl ally during the Depression and won election as mayor of Rogue River in 1932. He was a self-described "charter member" of the GGC and led the courthouse break-in of February 20.[23]

O. C. Train lived far up the Evans Creek Valley, where he owned a small, family-operated sawmill. Although very little biographical information is readily available, Train likely had lived in this remote area for over a decade. Train's sawmill served as a gathering place for local GGC members. An anti-GGC informant described him as "a very loyal member" and stated that, after the Medford violence of mid-March, Train held several nighttime "secret GGC meetings" at his mill.[24]

George Obenchain resided on a small farm outside of Central Point during the 1920s and 1930s. The son of hinterland pioneers in the Little Butte Creek Valley, he was born and raised in the county. Owning a small orchard until the Depression, by 1933 he made his living as a truck gardener. He knew of Banks's high reputation among those of his neighbors who marketed fruit through his operation. Obenchain considered Llewellyn Banks to be "one of the best men that ever come into Jackson County." Obenchain was an unsuccessful GGC candidate for sheriff in the post-rebellion election of 1934.[25]

Abner Cox was thirty-two years old in 1933. During the 1920s he had worked at the huge Toledo lumber mill on the central Oregon coast. Coming to Jackson County during the mill's Depression layoff, Cox lived in Medford and worked as a laborer in nearby orchards, pruning branches and spraying fruit on a part-time basis. He, too, was a charter member of the GGC and retained his faith in Llewellyn Banks after the 1933 crisis.[26]

May Murray had lived in Medford for fourteen years at the time of the GGC episode. Murray was a married woman, but her husband evidently resided elsewhere during 1932–1933. She and her married daughter, Effie Lewis (also a GGC member), lived together in the modest-income neighborhood of West Medford. She took in laundry, worked as a part-time cook at a Medford cafe, and did janitorial work at the Episcopal Church. She became a member of the GGC at its February 4 general assembly at the armory. She proudly stated that she "had attended all GGC meetings" after that. Murray proved to be a solid Banks supporter, apparently providing perjured testimony in his defense during his murder trial.[27]

Flora Becknell was another Medford resident. Her husband, who worked for Copco, had been either severely disabled or killed from a work accident with the power company. Becknell received a small monthly accident benefit from the state, which she supplemented by working in the bakery department of the Groceteria. An informant described her as remaining "much in favor of G. G. Congress et al." well after the 1933 crisis.[28]

May Powell had come to the United States from County Armagh, Northern Ireland, soon after World War I and to Jackson County in 1921. She had worked as a Red Cross nurse with British forces on the Western Front; she may have met her future husband in Europe before coming to the United States, but this is uncertain. The couple lived briefly in the Applegate Valley and then in Talent, where he worked as an auto mechanic at the Highway Exchange on the Pacific Highway. Mrs. Powell worked occasionally as a nurse and became very active in the Good Government Congress. She had known Banks personally since 1930. Powell visited Banks's home in mid-March 1933 to warn the publisher about threats to his life, and she later testified on his behalf.[29]

Ariel Burton Pomeroy owned a twenty-five-acre orchard near Central Point. She had first come to the valley in 1915. She preferred to be addressed as Mrs. Ariel Pomeroy, though her husband evidently was deceased or otherwise absent by 1932–1933. She first became personally acquainted with Banks in 1931 but proudly claimed to have "followed his editorials since the beginning." A charter member of the GGC, Pomeroy spoke on patriotic themes at a number of its meetings. She continued as a Banks loyalist long after the GGC movement had crumbled, circulating petitions for his release from prison and writing numerous letters on his behalf to the governor.[30]

Twenty-six-year-old Virgil Edington was one of Llewellyn Banks's bodyguards, and he pulled numerous late-night watches at the *News*. Edington became one of the so-called Greensprings Mountain Boys, several of whom came from the Greensprings Summit vicinity in the foothills east of Ashland. (The name of this group may have been favored by Banks so as to draw a parallel with Ethan Allen's Vermonter Green Mountain Boys of the Revolutionary War.) A native of Jackson County, Edington had worked for seven years after finishing grade school to help support his family. He graduated from high school in 1932 and was drawn into the GGC movement as a rural distributer of the *News*. Edington later remarked on the "power . . . manifested [by Banks] in meetings." He joined the GGC "believing it was fighting for a just cause." After his arrest for criminal syndicalism, Edington cooperated with the Oregon State Police in their anti-GGC investigations.[31]

OPPONENTS OF THE GGC: THE COMMITTEE OF ONE HUNDRED

Those most publicly associated with the fight *against* the Good Government Congress included attorneys such as Codding, Kelly, Reames, Neff, and Newbury, as well as editors Ruhl and Hall. American Legionnaires, merchants, and others joined the anti-GGC forces after these leaders had forged a countermovement. Few anti-GGC residents of the more remote rural districts participated openly, but their support was welcomed. Outside of official law-enforcement agencies, the most formalized component of the anti-GGC movement was the Committee of One Hundred, an ad hoc group that countered GGC "propaganda" with letters and statements published in the *Tribune*. Informally, its members became an influential network of anti-GGC organizers. Dominated by the Medford establishment, its ranks included men such as former mayor O. O. Alenderfer, who had crossed swords with Earl Fehl during past political battles. Alenderfer had longtime associations with the California-Oregon Power Company. In 1933 he owned the People's Electric Store, a large electrical appliance dealership located next door to Copco's Main Street offices. The very name of this group of GGC opponents, which indicated merely one hundred members, seemingly emphasized a self-chosen identity as a band of stalwart, courageous leaders.[32]

The Committee of One Hundred also included some of the valley's more prosperous orchardists, men whom Llewellyn Banks had challenged for leadership of the Fruit Growers League. Among these members were Henry Van Hoevenberg and O. C. Boggs. Van Hoevenberg owned extensive orchard land between Table Rock and Gold Hill. A 1902 graduate of Columbia University who had played end on the school's first football team, Van Hoevenberg apparently enjoyed close personal ties to several influential officials in Salem. Oliver C. Boggs, graduate of the University of Illinois law school and a Republican, owned more than one hundred acres of well irrigated, productive orchard land northeast of Medford. In 1933, Boggs, a major owner of the Jackson County Bank, became the leading force of the Committee of One Hundred.[33]

In February and March 1933, members of the Good Government Congress undertook direct action to eliminate the threat posed by opponents like the Committee of One Hundred. These events would lead instead to the GGC's defeat and the denouement of the Jackson County Rebellion.

7

"I Will Take the Field in Revolution"
The Tumult of Early 1933

Coming before the crowd at the Medford Armory on February 18, 1933, for the second general assembly of the Good Government Congress, Judge Earl Fehl acknowledged the approaching noon hour and his listeners' need for lunch. He spoke for about ten minutes. In addition to by-now-familiar scathing remarks about the "conspiracy" of *Mail Tribune* publisher Robert Ruhl, District Attorney George Codding, and circuit court judge Harold Norton to silence Jackson County's free press, Fehl stressed the threat to free assembly. He declared that the impending closure of the courthouse auditorium to the Good Government Congress by court order represented "the breakdown of the Constitution" in southern Oregon. Using the new building to symbolize the crisis in local government, Fehl swore that "we are opening the courthouse to the people. That courthouse belongs to you absolutely." Holding up his key to the courthouse auditorium for all to see, Fehl promised that, no matter "if all the lawyers in the state of Oregon . . . demands that the auditorium be closed," he would keep its doors open.[1]

The public struggle over the reins of government served to solidify forces on both sides of the battle line during January and early February. On the Good Government Congress side, by February, members' threats of the "hangman's rope" had replaced early January's more temperate call for appointment of a special prosecutor to expose the alleged gang conspiracy. Vigilante violence, including lynching, first suggested by Llewellyn Banks in private meetings, was openly demanded by unnamed members of GGC crowds at February rallies.[2]

Heightening the outrage of GGC members were speakers such as Adah Deakin, who read at one February rally her bitterly sarcastic "Legal Ten Commandments," among them, "Thou shalt praise the legal trust and the lawyers that separate you from your salary. . . . Thou shalt respect and honor an officer with a gun, that leaves the provider of your family dead in your dooryard."[3]

The embattled Banks and Fehl maintained a highly public loyalty to each other that served to cement the loyalty of followers. Banks praised Judge Fehl as "an iron man." Fehl commended Banks for his courage. GGC members in turn rallied to the two men, guarding their homes and forming protective escorts for their public appearances. Banks described his supporters as coming to his home prior to GGC meetings in several automobiles: "[The escorts] placed me in the rear seat between two people," taking him to meetings and walking him to the doorways of meeting places. These bodyguards "guarded me in and out." At meetings "where we had fifteen hundred or two thousand" people in attendance," Banks entered to "applause [that] was deafening because they knew I came at the risk of my life."[4]

At rallies, Banks spoke without notes and in a loud voice that could be heard from several hundred feet away. An anti-GGC listener remarked that Banks "knew how to work the crowd. . . . He'd get the tempo going, get them to nod their heads. . . . He could get them to do anything." At one meeting Banks stated that a friend had warned him that morning to "raise [his] foot off the peddle [sic]." He asked the assemblage, "Should I raise my foot or put it down harder?" According to an anti-GGC witness, the crowd resoundingly answered with its support of Banks's determination to fight the gang, to "give them hell."[5]

Titling his February 3 Daily News column "Wholesale Bloodshed," Banks warned of massive violence if the authorities attempted to deprive mortgage-ridden citizens of their property. His fight to retain the News symbolized to GGC members their own fight to hold on to farms, businesses, jobs, and homes. The Banks-Fehl alliance held strong throughout the next six weeks. Judge Fehl received undue credit in the News for newly elected state senator Edward C. Kelly's success in obtaining legislative approval to transfer $50,000 of state road moneys to the county's general fund. Once the money was under his control, Fehl allocated the funds to expand the county's relief commissary and to hire GGC members onto county road crews. When Medford constable George Prescott and other officers seized Banks's supply of newsprint by court order, he rebuked "Bandits on the public payroll . . . under the badge of the law . . . are in open violation of the law of this state." Some GGC members, hearing Banks's thinly veiled calls for direct action, saw extralegal measures as necessary to protect the people's rights from further insult.[6] In particular, the answer to the question of legal authority—of who would enforce the law in Jackson County—loomed with the impending sheriff's election recount. After numerous delays from Sheriff Schermerhorn, visiting circuit court judge George Skipworth, of Lane County (assigned to the case because of the Norton recall effort and other prejudicial matters), ruled on the afternoon of February 20 that the recount must proceed.

"CRIMINAL SYNDICALISM": THE BALLOT THEFTS

The Good Government Congress had scheduled a mass meeting at the court-house auditorium for the day of Skipworth's ballot-recount ruling, which doubtless gave many GGC members an increased sense of urgency. The hall was filled to capacity. People standing outside on the courthouse lawn listened through the auditorium's opened windows. GGC president Henrietta Martin began the meeting at 8:00 p.m., and Earl Fehl spoke first. His topic was the sheriff's recount, scheduled for the following morning. According to several witnesses, Fehl shouted to his audience, "Do you people want a recount?" and was met with a resounding "No!" from the crowd. He asked, "What are you going to do about it?" and, receiving a variety of shouted answers, Fehl urged his listeners to stand by him in the days ahead. Llewellyn Banks came to the podium twice that evening, warning of "secret service men" (plain-clothes state police officers) planted in the audience. His speeches brought further noisy approval from the crowd. Thomas Breechen spoke on a number of subjects, ranging from humorous "homespun" anecdotes to his alleged personal friendship with President-elect Franklin D. Roosevelt. Stoking a bit of xenophobia, twenty-two-year-old Jean Conners, GGC vice president, spoke on America's problems with "the foreign population." The meeting ended at around 11:30 p.m. [7]

Miner editor Leonard Hall, *Tribune* writer Art Perry, and a few other anti-GGC observers listened to the February 20 GGC speeches from the auditorium vestibule and from the opened ground-floor windows along the auditorium. During the meeting, Hall and others noted the "comings and go-ings" of a number of GGC leaders, members, and *News* employees near the southwest corner of the courthouse. These people were evidently entering and exiting from the rear entrance of the courthouse. Hall surmised that "from the amount of trips made back and forth," that there must have been "a [liquor] jug around someplace." Anti-GGC observer A. R. Hoelting thought the activ-ity was "rather peculiar," but walked home without giving it further thought.[8] On the following morning, deputy county clerk Nydah Neil prepared to enter the ground-floor records vault. She had secured the ballots there the previous day because the recount was to take place in that room. Accompanied by Judge Skipworth, attorneys, and other officials involved in the recount, Neil and the others first stepped outside the rear door of the building at the request of one official visitor in order to examine some construction details of the as-yet-unfinished courthouse structure. While outside they noticed the record vault's broken window. They quickly entered the room and immediately realized the room had been burglarized. Thirty-six of the ballot pouches were missing. The thieves had obtained entry to the vault, which had thick concrete walls and a sturdy combination-locked door, by breaking the window. (Among other unfinished construction details of the new courthouse, steel bars had not yet been installed outside the vault's glass windows; their only security was the wire mesh encased within the frosted glass itself.) When informed of the theft, Fehl expressed outrage and attempted to cast suspicion on former sheriff Ralph Jennings's son, Paul. Sheriff Schermerhorn pledged a full investigation.[9]

Numerous corroborative accounts provided by the burglary participants, which they gave as statements and affidavits during the Oregon State Police (OSP) investigation of the ballot-theft case, provide a detailed narrative of the theft. Earl Fehl and other GGC leaders had decided, as early as the day after the November 1932 election, to take any action necessary to ensure that Ralph Jennings did not displace Schermerhorn as Jackson County sheriff. During December and January, Fehl and others had surreptitiously "picked at" some of the ballot pouches on several occasions in an effort to show evidence of tampering and thereby avoid the recount. When Judge Skipworth's ruling seemed inevitable, GGC leaders began actively planning the removal and destruction of the contested ballots. The Good Government Congress's loud, standing-room-only meeting in the courthouse on February 20 provided a fortuitous cover for the ballot theft taking place down the corridor from the auditorium.[10] GGC members Mason Burl Sexton and Milton (aka Wilbur) Sexton, aged twenty and seventeen, respectively, had been released from the county jail in mid-January after the grand jury returned a "no true bill" on charges of disorderly conduct. The brothers were invited by Sheriff Schermerhorn and county jailer John Glenn to room in the courthouse's "penthouse," a small storage area next to the courthouse's top-floor jail, in return for performing daily janitorial chores. Shortly before the start of the February 20 GGC meeting, the Sexton brothers met in the ground-floor corridor with Judge Fehl, Rogue River mayor Walter Jones, county shops foreman Chuck Davis (a Fehl appointee), and several other GGC leaders, who asked the brothers if they had been able to learn the combination to the vault's door from deputy clerk Neil. Replying in the negative, the Sextons remained behind with the others as Judge Fehl left for the GGC meeting down the hall with the parting words, "Now I would hate to see you boys have to break a window to get those ballots out of the vault."

Jailer John Glenn, telling the Sextons that Sheriff Schermerhorn had confidence in them, persuaded the young men to try to force open one of the ground-floor vault's outside windows. When that effort failed, Mason Sexton obtained a fire axe. At about 9:30 p.m., while Banks was speaking to a crowded auditorium, Mayor Jones arranged for R. R. Cummings, at Jones's hand signal, to race the engine of a nearby parked Ford coupe simultaneous to loud applause from the auditorium. During the noise, Sexton broke the window with the axe and then crawled inside. More than fifteen men participated in removing three dozen ballot pouches to waiting automobiles. Among the lookouts was Sheriff Schermerhorn, who stood discreetly on a nearby corner with a view of the courthouse's south and west (rear) faces, ready to signal with a flashlight of possible danger.

The Sextons and R. C. Cummings, loading four of the pouches into Cummings's Ford, drove to the Pacific Highway and then Table Rock Road, which they followed north to the Rogue River. Crossing onto the Rogue's Bybee Bridge, the men slit open the containers, put rocks in them, and tossed the pouches over the railing of the bridge and into the river. Returning to the courthouse within an hour, the Sextons were directed to load more pouches into a delivery truck owned by E. A. Fleming. The elderly Banks supporter had stumbled on the burglary in progress; when told that the men were "hauling away those damn ballots so they can't be counted," he volunteered to help dispose of them. He and three other men put several pouches into Fleming's van and drove to the brushy hills between Phoenix and Jacksonville, where they spent several hours burning the ballots in a hastily built bonfire.

Banks's circulation manager, Arthur LaDieu, and another group of GGC men had driven another load of ballots to the Rogue River home of *News* guard Wesley McKitrick, where McKitrick's mother permitted them to be burned in her woodstove; Mayor Jones had provided some pitchy-pine firewood especially for the purpose. During their return drive on the Pacific Highway to Medford, the men threw more weighted ballot pouches into the Rogue River, near the mouth of Gall's Creek. With the GGC rally close to ending, the Sexton brothers took a final fifteen to twenty pouches of ballots down to the courthouse basement, burning them in the new furnace before retiring to their upper-story quarters for the night.

After discovery of the courthouse burglary, while Earl Fehl continued to blame anti-GGC individuals for the theft, the campaign of GGC opponents gathered momentum and attracted attention outside of southern Oregon.[11] Oregon's prominent conservative-Republican commentator C. C. Chapman, a longtime member of Portland's business elite, acidly wrote that "Banks is vermin" in his influential political newspaper, *Oregon Voter*. Reginald Parsons, a wealthy Rogue River Valley orchardist then living in Seattle, compared Jackson County's danger to the time when he had lived in Colorado during the violence-ridden "old days of the Western Federation of Miners and the [William 'Big Bill'] Haywood and [Charles] Moyer regime." Parsons urged "the leading men of the valley" to organize quickly in support of law and order. The pleas of A. R. Hoelting and others to Governor Julius Meier to mobilize the National Guard had some effect: a small contingent of local guardsmen went on "alert," ready to report to the Medford Armory in case of an "uprising."[12]

Of more immediate use than calling out the guard was Meier's dispatch of additional Oregon State Police from Salem to help with the investigation; OSP captain Lee Bown, assisted by Medford chief of police Clatous Mc-Credie, headed the team. Some of the ballots had been found floating in a back eddy of the Rogue River just below Bybee Bridge. Careful sifting also revealed ballot-pouch fragments among the ashes in the courthouse boiler room. State police detectives found a torn piece of fabric on the vault's broken window. Observing the crowd of onlookers outside the courthouse, McCredie noted Mason Sexton wearing torn trousers of the same material. Quickly and quietly arresting the Sextons out of sight of other GGC supporters, McCredie took them to the city jail, where the brothers were held without bail or benefit of counsel. After waiting four days without any word of support from his GGC allies, Mason Sexton confessed to his part in the theft and implicated numerous others. The brothers agreed to assist the police further.[13]

On February 27, Judge Fehl, Sheriff Schermerhorn, Mayor Jones, jailer Glenn, Davis, Breechen, Conners, McKitrick, Edington, and a number of other GGC members were arrested on charges ranging from "criminal syndicalism" to "burglary, not in a dwelling." Fehl posted bond almost immediately, but many suspects remained in custody for much of the day.[14] The suspects were held in the city jail, and the state police arranged to hold each of them separately.

As yet unaware of the Sextons' confession and cooperation with the police, each one of the suspects was placed temporarily in the women's ward with the two brothers during the course of the day. There, Mason Sexton, casually assuring each new arrival that they could not be overheard by the police, engaged each temporary cellmate in conversations about the theft. In an adjacent locked restroom, able to hear all that was being said, were Oregon State Police sergeant James O'Brien, deputy district attorney George W. Neilson, and court stenographer Walter Looker. Schermerhorn and Breechen both feared entrapment and refused to incriminate themselves. Schermerhorn alerted the Sextons of the likelihood of "dictaphones," and Breechen warned that "the walls have ears." Others were less discreet.[15]

County shop foreman Chuck Davis at first denied his involvement. Within a few minutes, however, an angry Davis, who had been appointed a special deputy by Schermerhorn, talked openly of the theft, adding that, after he was released, "these prosecuting attorneys [had better] make themselves scarce," threatening to "go and get the Luger and start gunning for some of

those sons of bitches, . . . to do something to put me in for." Davis admitted that
the county seemed headed for military rule. He then speculated about making
"enough bombs to blow up the whole town." During his jail-cell discussion
with the Sexton brothers, the bombastic Davis even proposed forcing at
gunpoint Henry "Heinie" Fluher, proprietor of southwestern Oregon's largest
bakery and owner of an airplane, to fly over the town while Davis tossed out
sticks of dynamite.[16]

That evening, reported the Ashland *Tidings*, a crowd of GGC members
gathered near the county courthouse, threatening to march on the city jail and
free their friends. As a result, members of the local National Guard unit reported to the armory, and state police officers, armed with submachine guns and
"[tear]gas bombs," stationed themselves visibly at the jail. No confrontation
ensued. Elsewhere in Medford, Leonard Hall, having satirized GGC president
Henrietta Martin in the pages of the *Miner*, was accosted by congress members
on the street. They pinioned the editor's arms behind his back while Martin
lashed him several times across the face with a horsewhip.[17]

Good Government Congress members provided the bond for Fehl's
freedom. With George Codding attempting to re-jail him and declare the position of county judge vacant, Fehl desperately attempted to hold on to political
power. Issuing habeas corpus writs for release of the jailed ballot-theft suspects
as well as an arrest warrant for Chief McCredie, he ordered Schermerhorn, out
on bail, to appoint "50 deputies" to counter the state police and keep up "the
struggle for justice." The sheriff, evidently sensing futility in further resistance,
temporized and then refused. In an apparent attempt to heighten local panic
during the national banking crisis then rocking the country, Fehl's *Record Herald* published an unsubstantiated story on March 3 claiming that Medford's
Fruit Growers' Bank had secretly removed its deposits.[18] Hounded by creditors and a criminal investigation, Llewellyn Banks now proposed expanding
the Good Government Congress into a state and even national movement.
He sent a letter on March 7 pleading for personal intervention in the Jackson
County situation by his political hero and counterpart on the national stage,
Senator Huey Long.[19]

On March 6, Banks had addressed another mass meeting of the GGC.
The rally—which, unknown at the time, would be the last such gathering—
attracted approximately two thousand people to the front lawn of the courthouse on Oakdale Avenue. GGC speakers stood on the top steps of the main
entrance, giving them a good view of the crowd. Directly across Oakdale from
the courthouse lawn, standing among the oak trees near Medford's Carnegie
Library, were several staff members of the *Tribune* and anti-GGC observers.
Henrietta Martin sarcastically drew her audience's attention to the onlookers

on the other side of the street, pointing and saying, "There, that is some of that 'brave one hundred,'" before she went on to speak of Franklin Roosevelt's inauguration two days before. She dwelt particularly on the mid-February assassination attempt in Miami, Florida, that had taken the life of Roosevelt's visitor, Chicago mayor Anton Cermak, stating that the assassination was part of a much larger conspiracy. [20] Earl Fehl used Roosevelt's inaugural speech as a theme, paraphrasing the new president's words about the "people's mandate for direct vigorous action." Gesticulating forcefully, Fehl heaped scorn on the "Committee of One Hundred" and the "display of the State Police.[21] Llewellyn Banks spoke last. The *Daily News* was about to be repossessed, and Banks reminded his listeners that "you were told . . . that if they could close the *News* that you would have peace in Jackson County." You were told that Llewellyn A. Banks was a "disturber of the peace" (a voice from the crowd added, "A riotous man!") "Yes, a 'riotous man.' Now, my friends, the Medford *Daily News* was stolen . . . deliberately stolen into the hands of thieves. . . . I see some of the criminals in this crowd." Concluding his brief speech, Banks turned a defiant gaze over the heads of supporters toward his enemies across the street and stated that "unless we can have justice, I will take the field in revolution against you people—now make the most of it."[22]

LLEWELLYN BANKS, THE "TIGER" AT BAY

By mid-March, Banks feared capture and destruction at the hands of his enemies. Robert Ruhl characterized Llewellyn Banks as "cunning . . . and dangerous as a . . . tiger." At first not among those indicted for the ballot-theft conspiracy, Banks confronted many creditors who closed in with civil suits. By court order, the *Daily News* was transferred to its creditors on March 15. The procedure took place in the *News*'s Main Street building. Although GGC members and others packed the lobby, plainclothes policemen kept order. Banks's orchards and packinghouse were also seized. He reacted to such defeats with accusations that "gang" members plotted his death. At times hiding for extended periods at the homes of supporters, such as Dr. Swedenburg in Ashland, during February, Banks remained in his West Main Street house in Medford through the second week of March, unwilling to venture out without an armed guard. A barber (a GGC member) came to Banks's home to give him a haircut. Other supporters came to the publisher with warnings of possible assassination.[23]

Banks also responded with a counterthreat. In February, he and Fehl had urged Schermerhorn to arrest George Codding and other unfriendly county officials. Initially their plan involved simply holding the men incommunicado somewhere just beyond the county or state line until the GGC had asserted full control over county government. Soon, however, the scheme evolved into holding Codding for ransom or, "if necessary," killing him. When Schermerhorn balked, Banks met with hard-core GGC members from the Evans Creek Valley to organize a "secret group of fighting men." Guns were to be cached at two abandoned mines and at a "log-house" redoubt in the hills. Banks told the men that he "meant business. . . . If anyone did not want to go through [with the plan,] this was the time to drop out."[24]

At about 8:30 a.m. on March 16, sixty-three-year-old Medford constable George Prescott joined Detective Sergeant James O'Brien of the state police at city hall. The OSP contingent operated from a temporary command post at the building. Prescott and O'Brien had worked together serving arrest warrants on the ballot-theft suspects and other tasks related to the recent turmoil. On this day, they were to go to the home of Llewellyn Banks to arrest him as a conspirator in the ballot theft; the ongoing investigation had recently provided sufficient evidence to implicate Banks in the courthouse break-in.

Sheriff Schermerhorn's arresting authority had been revoked by the circuit court, as had that of his deputies. Prescott, who had been delegated the responsibility within the city limits, was a former traffic officer, now nearing retirement, and a familiar figure on the streets of Medford. Called a "bandit" by Banks for his part in confiscating rolls of newsprint, Prescott was known to friends as a quiet married man who shouldered his duties during the excitement of 1932–1933 without complaint. Some GGC supporters later accused him of calling them "anarchists," and even of threatening to kill Llewellyn Banks, but there is no credible evidence to substantiate the latter claim. However, Prescott doubtless shared the anti-Banks sentiments of the Medford legal establishment.[25]

Prescott expressed to O'Brien his misgivings about the impending arrest. Banks had publicly threatened to shoot any officer that attempted to enter his home. According to O'Brien's written statement later that day, the two joked a bit about the subject. O'Brien said, "George, you never want to get nervous until it is all over with—then . . . you'll eliminate a lot of nerve trouble." Laughing at O'Brien's assertion that "only the mean die young," the elderly Prescott responded with a joke, "Yes. . . . And there's one thing that is certain . . . the old never die young." The two men, after retrieving O'Brien's large-caliber service revolver and arranging for two other state police officers to cover the rear entrance of the house, left for the Banks residence at about 10:00 a.m.[26]

At home that morning, Llewellyn Banks had determined to elude arrest by fleeing to the mountains. With the *News* now gone, and having received word that a new arrest warrant would be served on Earl Fehl that day, Banks's position seemed desperate. Unknown to Banks, however, Fehl had escaped immediate arrest by hiding at downtown Medford's Holland Hotel for two days. A few days before, Banks had arranged for refuge: an elderly miner and GGC member named Geiger invited Banks to hide at his remote log cabin on Forest Creek, in the hills west of Jacksonville. Preparing to leave for Geiger's cabin later in the day, Banks packed a valise of "mountain clothing" and dressed in his "golf suit" of plus-four knickers and heavy sweater. In the home's foyer, Banks set out a holstered .44 Smith and Wesson revolver and a 30.06 Newton hunting rifle, a "hard shooting gun" he had purchased years before for cougar hunting in the southern Sierras.[27]

Early in the morning, Banks dictated a letter to his secretary, Janet Guches, returning the quit-claim deed for a small orchard to GGC supporter Reverend L. F. Belknap, who Banks hoped would help raise additional funds for any forthcoming bond. Edith Banks, out meeting with another GGC leader, previously had left a note for her husband, pleading for Banks not to issue a "written bulletin . . . to the gunmen" for assistance during any imminent "fight." She counseled him to use "word of mouth" instead and thereby possibly avoid arrest for criminal syndicalism. Mrs. Banks returned home around 9:30 that morning. Shortly afterward, Guches left the house to deliver the Belknap note. Banks also penned two brief notes, one to Medford's police chief and another to the head of the Oregon State Police, informing them that he would refuse to submit to arrest. Banks loyalist E. A. Fleming arrived unannounced around 9:45 a.m. to discuss GGC plans to raise bond money for some of the ballot-theft suspects, thereby delaying Banks's departure to Forest Creek.[28]

Officers Prescott and O'Brien arrived at the Banks residence around 10:15 a.m. They parked the Nash police sedan on West Main Street, directly in front of the home. O'Brien, carrying his small pistol in his coat pocket, left the large service revolver in the car. Officers C. A. Warren and A. K. Lumsden turned off onto Peach Street and drove up the alley to the rear of Banks's house. After some reassuring words outside the car about Banks "just making a lot of noise," Prescott and O'Brien mounted the steps of the front porch, where Prescott used the heavy iron door-knocker to announce their presence.

The two officers were plainly visible through the door's paneled-glass window. Edith Banks opened the door with the burglar-chain latched and tossed her husband's two notes out onto the porch, saying, "Here's two letters for you." Prescott responded, "I am sorry, Mrs. Banks, but I have a bench warrant for your husband." Before she could attempt to shut the door, Prescott placed his foot in the threshold to keep it ajar, and said, "Just a minute, I will give you that warrant and let you read it." As Prescott reached into his overcoat pocket for the papers, the woman stepped back and Llewellyn Banks appeared with his hunting rifle leveled at Prescott, pointed through the slightly open doorway, and fired. Prescott fell back into O'Brien's arms and both men toppled to the floor. Prescott died almost immediately, and O'Brien retreated from the porch.[29]

E. A. Fleming, who had unexpectedly witnessed the shooting from Bank's living room, fled out the back door and was arrested by Warren and Lumsden. O'Brien, fearing that he might be shot before he could speak to fellow officers, scrawled a note: "10:20 Officer Prescott killed . . . Banks shot with a rifle from doorway." O'Brien ran to the car, where he strapped on his service revolver and put a tear-gas bomb into his coat pocket. He then went to a nearby apartment house and telephoned his superiors to report the shooting and request reinforcements. Within minutes the sirens of police cars brought a crowd of onlookers to West Main Street. O'Brien and other officers cleared the street of bystanders and were preparing for a tear-gas assault of the house when Edith Banks telephoned police headquarters, stating that her husband would peacefully submit to arrest but only to county deputy sheriff Phil Lowd. When state police captain Lee Bown and the former Banks supporter Lowd entered the front door to make the arrest, Banks shook the captain's hand and explained that because Prescott had tried to force his way into the house, he had justifiably shot him "just like any burglar."[30]

Bown escorted Banks out to the waiting police sedan. Concluding that incarceration of Banks within Jackson County held too high a risk of further violence, state police officers took him to the Josephine County jail in Grants Pass. Banks sat between Bown and Lowd in the rear seat of the car. During the trip, Banks talked about guns, mentioning in particular how he had always wanted to shoot a mountain lion with the Newton. He expressed regret at the death of George Prescott but reflected that the constable, as "an old timer," had acted stubbornly, and simply did not "know when to leave well enough alone." Before arriving in Grants Pass, Banks asked for one favor: "I am used to having things clean, and I would like you to put me in a clean cell. I was never used to dirt."[31]

The day before the shooting, Captain Bown, worried about an insurrection by GGC members, had sent an emergency request to Salem for thirty more officers. One of the state police cars, speeding south to Jackson County with sirens wailing, collided with another automobile. The driver, a Portland realtor, died of his injuries. Immediately after the shooting, uniformed officers appeared in force on the streets of Medford, armed with tear gas and shotguns. Warrants for an additional twenty-three suspects in the ballot theft were issued that afternoon. "Wholesale arrests" of GGC members soon followed.[32] Sergeant O'Brien stated that "agitators were quickly clamped in jail without warrant, warning or ceremony; we were determined to clean it out to the very core."[33]

Two days later, Governor Meier instructed Oregon attorney general I. H. Van Winkle to conduct a special investigation of the Jackson County affair and to prosecute all those charged with criminal syndicalism or related crimes. Meier also sent by airplane a special order to the southern Oregon circuit court for Sheriff Schermerhorn's removal from office. Robert Ruhl wrote immediately to Meier with his thanks, particularly the "incalculable assistance" of the state police, whose "aloof[ness] from local dissensions" allowed them to keep order when an "actual reign of terror threatened."[34]

The violent turn in southern Oregon received wide press coverage, with the wire story appearing in newspapers from San Francisco to New York City. As a result of the news, executives of a Massachusetts bonding insurance company became worried about conditions in distant Jackson County, sending a telegram to its Oregon representatives revoking the surety bond for Gordon Schermerhorn. The *Oregonian* gave the shooting and related events much front-section and editorial attention over the next few weeks.[35]

Many Good Government Congress members had drifted back to their homes and farms by the time of the March 19 funeral for George Prescott. According to the Portland press, more than three thousand people, headed by the Elks Club band and the American Legion, filed down Main Street to the Presbyterian Church to pay their last respects to the slain officer. After two weeks in Grants Pass, Llewellyn Banks was transferred to a cell in the Jackson County jail, on the upper floor of the courthouse. Banks reportedly kept his cell in meticulous order throughout his stay. The new county jailer, Fred Kelly (twin brother of attorney E. E. Kelly), kept daily notes of Banks's demeanor, which he consistently recorded as "calm," "cheerful," or "remorseless." GGC admirers visited Banks often, bringing him candy and cakes, as well as the cigarettes he smoked constantly. Banks's attorney, William Phipps, also made regular visits, earning Kelly's ire as a "bull artist . . . coarse as a rasp." Although admitting that Banks was the most "rational, intelligent, and least troublesome" of his GGC inmates, Kelly at one point opined that Banks, so "vain of appearance and cold-blooded," was "hardly human."[36]

While imprisoned in the county jail, Banks received a brief note from Senator Huey Long. Long stated that he had found Banks's early March letter "quite interesting." But, while admitting that he, too, had experienced a "stormy career," the Louisiana senator declined to inject himself into the Jackson County situation.[37]

8
Rebellion Crushed

Despite Llewellyn Banks's repeated evocation of the American Revolution as the guiding spirit that propelled the Good Government Congress movement, and despite the coast-to-coast news coverage of the shooting, the killing of George Prescott was not, in the end, a "shot heard round the world." Outside of the Pacific Northwest, it was barely audible. Nevertheless, the climax of Jackson County's turmoil reflected the dangerous level of social unrest elsewhere in the Pacific Northwest and the nation.

During April 1933, Oregon newspapers brought word of violent protests to the north and far to the east. In Seattle a crowd of unemployed men, demonstrating against the eviction of a family, rioted and injured the King County sheriff and eight deputies. In Iowa the governor declared martial law in the town of Le Mars after a crowd of angry farmers dragged a foreclosure judge from his courtroom and threatened to hang him. Possibly inspired by the actions such as those of the Iowa farmers and the Good Government Congress, the People's Protective League of Vancouver, Washington, attempted to block farm foreclosure sales by marching on the Clark County courthouse. With an eye toward these events outside of Jackson County, an *Oregonian* editorial piece blamed Llewellyn Banks for inciting anger and violence among deluded followers.[1]

FRAGMENTATION AND COLLAPSE

In Jackson County, the Prescott shooting vindicated community leaders who had warned of violent outcomes from Bank's demagoguery. Titling his March 16 editorial "Too Late!," Robert Ruhl wrote that "the tragedy that the *Mail Tribune* has feared—that it has fought with everything in its power for months has at last happened."

> Thus ends the dastardly campaign of inflammatory agitation, the contemptible circulation of lies . . . which has been going on in this community for so long, with just one purpose in view—to destroy the community, to allow one man to dominate it . . . by armed forces, threats and blackguardism.[2]

More important, the tragedy split the ranks of the Good Government Congress into apostates and hard-core loyalists. Appalled by the shooting and frightened for their personal reputations, many GGC people renounced their memberships while others rallied behind Banks and Fehl as the true martyrs. According to a front-page article in the *Mail Tribune* published on the afternoon of the shooting, a "virtual stampede of Good Government Congress members to get out of the lawless organization" began that day.[3] The death of George Prescott caused many GGC sympathizers to abandon the organization within hours of the news. Immediately after the shooting, L. E. Fitch, a GGC loyalist, met another GGC member on Medford's Main Street. A brawl ensued when the other man decried the shooting and Fitch called him a "stool pigeon." Fitch received a pistol-whipping that required hospitalization for head injuries. Courthouse staff took telephone memoranda shortly after the shooting from a number of GGC members who called the district attorney, urgently attempting to distance themselves from the organization.[4]

When Codding and private attorneys advised such people to announce their withdrawals publicly, the editorial pages of the *Tribune*, beginning the afternoon of the shooting, printed many letters from Banks's former supporters. Dave Gould, of Medford, complaining to Ruhl that GGC officials refused to return his membership card, wrote on March 16 to announce his "absolute withdrawal, to take effect at once." The following day, the *Tribune* carried similar renunciations from more than twenty GGC members. Members of the Applebaker family and other residents of the Applegate Valley signed a letter stating that, "whereas, by reason of misrepresentation made ... as to the grievances to be remedied and the purpose and scope of the so-called Good Government Congress" they originally had become unwitting members, they now publicly resigned from such organization and pledged their support "to the upholding of law." Other writers voiced support of the stated principles of the GGC even as they denounced the violent actions of its leaders.[5]

A group of eight GGC members from Talent provided Codding with a copy of their letter to the organization's secretary, demanding return of their cards in light of "the agitation of the Good Gov't Congress Leaders." (This particular note, dated March 14, may be genuine evidence of a tide of abandonment prior to the shooting; alternatively, it may have been backdated to strengthen the signers' anti-GGC appearance.)[6]

One Evans Creek family appealed to Codding to force the return of their GGC cards, stating that the cards "were sent to us by the bus driver of the school and we, like most of our good neighbors, thought it was a nation[wide] affair." Pointing out that they lived "39 miles from Medford, at the forks of the Creek," they had had no chance "to hear all you people in town knew" and that

"it was all misrepresented to us." Codding replied, thanking the family for joining the "large number of good people" who, "misled and unduly influenced by
vicious propaganda," had now abandoned the GGC. He added his hope that
"all the substantial and reliable citizens" who had been so duped would now
become thoroughly informed about the organization's real purposes.[7]

Some signers of GGC petitions, who claimed never to have joined the
organization, urged Codding that their names be struck from the documents.
Several prominent GGC members, such as Orlen R. Kring and Edwin H. Malkemus, both Protestant ministers closely associated with Banks, quickly joined
the chorus of ex-members. Kring, who claimed to have joined the movement
"for the purpose of helping the common class of people and rehabilitation for
the working man," told Ruhl that he was "for law and order always but not the
kind where one person wants full control."[8]

Other Good Government Congress supporters still believed in the cause
and its leaders. A day after the shooting, Mrs. Arthur LaDieu was taken into
custody after claiming that Constable Prescott "got what was coming to him"
and warning that "there will be more of this." Shortly before the shooting, her
husband had pledged that, "sink or swim," he would "stay with Mr. Banks."
Regarding the forthcoming trials of Banks and Fehl, one anonymous GGC
supporter warned Ruhl to "change your ways; Prosecute all criminals, not
upright citizens." Within days after the shooting, L. M. Sweet, the adamantly
pro-GGC mail carrier of Sams Valley, distributed petitions demanding Sheriff
Schermerhorn's retention in office despite his obvious participation in the ballot theft.[9]

The towns of Rogue River and Gold Hill held a hard core of active
GGC loyalists. One Gold Hill man, according to the district attorney's local
informant, continued to "preach sedition to . . . boys and young men" and
claimed that he could "take 25 men to Medford and clean out the Gang."
Another informant stated that, during April and May, one Evans Creek resident welcomed local GGC insurgents to his property for nighttime political
discussions around a bonfire. Several Rogue River citizens continued to speak
openly of their belief that Banks was "justified in killing officer Prescott." They
emphasized their disgust with law enforcement officers generally and the state
police in particular.[10]

In May, Codding's Rogue River informant reported that some local
insurgents, who frequented "bootlegger Corey's new log-cabin dive and
GGC headquarters," had met with fellow "[guer]rillas" from Douglas County
to discuss "dynamiting D. H. Ferry's [mining dredge] operation or Copco's
hydroelectric plant on the Rogue River." Rather than warning of further
violence, some of Codding's informants simply desired to settle old scores.

One Ashland resident offered to stand as a character witness against realtor and would-be politico Thomas Breechen, one of the ballot-theft defendants, whom he described as a "crooked Old RATTLE SNAKE."[11]

In his March 17 editorial, "The Challenge Is Accepted," Ruhl called for peace. Although he attempted to shame some rural areas for their GGC support—admitting that the *Tribune* had failed "to appreciate the depths of depravity to which certain sections of Jackson County had fallen"—Ruhl also appealed to rural people living in widely separated sections of the county for unity, calling on "an aroused and militant citizenship . . . that will stand 100 percent" behind constituted authority. He vowed that the people of Jackson County would not rest "until this section of Oregon, from Ashland to Rogue River and from the Applegate to Roxy Anne, is cleaned up." Ruhl urged southern Oregon to be "freed of these ballot burners, horsewhippers and murderers . . . freed of them FOREVER!"[12]

With their leaders in jail, and with anti-GGC feelings rising, holdout members of the Good Government Congress faced isolation. Given the changing local sentiment, there could be no more mass rallies on the courthouse steps. On the very afternoon of Prescott's death, the American Legion announced plans for a suitable memorial to the officer. Contributions poured in, stated the *Tribune*, from Medford residents "who represented many classes of people." A large granite boulder, quarried from the Siskiyous just south of Ashland, held a bronze plaque honoring "George J. Prescott, who gave his life in the discharge of his duty." The Legion placed the stone in the small city park facing West Main Street, one block from the county courthouse. At Ruhl's private urging, the memorial was kept extremely simple so that most contributions would go into a trust fund for Prescott's widow. According to Ruhl, the monument—unveiled a few days after Llewellyn Banks began trial on charges of first-degree murder—was tribute to one who had tried to "protect [the people's] privileges under democracy, whatever the cost."[13]

ESTABLISHMENT'S TRIUMPH: THE GGC TRIALS

Llewellyn and Edith Banks, both incarcerated in the Jackson County jail by late March, each faced charges of first-degree murder. Llewellyn Banks occupied an isolated cell that permitted no communication with his fellow GGC defendants. Supporters of the Banks couple came regularly to the courthouse. Most of them seem to have been women, including May Powell and Henrietta Martin. Ariel Pomeroy visited often, bringing encouragement and, on Good Friday, an Easter lily for Edith Banks. As his trial neared, Banks told Pomeroy of his detachment from the course of events: "We are bound to . . . view this drama as though we are not part of it."[14]

The former publisher's legal defense strategy indicated that Banks, facing the death penalty, intended to struggle for freedom and exoneration. One of his brothers, W. A. Banks, came to Medford from southern California to help arrange the legal defense. Rumored to be wealthy, the Los Angeles resident nevertheless encouraged Pomeroy in her efforts to raise a legal fund for his brother. Joined in Medford by Banks's sister, Evelyn Banks Moran, and her husband, prominent Cleveland businessman George F. Moran, W. A. Banks hired a battery of five attorneys for the couple's defense. Providing local knowledge were Thomas J. Enright, the 1932 Banks-Fehl candidate for district attorney, and William Phipps, the aging former Populist and Klan supporter. Upstate defense lawyers Frank J. Lonergan, Charles A. Hardy, and Joseph L. Hammersly were expected to provide the polished courtroom experience needed for the upcoming trial. Hammersly's large retainer of $2,500 earned jailer Kelly's comment as "some fee, even in Los Angeles."[15]

At first, Llewellyn Banks attempted to construct his defense around the supposed existence of a private detective he claimed to have hired in March. This man, whose real name Banks said he could not recall, purportedly served as the publisher's special bodyguard; Banks claimed that this phantom-like figure actually fired the fatal shot and escaped during the ensuing confusion. At his attorneys' insistence, Banks dropped this line of defense. Admitting that their client had fired the shot, they instead intended to concentrate on a history of persecution and threats by his enemies, including Prescott, and to portray Banks's deed as an act of temporary insanity. Although strenuously objecting to this plan as undignified, in late April Banks accepted its wisdom.[16]

The prosecution's team, under the direct supervision of Attorney General I. H. Van Winkle, included Assistant Attorney General William S. Levens, aided by Jackson County's Codding and Neilson. Ralph P. Moody, appointed as an assistant attorney general especially for the Banks trial, was a veteran Oregon corporate lawyer and a special assistant US attorney general during the 1920s. He had come to Medford in the early 1930s to represent the legal interests of the Southern Pacific Railroad and, on occasion, the California-Oregon Power Company. An experienced courtroom debater, Moody had assisted Codding during the GGC turmoil.[17]

The defense, providing an exhibit of clippings from the *Mail Tribune*, moved for a change of venue on the grounds that "the inhabitants of [Jackson County] are so biased and prejudiced . . . that a fair and impartial jury cannot be selected." Judge Skipworth agreed and moved the trial to the state circuit court for Lane County, in Eugene. A jury of six men and six women, most of them of working-class or farming backgrounds, was chosen during late April, and the trial was set to open in the Lane County courthouse on May 3. On

May 2, during his closing examination of prospective jurors, the sixty-year-old Levens complained of chest pains and was aided into Judge Skipworth's chambers. Rushed by state policemen to a doctor's office, Levens died of cardiac failure within an hour. Moody took over as head of the prosecution and the trial began on schedule the following day.[18]

Because of the trial's sensational nature and the heavy press coverage, the large upstairs courtroom in the ornate brick courthouse was filled to capacity for the opening statements. Moody portrayed Banks and his wife as cold-blooded killers who deserved punishment for murder in the first degree: "Banks laid in wait for Prescott and took dead aim at him through the partly open door." Defense counsel Hammersly countered that Llewellyn Banks had fired "as a warning to marauders who were trying to force their way in." Edith Banks, stressed the defense, literally had "been in the kitchen" just prior to the shooting; "she was at home where a good wife and a good mother should be." Hammersly, projecting Banks's populist appeal toward the jurors, also underlined the wealth and power of the defendant's enemies.[19]

The state's case entailed testimony from more than sixty witnesses and accounted for more than two weeks of the three-week-long trial. The old courtroom's acoustics were poor, and opened windows meant that the noise of traffic and barking dogs regularly forced witnesses to repeat themselves. Still, public attendance remained heavy throughout the trial. Moody's prosecution moved from two eyewitnesses of the shooting, Sergeant James O'Brien and a cooperative E. A. Fleming, through to the coroner who performed Prescott's autopsy. Moody exploded the defense's opening assertion that Prescott had been holding a gun by demonstrating that the fatal wound, which had passed through Prescott's left hand, could have been inflicted on the officer only as he was reaching into his coat's inside pocket with his right hand while holding the coat open with his left.

The defense called twenty-four witnesses. Several of them were prominent character witnesses such as Dr. Francis Swedenburg and retired Medford banker William Gore. Others included physician "alienists" who testified to Banks's "transitory mania," but most witnesses recounted either having heard George Prescott threaten the life of Banks or having seen Prescott mount the front porch with a gun aimed to fire. The prosecution's numerous rebuttal witnesses cast serious doubt on the veracity of this line of Banks's defense. As a result, jurors probably discounted much of the defense's case as perjured testimony.[20]

The defense's star witness was Llewellyn Banks, who spent a full day on the stand under the gentle prodding of attorney Lonergan. The defendant, wearing his customary Norfolk jacket, spoke at great length and with little prompting. One anti-Banks observer had warned the prosecution to beware of the man's ability "to hypnotize [the jury] with twisted half-truths." And Banks—after proudly tracing his genealogy directly back to "John Alden of the Mayflower" and reviewing his formative childhood experiences on the Ohio farm—recited the full litany of injustices he had suffered at the hands of the "Medford gang." Occasionally shouting and pounding on the arm of his chair in anger, Banks told jurors in detail of the conspiracy that took shape after he first challenged the fruit-packers' Traffic Association.[21]

Lonergan then questioned Banks about his "dizzy spells" and "visions." Banks readily admitted to having experienced a number of powerful visionary dreams that later had come true. One of them was young Banks's 1898 vision of a naval battle on Lake Erie, which he took as prophesy of the American victory over Spain at the Battle of Santiago. Lonergan brought the witness to the morning of March 16 with testimony about the defendant's fear for his life. Describing the moments of the shooting, Banks stated that, as the front door was "gradually opening, . . . I saw what I believed to be a pistol. . . . I believed at that instant that that door would break open." Banks portrayed his wife as struggling to hold the door shut against the intruder and shouting, "You shall not come in," as he raised his rifle and shot in desperate self-defense.

The prosecution stunned the courtroom when its long-awaited cross-examination ended after less than five minutes; Moody evidently hoped to impress the jury with his utter contempt for the defendant's story. Although Edith Banks's subsequent testimony repeated the story of Prescott's threatening gun, Moody's thundering closing argument dismissed Llewellyn Banks "as a coward hiding behind a woman's skirt," and accused the couple of acting with premeditation and in concert to take the life of George Prescott. He waved the bloody warrant taken from Prescott's coat pocket and demanded the death penalty for both. Lonergan closed with a plea to the jurors for mercy and understanding of the extraordinary situation in Jackson County.[22]

The jury deliberated for ten hours and returned its verdict on the afternoon of May 21. Although acquitting his wife of the charges, the jurors found Llewellyn Banks guilty of murder in the second degree, which carried a mandatory sentence of life imprisonment. Banks took the verdict without outward emotion. He issued a brief statement to the press: "I am undismayed. I have implicit faith in the eternal cause of righteousness. I have been persecuted, prosecuted, and convicted by the . . . special privilege interests."[23]

Following the trial, the prosecution immediately opened a probe on perjury by seven of Banks's defense witnesses. The *Oregonian* reflected that the outcome was "doubtless as just . . . for this unhappy affair as could be achieved." The newspaper reflected that, although Banks probably was insane, he deserved "permanent confinement." A first-degree verdict with a life sentence would have been far more appropriate, but the paper admitted that the end result of the jurors' decision was the same.[24]

The state held the remaining GGC trials throughout the summer of 1933, with Jackson County serving as the venue for most of the court proceedings. Although twenty-three individuals had been indicted for the ballot theft, other criminal acts also led to trial. Henrietta Martin and three accomplices in the Main Street assault on Leonard Hall stood accused of "riotous and disorderly conduct." Martin's horsewhip was the prosecution's main exhibit.[25] Other GGC members, involved in brawls or threats during February and March, faced similar charges. The ballot-theft suspects provided the main grist for the legal mill. The succession of trials for burglary and criminal syndicalism, presided over by Judge Skipworth and prosecuted by Moody, lasted into August, with the sentencing of the defendants delayed until the end of the proceedings.

News manager Arthur LaDieu's trial led off the series in early June. Testimony from the Sexton brothers, Virgil Edington, and other participants convicted LaDieu as one of the main leaders in the theft. The trial of Rogue River mayor Walter Jones followed in mid-month, with the same testimony that had been presented in LaDieu's trial. The jury quickly found Jones guilty. The third trial, of former county jailer John Glenn, came to a temporary halt when one juror was found to have stated that Banks was "justified in killing Prescott." Skipworth dismissed the entire jury. With the original jury list all but exhausted, an entirely new list of potential jurors was assembled. The prosecution proved even less selective with the second jury, which found Glenn, a Spanish-American War veteran, innocent. The district attorney's staff, describing the largely rural group as "a poison-oak jury . . . [composed of] wood choppers," noted that it contained at least three GGC sympathizers.[26]

Former sheriff Gordon Schermerhorn's trial began after the July 4 holiday. Schermerhorn, who had been replaced at Governor Meier's repeated order by acting sheriff Walter Olmscheid, continued the struggle to regain office during his trial. When Olmscheid's emergency appointment expired on July 10, Schermerhorn unsuccessfully demanded to resume duty as county sheriff. After testimony from fifty prosecution witnesses implicating the former sheriff in the theft as well as in suppressing evidence during the investigation, the jury found Schermerhorn guilty. The proceeding's length, combined with Medford's summer heat, may have increased the trial's rancorous atmosphere. Prosecutor Moody, said to have been drinking heavily, angrily shouted, "You are lying!" at pro-GGC defense witnesses from places like the Applegate Valley.[27]

The trial of Judge Earl Fehl promised to be the capstone of the prosecution's campaign. By mid-July, most of the other defendants had either pled guilty or, having played very minor roles in the theft, would likely have their cases dismissed. Fehl's attorneys requested a change of venue, due to widespread prejudice against their client, and Judge Skipworth admitted that it was "getting to be a battle of wits to select a jury in this county." Adding to the charged atmosphere, Medford radio station KMED asked permission to broadcast the Fehl trial. Denying the station's request, Skipworth agreed to move the trial to Klamath Falls.[28]

Earl Fehl's trial lasted less than two weeks. As in the previous trials, the state paraded numerous witnesses who placed the defendant at the crime scene just prior to the break-in. The Reverend Orlen Kring testified to incriminating statements made by Fehl prior to the theft. Although Fehl had not actually removed any of the ten thousand ballots himself, Moody convincingly portrayed him as "the mastermind" of the theft. Fehl spent more than eight hours on the stand, denying his involvement and explaining the conspiracy against him. The Klamath County jurors took only twenty minutes to find him guilty. Upon Fehl's conviction, Governor Meier immediately appointed Republican state legislator Earl B. Day as new county judge.[29]

Judge Skipworth sentenced the ballot-theft defendants in early August. Fehl received the maximum penalty of four years in the state penitentiary, as did LaDieu and Jones. Schermerhorn was sentenced to three years, and Breechen received an eighteen-month sentence. Skipworth gave several other participants penalties ranging up to a year. GGC secretary and Greensprings Mountain Boy Jean Conners received a suspended three-year sentence, contingent that he "stay out of Jackson County for at least one year." Moody, stating that he did not want to carry on the prosecution "to the degree that it will become persecution," recommended leniency for the remaining ballot thieves; Skipworth either dismissed their cases or granted them immediate parole.[30]

Fehl immediately proclaimed his innocence from the Klamath County jail. His lengthy letter, printed in the Klamath Falls *Evening Herald*, contained familiar themes. Fehl, who previously had compared his tribulations to the crucifixion of Christ, stoically accepted his fate: "The cross that I am called upon to bear must be borne alone. The jury has spoken." Still, Fehl urged his friends "to take steps to protect life, liberty and property" by calling public attention to the "awfulness of the grasp of a conspiracy."[31]

Such sentiments probably spurred GGC supporter Joseph B. "Budd" Johnston when he accosted Chuck Davis, the Fehl-appointed county employee who had testified against the judge in Klamath Falls. The sixty-two-year-old Johnston confronted Davis on a Medford street the day after Fehl's conviction, hurling insults at the turncoat. During the brief fistfight that followed, Davis, a former professional boxer, struck the older man and knocked him to the pavement. His head hitting the concrete curb, Johnston lost consciousness and died of a fractured skull within a few minutes. The *Oregonian*, commenting that "tragedy again stalks at Medford as a result of hatred engendered by the Banks case," put the blame for Johnston's death squarely on the shoulders of the former publisher:

> Never has there been in the life of Oregon another man who has done such widespread harm as Banks. His megalomania, his obsession of persecution, his violent hatred of all who crossed his purposes, his terrifically perverted leadership, have spread untold harm. Now he sits smugly in a cell, boasting of his comforts. . . . The Johnston tragedy must be counted another to be laid on the doorstep of Banks.[32]

Johnston's widow took a different view. In a letter referring to her husband's family members back in his home state of Pennsylvania, she claimed that they could not understand "why Davis alone, who should have been taking his medicine with the rest [of the ballot thieves], was permitted by the State . . . to roam the streets freely." The Johnston family, who had read "Eastern newspaper accounts of the [county's] political fracas," had been dumbfounded by the events.[33]

The events of February and March 1933 gained Jackson County brief nationwide notoriety. The local establishment, on the offensive since mid-March, seized the opportunity offered by the GGC trials to declare triumph and rally the forces of order. Shortly after the shooting, Ruhl told Governor Meier that the "vast majority of the people" in southern Oregon, "including the deluded members of the Good Government Congress, at last see the light clearly." Ruhl was sure "the victory has been won—the mopping up process alone remains to be done." The anti-sedition mood became widespread. During the Banks trial, Moody claimed to have received many supportive letters "from all portions of the State." The establishment's momentum was real enough. However, the public confidence of establishment members such as Ruhl and Moody masked the urgency of the campaign that had been waged against the Good Government Congress throughout the spring and summer of 1933.[34]

George Codding led the unpublicized effort to repress the insurgent threat once and for all. Codding's notes and correspondence during 1933 indicate that the district attorney's office coordinated the anti-GGC activities of law enforcement officials and encouraged influential private individuals to undertake similar but informal efforts. Codding and his assistants compiled what they called the "Jackson County Black List," which held the names of all known GGC members and sympathizers (the latter drawn largely from the

Norton recall petition). The district attorney's office scanned the venire lists of potential jurors for such persons and eliminated them through challenge. Codding worked with his counterparts in Lane and Klamath Counties to ensure acceptable juries for the Banks and Fehl trials. Although, as in the case of the John Glenn jury, the district attorney's effort did not always succeed, the legal establishment put forth a sustained and widespread effort to cleanse the juries of any "radical" taint. A network of local informants provided individual assessments of potential jurors. In addition, some of them cautioned against accepting any jurors from certain communities. One informant recommended that "absolutely no person from the town of Rogue River or the remote Evans Creek hamlet of Wimer be accepted on ballot theft juries, except possibly Victor Birdseye."[35] Another informant urged Codding to "lookout for all Owen-Oregon [Lumber Company] employees and for any residents of Butte Falls."[36]

A Miss Johnson of Ashland assessed potential jurors from the county's southern section. Eliminating one man from consideration as a "Bolshevik," she encouraged selection of another Ashlander, a carpenter, as "a splendid, substantial middle-class type . . . utterly remote from either the GGC or the 'Committee of 100.'" Johnson found a third venireman to be "acceptable . . . because of his natural temperament," but also "sufficiently silent" about his anti-GGC feelings to be unobjectionable to the defense. She concluded that the wife of a railroad employee, "one of the Daughters of the Nile Queens . . . [who sought] vainly to lead in society," would prove to be "righteously fair." Johnson described one of Ashland's more prominent businessmen, a Kiwanis leader, as "an old maid type . . . who plays golf religiously," but felt that he "would have the right sort of attitude toward ballot stealing."[37]

The effort of the district attorney and the state police to collect unwitting confessions from ballot-theft suspects involved well-planned eavesdropping and transcription of jail-cell conversations. The district attorney's office continued its tactic of audio surveillance throughout the summer, evidently even listening in to daily client-attorney conversations that took place at the courthouse (where Earl Fehl, out on bail, still maintained an office). Court stenographers Looker and Cuffel may have used microphones or other devices hidden in the new courthouse's system of heating ducts that enabled them to overhear and record in shorthand the intimate legal discussions of Fehl, Jones, Enright, and others. Telephone conversations were similarly subject to eavesdropping. Some clandestinely transcribed conversations yielded little more than blustering dialogue that may have owed much to contemporary gangster films. For example, Fehl's defense attorney Enright, who repeatedly called Codding's assistant a "dirty rat" and "lowdown skunk," was overheard threatening to "beat up" assistant DA Neilson at the first opportunity. Although these conversations, evidently obtained illegally, did not appear as evidence in the trials, the prosecution no doubt used such privileged information to design its own courtroom strategy. Codding's office also obtained copies of confidential telegrams and personal letters sent to Banks and other defendants while incarcerated. It is possible that the district attorney received word about the content of other telegrams that were not subject to the jailer's inspection.[38]

The district attorney's efforts were not confined to those actually charged with the crimes of February and March. Upon learning during the Fehl trial that one young Jacksonville man continued to spout publicly the anti-gang line of the Good Government Congress, Codding suggested to his assistant "that a jolt might do this boy good."[39]

Although the state's behind-the-scenes legal, and possibly extralegal, campaign against the GGC certainly was no "white terror" of repression, it reflected little credit on the professional integrity of the participants. No doubt Codding felt that extraordinary times demanded extraordinary measures. In using such measures, however, he gave at least some, albeit after-the-fact, substance to the GGC's charges of a conspiracy by the county's legal officers.

The question of conspiracy brings up Banks's and Fehl's broader indictment of "the gang" as a clique of powerful and corrupt officeholders, attorneys, and business executives. Jackson County undeniably possessed an influential establishment, a coterie of professionals, executives, and merchants based in Medford. Like countless local establishments elsewhere in the nation during the early twentieth century, this group was relatively fluid, not formalized, and contained numerous competing subgroups. Nevertheless, by means of fruit-packing associations, private utility companies, and other institutions, Jackson County's establishment worked as a unit to incorporate southern Oregon into the system of big-business capitalism that had reigned triumphant in America since the late nineteenth century.[40] Medford was a small but important regional outpost in this national system. Establishment members obviously benefited personally, in terms of economic status and social prestige, from this process of incorporation. Members of the county's professional and commercial establishment, although often divided into factions, shared a consensus that ensured the continued dominance of this modernization process over the region's older, more rural-based politics.

Members of the establishment not only formed a "community of interests," they also interacted socially, regularly sharing comfortable middle-class pleasures such as golf and bridge. Such personal connections strengthened the web of their associations in business and politics. Concomitantly, some members of the elite probably felt considerable social distance from, if not disdain for, rural and working-class residents of the region.

However, Jackson County's establishment was neither a monolithic conspiracy nor was it a "corrupt gang." It is likely that some members did indulge in unethical or illegal practices to advance personal interests. Medford accountant A. R. Hoelting, the anti-GGC establishment loyalist, admitted as much in his letter to Governor Meier: "There is much rottenness, no doubt, in any community to stir up a stink over." But, aside from the repeated allegations of Banks and Fehl, there is nothing to suggest frequent, let alone systemic, corruption as a group endeavor. Regarding conspiracy, actions that, to Banks, seemed evidence of the Traffic Association's monstrous collusion was simply the packers' defensive reaction to an audacious newcomer's challenge. Most of Banks's financial woes originated with the Depression's financial collapse or his own intemperate behavior. The local establishment, although shedding few tears over his predicament, probably did little, in terms of premeditated actions, to create it. The pejorative term "gang" resonated among people who viewed the local elite from the outside looking in. To members of the establishment, having long enjoyed the view from inside, the term was both insulting and laughable. Their own political goals, although rarely without self-interest, were seen by them as fundamentally beneficial to the community at large.[41]

To supporters of the Good Government Congress, Robert Ruhl seemed the quintessential establishment figure. Originally reluctant to engage in open editorial combat with a competitor whom he privately despised, Ruhl proved a vocal and implacable foe of Llewellyn Banks after the Prescott shooting. He spearheaded the opposition to subsequent attempts to obtain pardon or parole for Banks. Ruhl, who had become the lightning rod of antiestablishment anger during the height of the turmoil, emerged from the fight with enhanced prestige and with his newspaper intact. Although the fortunate result was hardly something over which Ruhl had any personal control, the Mail Tribune found itself, in the words of the United Press Association's Pacific Division manager, "in sole possession of the field." Preparing to reestablish his company's interrupted franchise in southern Oregon with the Tribune, the wire-service man congratulated Ruhl on his newspaper's improved financial prospects: "The fight is over at Medford; the wrecking crew has departed. . . . Your situation is better than it has been in some years."[42]

THE PULITZER PRIZE—AND HISTORY'S VERDICT

In New York City on the evening of May 7, 1934, Columbia University president Nicholas Murray Butler announced the recipients of the Pulitzer Prizes for 1933. Speaking to the annual banquet gathered at the faculty club, Butler told the group that the Medford Mail Tribune had been awarded the Pulitzer's meritorious public service prize in journalism, "for stemming a rising tide of public insurrection which was the growth of a bitter political fight." The *Mail Tribune*, under Robert Ruhl, "took the leadership in pleading for straight-thinking and peace." The *New York Times* described how the *Tribune*, "under armed guard day and night, and in the face of constant threats of violence," conducted a vigorous editorial campaign against a rising "dictatorship in Southern Oregon."[43]

The Pulitzer story received a banner headline in the *Mail Tribune*. In his column the day after the award, Ruhl expressed surprise and deep pleasure that "this 'small town' daily" had been honored. He acknowledged his fellow journalists, particularly Leonard Hall, who had fought the GGC fight, and thanked all those in the community who had helped the *Tribune* through the difficult time of 1932–1933.[44]

When Ruhl had forwarded a scrapbook of *Tribune* articles and editorials for consideration by the Pulitzer committee in September 1933, he had titled the Good Government Congress episode as the "Jackson County Rebellion." Ruhl wrote to Dean Carl W. Ackerman of Columbia University's School of Journalism that his main purpose in submitting the material was, like any good journalist, to "get the story out," particularly to fellow newspaper editors outside of Oregon:

> I would certainly not claim [the "most distinguished service"] distinc-tion for the *Mail Tribune*. On the other hand, the local situation was so unusual—so incredible in fact—and the [*Tribune*] was for so long on such a hot spot, that I am sure the details . . . would be interesting to any newspaperman, if not to the country at large.[45]

Although Ruhl openly doubted that the Pulitzer award would go "to a small newspaper like this," especially for such a tumultuous news year as 1933, Dean Ackerman replied that, on the contrary, the Pulitzer jury regarded such papers with "sympathetic interest." Ackerman's assurance was well-founded. Since its establishment in 1917, the Pulitzer Prize meritorious public service award had often gone to small-town dailies for editorial crusades against local corruption and political extremism.[46]

When given advance notice of the prize, Ruhl begged off on Ackerman's invitation to attend the awards ceremony. The editor would have had to travel to New York by airplane, and Ruhl hated flying, but a more central reason was his self-admitted lifelong aversion to public speaking. Ruhl closed his letter of thanks with some general thoughts on "the small-town newspaper . . . as a force for good":

[Although their] field is so limited, opportunities so few . . . these papers, plugging along from day to day, do, as a whole, render a real service to their communities and to their country—and it is well to recognize the fact—good for the profession and good for the country.[47]

Ruhl's fellow Oregon editors offered more laurels to their colleague. Commenting on the *Mail Tribune*'s Pulitzer, the *Oregonian* praised its "editorial courage and judgment of a high order," and the Albany *Democrat-Herald* found Ruhl's "courage . . . and honesty" in keeping with "the best newspaper tradition."[48]

The Eugene *Register-Guard*, condemning the "fanatic Llewellyn Banks," noted that, "For a long time, Mr. Ruhl displayed great tolerance toward this strange opponent . . . [making] all possible effort to treat him with the courtesy which the unwritten law of newspaperdom requires one to show a competitor." It continued, "The Pulitzer award to the *Mail Tribune* is a warning to demagogues in and out of the business that quackery has become a tiresome fashion."[49]

Local reaction to the prize varied from pride to resentment. The county establishment saw the award as national recognition of its righteousness in the fight for law and order. On a more personal level, Ruhl's friend and former partner, Sumpter Smith, dismissed those who had criticized the *Tribune*'s initial reluctance to do battle; Smith felt that Ruhl's "conservative . . . line of attack [during] the unpleasantness in Jackson County was correct, and [it] won."[50]

However, in what might have stemmed from a long-term sense of grievance against Medford—and despite Ruhl's repeated acknowledgment of Leonard Hall's journalistic courage during the events of early 1933—some Jacksonville residents felt pique that the often-inflammatory *Miner* did not share the Pulitzer award.[51]

Other resentments went far deeper. Adah Deakin, a GGC stalwart, wrote with bitterness to Ruhl about the continued miscarriage of justice in a county where "cold-blooded murderers [i.e., Prohibition officers involved in the Dahack shooting] . . . have not yet been brought to trial." Referring to Prescott's memorial, Deakin sarcastically suggested that Ruhl, whom she called "old Prize Truth-twister," go on to "rear a few monuments . . . to the honor of our protected murderers." Henrietta Martin, angered by her treatment in the anti-GGC press, admonished the editor that the *Tribune*'s masthead, alongside its prideful mention of the Pulitzer Prize, would do well to include the words of the Golden Rule. After the trials, Ariel Pomeroy, the most active Banks-Fehl loyalist, continued to barrage the *Tribune* with lengthy letters and articles on various issues, demanding that they all be printed in their entirety. Ruhl rarely did so. Two days after the Pulitzer announcement, she complained to Ruhl about his refusal to print several of her articles on the proposed Oregon sales tax. Signing her letter "Yours for good government," Pomeroy pointed out that, as a Pulitzer Prize winner, Ruhl had "a great responsibility to live up to," and charged that the *Tribune's* unwillingness to print her letters made a mockery of the free press. If Ruhl still declined to publish her pieces, Pomeroy threatened to inform the "Pulitzer Prize award jury and . . . other authorities" of his refusal. Ruhl, pointing out the excessive length of her communications, courteously informed Pomeroy that she was welcome to refer his "refusal to print . . . to any committee of reputable newspapermen."[52]

The Pulitzer Prize served as an imprimatur for the local establishment's interpretation of the Jackson County Rebellion. Ruhl chastised his counterparts at the *Oregonian* for suggesting that the Good Government Congress tumult sprang largely from the Depression's economic distress. For Ruhl, the episode clearly originated from the amazing personal magnetism of Llewellyn Banks, a man whom Ruhl considered to be not only "thoroughly dangerous and sinister" but also "one of the cleverest and most resourceful" he had ever known. As this emphasis on personality—on Banks as a Svengali—replaced more complicated and thoughtful assessments of its causes, Ruhl's very term "Jackson County Rebellion" (along with similar phrases such as "Jackson County War") soon faded. The establishment's original fear of mobs of "Bolsheviks" and radical farmers soon was supplanted by its cautionary tale of one-man rule. Moody warned the jurors of one GGC trial that Banks, with his henchmen, had attempted to subvert the will of the people to the will of "a Mussolini . . . a dictator."[53]

The Banks-as-dictator interpretation of southern Oregon's turmoil continued to hold sway. Some years later, the national radio drama series *Pulitzer Prize Playhouse* (featuring James Dunn as Banks and Everett Sloane as Ruhl) portrayed the "political machinations of Llewellyn A. Banks," whose cynical hold over "disgruntled citizens" permitted him to take power. By the late 1950s, Pulitzer administrator John Hohenberg's heroic version of the tale had transformed Ruhl, who was over fifty years old in 1933, into an "energetic young editor" who had "alone opposed . . . the overthrow of a town's free, democratic government by a corrupt, totalitarian regime."[54]

Fig. 22. February 1933 Oregon State Police photograph of ground floor of Jackson County Courthouse, showing the auditorium (at far end of hall) and the "vault" room (nearest door on the right), from which the 1932 election ballots were stolen the night before the scheduled recount of votes. (Author's collection)

Fig. 23. OSP photo of the courthouse's rear window, broken to gain entry to the ballots; an OSP detective examines evidence inside the vault room. (Author's collection)

Fig. 24. Fehl's image appears here on the front page of one of the final issues of his weekly newspaper, in which he protests the March 1933 move to have Oregon's governor remove him as county judge. (Author's collection)

Fig. 25. Medford police officer George Prescott; ca. 1930. (SOHS #9154)

Fig. 26. Front door of Banks home. (SOHS #14708)

Fig. 27. Medford police officer directing onlookers to make way for the ambulance crew carrying litter that held Prescott's body. (SOHS)

Fig. 28. Interior of the Banks home soon after the killing of George Prescott; on the left, the Newton hunting rifle is on top of the card table; to the right is the vestibule of the house's front door. (Author's collection)

9
The Echo Fades
The New Deal and After

The Good Government Congress trials left many Jackson County citizens emotionally exhausted. Expenses directly associated with the legal proceedings drained an already impoverished county treasury of more than $68,000. The room-and-board bill for Banks' Eugene trial alone cost nearly $8,000.[1]

The Roosevelt administration's relief and recovery programs began to arrive in southern Oregon by late summer of 1933. The Forest Service's first Civilian Conservation Corps (CCC) camp in the Pacific Northwest sprang up on the banks of the Applegate River that August. Many other CCC camps soon followed, housing hundreds of young enrollees arriving from across the nation to work in the forests of southern Oregon. Medford became the CCC's administrative headquarters for a vast section of Oregon and northern California. The contingent of regular US Army officers that set up the camps occupied space at city hall recently vacated by the state police. Soon the corps built its own large administrative complex on the south edge of town. One major project of the Civilian Conservation Corps was Medford's new George Prescott Park, an extensive development of equestrian trails and picnic areas on the oak-covered slopes of Roxy Ann Peak, just northeast of the city and visible from Main Street.[2]

Many older men found jobs on New Deal–funded highway construction projects in the county. Private industry also offered increased opportunities for employment. Medford Corporation, inheritor of the bankrupt Owen-Oregon sawmill, subscribed to the National Recovery Administration (NRA) Lumber Code, which involved self-imposed restraints on production and commitment to the concept of sustained-yield forestry. The Medco operation began to make slow, steady gains, even reopening an evening shift before the end of 1934. In Ashland, the much smaller Moon Lumber Company began to receive sufficient orders to restart sawmill operations that spring. NRA-sponsored price-controls for Pacific Northwest fruit likewise encouraged the Rogue River Valley orchard industry toward recovery from its previous devastation. In early 1934, Democratic attorney Porter Neff, one of Banks's legal nemeses, went to Washington, DC, and secured government loans for the county's hard-strapped irrigation districts. Although the mid-1930s in southern Oregon certainly brought no boom, by late 1934 the intense desperation of the previous few years had passed.[3]

Robert Ruhl abandoned what he called the "moth-eaten pachyderm" of Republicanism and emerged as a committed New Dealer. He supported Franklin Roosevelt's economic reforms because they benefited the West and because Ruhl detested what he saw as the smug, narrow agenda of hidebound elements in the old GOP. Although maintaining a warm relationship with progressive Republican senator Charles McNary (whom he addressed in personal correspondence as "My Dear Charlie"), Ruhl vigorously endorsed a Democrat, congressman and former army general Charles H. Martin, in the 1934 gubernatorial election. Martin, who would prove himself to be a reactionary anti–New Dealer, appointed Ruhl to the State Board of Higher Education soon after the election.[4]

In an ongoing exchange of letters, Ruhl privately debated the merits of the New Deal with Kansas newspaper publisher William Allen White. Like Ruhl, the nationally renowned "Sage of Emporia" was also a small-town editor and a progressive; he and Ruhl's older brother had been college friends. Both men supported much of Roosevelt's reform program, but White distrusted the president's alleged pandering to the downtrodden for votes while Ruhl defended his Harvard schoolmate's political instincts.[5]

The happier days of the mid-1930s notwithstanding, Ruhl and other members of the establishment still faced the dogged efforts of Good Government Congress loyalists to revive their organization and free their imprisoned champions. The obstinate refusal of Banks, Fehl, and their hardcore supporters to accept the new order of things, although never seriously threatening renewed rebellion, sounded a protracted echo of the turmoil.

FIRST AS TRAGEDY, THEN AS FARCE

The spring primary of 1934 brought hopes of renewal to remnants of the Good Government Congress. With her husband in the state penitentiary, Electa Fehl attempted to restore his rule by proxy. She filed as a candidate for county judge, pledging to "carry out the sacred promises of . . . Earl Fehl to the electorate of Jackson County." Even Henrietta Martin, noting Electa Fehl's incompetence for the position, criticized her mudslinging as counterproductive; her brief campaign sputtered to a close with the primary election. Former GGC secretary C. H. Brown petitioned for appointment as Medford postmaster. George Obenchain, the prominent Banks loyalist from Butte Falls, filed as a candidate for sheriff in 1934. Both lost their bids for office.[6]

Hoping to revitalize the organization, Martin, Brown, and several associates filed articles of incorporation for the GGC in April 1934. Other than at-
tracting a few diehard believers, the first meeting, held at the Medford Armory,
was a disappointment. The organization evidently disbanded by the end of the
year, although Martin continued her unsuccessful attempt to gain local office
as late as 1936.[7]

Llewellyn Banks's tangled financial dealings left the remnants of his
Jackson County properties in the control of federal bankruptcy court. William
Phipps, the orchardist's former defense counsel, represented his creditors in
the proceedings. Banks's once-extensive holdings passed into the hands of
others while he served the first two years of his life sentence in Salem.[8]

Banks's first few months in prison were quiet ones. He worked in the facility's laundry and later was transferred to the prison library. During 1933 he
completed a book of essays, *Weighed in the Balance: A Famine Foreseen.* Privately
published (probably with funds furnished by his siblings), the antimodernist
jeremiad, sprinkled with scriptural verse, followed some of the main themes of
his "Once In A While" columns. He saw a formerly Christian America declining rapidly into "Pagan Dictatorship." Whereas Herbert Hoover had borne the
brunt of Banks's attacks before 1932, now Franklin Roosevelt stood forth as the
nation's dictatorial traitor. Incensed at New Deal agricultural policies, Banks
asked his readers, "Did not we Pagans demonstrate that millions . . . starved
beneath the bursting granaries? Did not we pagans burn our grain? Did not we
feed it to swine?" Banks continued with sarcastic allusions to the New Deal's
restrictions on acreages planted to crops, on its removal of livestock from the
West's rangeland: "Have not we proven our power over those shepherds, those
hillbillies, those gleaners of the herbs of the earth?"[9]

In addition to proclaiming the producerist ideology of old-style agrarian populism, Banks warned of military takeover: "Those uniforms, THOSE
ENDLESS UNIFORMS. The uniformed State Police, armed to the teeth, the
uniforms of our State Militias." In particular, Banks saw the army-run Civilian Conservation Corps camps then springing up across the West, with their
"military trucks passing, re-passing," as the prelude to military rule. He saved
particular scorn for "Ye Dishonorable Lawyers," assuring these "profiteers on
the tribulations of [their] brother" that a special place awaited them after the
day of judgment.[10]

Banks also castigated Jews, that "usurer class which lives on the virtue
of the labor of the Gentiles," as the real power behind the New Deal, and he
propounded "British-Israelism"—a variety of anti-Semitism that denied that
the Old Testament Israelites (and, by implication, Jesus of Nazareth) were
Jews. According to British-Israelism, the true Israelites of the Bible instead

were "British Israelites," direct ancestors of the Anglo-Saxon peoples; the Jews had never been "God's Chosen People." (Indeed, by the 1950s, the American branch of British-Israelism had evolved into the Christian Identity movement, which held to a "biological" form of anti-Semitism that claimed that Jews were literally the children of Satan.)[11]

* * *

Banks ended his book with some of his personal "visions." In one dream, he recounted, while "walking alone on a trail" high in the mountains, he had faced a "huge lion, ferocious in appearance, rushing toward [him] with tremendous speed." In the dream Banks stood his ground, "without fear regardless of the outcome," and thus the beast rushed past without harming him. Although the Oregonian's editor scorned the "orotund, ponderous" essays of Weighed in the Balance as those of a "poor fatuous scribbler," Banks soon set about compiling an autobiography.[12]

With Julius Meier soon to leave office in 1935, Banks's brother-in-law George Moran undertook an intensive lobbying effort with the outgoing governor. Pointing out the imprisoned man's potential to arouse still further social, religious, and ethnic division, Moran persuaded Portland's Roman Catholic archbishop, prominent Jewish representatives, a former US senator, and many other influential Oregon citizens to plead for Banks's pardon on the condition that he leave the state forever. Meier indicated some receptivity to the idea until Ruhl and others launched a countereffort from southern Oregon. During the Christmas season, Moran wrote directly to Ruhl, importuning him to support the pardon. He warned the editor that "as long as [Banks] is in Oregon there will be a controversy." Moran influenced two Cleveland attorneys, Ruhl's friends from student days, to write similar letters on Banks's behalf. Ruhl refused to entertain the requests. He wrote to Judge Skipworth that the "idea of even considering a pardon or parole for a killer like Banks, with only 15 months of his life term served" impressed him as "incredible." To Governor Meier, he insisted that "every right thinking citizen of Jackson County ... [was] opposed to any such action." He included not only the businesspeople of Medford, but "prominent people throughout the country districts."[13]

The initial campaign for Banks's pardon ended on Christmas Day, with Moran's death in Ohio from a heart attack. Oregon's new governor, Charles Martin, was not inclined toward clemency, but Ruhl surmised that the effort was merely stalled "until the time appears opportune for it to break out again." Indeed, Ariel Pomeroy renewed the struggle for Banks's release in July 1935. Claiming that Banks's life was endangered by hired assassins within the walls of the penitentiary, she petitioned Governor Martin to place Banks in special protective custody while considering his pardon. The tireless Pomeroy traveled the state, meeting with many persons of influence in an effort to build momentum for a special inquiry. Demanding an investigation, she wrote to Governor Martin that Banks's "vast estate" in southern Oregon was being looted by those who had destroyed him. Pomeroy returned to Medford from Eugene with word that the dean of the University of Oregon Law School had agreed to join her cause. When apprised of the claim, the school's dean (later US senator) Wayne L. Morse promptly took pains to inform Martin, Ruhl, E. E. Kelly, and others that he had never indicated any such support and that he was not in favor of a pardon for Banks.[14]

Pomeroy's pardon effort had better success with another future US senator, young Richard L. Neuberger. Neuberger, then beginning his career as a liberal journalist, supported her call for a "sincere and exhaustive investigation" of Banks's prejudicial trial and signed the petition. On the Jackson County district attorney's copy of the petition, Codding scrawled, next to Neuberger's name, "U[niversity] of O[regon] journalism student, very radical." Pomeroy also enlisted the support of Portland's Republican leader Rufus B. Holman. Unlike Neuberger, Holman was a bigoted reactionary, but, as with Neuberger, Holman's motive may have been more to embarrass Governor Martin than to secure "justice" for Banks.[15]

In addition to several other prominent upstaters, the petition garnered the signatures of ninety local people, most of them residents of Medford, Rogue River, and Gold Hill. Pomeroy and other Banks loyalists kept up the pardon crusade across the state. Editorial support came from small "country weekly" newspapers as distant as the Harney County *Free Press*. Jackson County's establishment geared up once again to keep Banks behind bars. Medford's American Legion post protested the pardon endeavor to the governor, as did separate petitions from Medford schoolchildren and Jackson County voters. County and city law officers took a lead in circulating the petitions, and Moody presented them to Martin.[16]

Banks's pardon campaign unraveled dramatically during the August hearing in Salem, when Assistant Attorney General Moody pointed his finger at former state parole officer Dan Kellaher and accused the man of having entered into an illegal contract with the Banks family. Shouting at the "pale and silent" Kellaher and holding up a copy of the secret document for a hushed court to see, Moody charged him with accepting promises of $50,000 in return for "prostituting his oath of office" to gain Banks's release. Kellaher was arrested on bribery charges within the week.[17]

During 1935, Banks attracted further publicity when he alleged that several attempts had been made on his life while in prison. He also claimed that prosecutor William Levens's 1933 death during the Eugene trial actually had been arranged by Ralph Moody. One late-December 1934 incident in particular, a supposed poisoning attempt in the prison, became the centerpiece of Banks's campaign for release, or at least for transfer, from the penitentiary. As prisoner #12697, Banks occupied cell 430 in block C. Bowing to Banks's forceful persuasion, prison officials allowed him to wear a custom-tailored, white outfit. Earl Fehl, prisoner #12698, served as an inmate trustee for that block, and on the evening in question, as he had customarily done each evening before, Fehl stopped at Banks's cell to chat and to bring a pot of boiling water for Banks's nightly cup of hot chocolate. The two men talked as Banks added sugar from his personal supply to the mixture. Noticing that the "sugar" created an unusual appearance in the beverage, Banks allegedly tasted the mixture and became nauseated. Analysis of the sugar by prison authorities confirmed the presence of lethal amounts of bichloride of mercury crystals. Banks and Fehl both provided statements that pointed to attempted poisoning by an unknown third party. Governor Martin's special secretary conducted an investigation of the affair, which instead indicated "Banks himself as being the person who crumbled the ... tablets into his own sugar." Prison officials theorized that Banks had done so either because of his severe depression following Moran's failure to secure his pardon or, more likely, as a staged "assassination" attempt.[18]

According to prison medical reports, Banks had become extremely depressed during December. Dr. R. E. Lee Steiner, superintendent of the state hospital for the insane, later examined Banks and agreed as to the inmate's temporary melancholia. However, Steiner argued against his transfer to the state hospital. He reported to Governor Martin that Banks was a dangerous man, a "psychopathic personality with strong paranoid trends" who might again take human life. Steiner added that during his interview Banks had spoken of his "duty to be out ... running the State on military lines and ... a lot of other foolishness."[19]

*　*　*

Adding to Banks's sense of isolation and hopelessness was the departure of his wife and daughter from Salem. Edith Banks had spent more than two years in Salem, renting a small apartment and visiting her husband regularly. Sometime in late 1935, her visits became much less frequent, eventually ending entirely. Ariel Pomeroy remained Banks's steadfast link to the outside until her "disturbing influence" on the prisoner caused the warden to end her visits "for the mental good of Banks." Pomeroy shared Banks's visionary belief in divine retribution. In a letter titled "The Feast of Belshazzar," she described a formal dinner given for Governor Martin in Medford on April 25, 1935, the evening that the Oregon State Capitol burned to the ground. Pomeroy's allegory indicated that the destruction of the state house "represented the judgment of God [on the people of Oregon] for their attitude toward Llewellyn Banks." Her letter (quite possibly written by Banks himself) read,

> Even then, the prophet of his time and place was gazing through prison bars at the flaming dome of the Capitol—the Capitol of the State for which he had sacrificed all earthly possessions, even liberty itself. As he gazed, the great dome crashed inward to its base. The treasures of his people consumed, destroyed before his very eyes.[20]

Some of the GGC figures incarcerated for ballot theft began to be released during 1934. The terms of Thomas Breechen's eighteen-month sentence allowed him to be paroled in July. The state parole board recommended conditional release of the contrite former sheriff Gordon Schermerhorn the following summer. Ruhl, asked for his opinion by Governor Martin, indicated that Schermerhorn had been led astray by Banks and Fehl, and he thoroughly approved of the parole board's decision. Walter Jones, ex-mayor of Rogue River, gained his freedom in April 1936. Jones's good behavior in the penitentiary lessened his term by eighteen months.[21]

Acting at the strenuous urging of Ruhl and others, Governor Martin rejected Earl Fehl's 1935 pardon request. As she did with the Banks pardon campaign, Ariel Pomeroy promoted the Fehl effort. Stiff-necked Fehl, referring to himself in letters with sardonic pride as "County Judge and Convict No. 12698," had refused to admit to any wrongdoing, insisting that the "gang" had cunningly engineered his imprisonment. Through his wife and other representatives, Fehl fought successfully to save some of his real estate holdings from mortgage foreclosure. In early 1934, a few months after his imprisonment, Fehl and his wife printed several thousand copies of a handbill titled "Black Political Plot Exposed: Who Stole the Ballots?" Distributed throughout Jackson County and in the capital, the sheet accused the Jackson County district attorney's office of forcing perjured testimony in order to convict Fehl. Codding had Electa Fehl and other Medford handbill distributors indicted and arrested for libel. Behind Codding, according to Fehl's broadside, "lurk[ed] the REAL CONSPIRATORS—namely: The Invisible Government; the Power Company, the Gang and the SUBSIDIZED PRESS, who for years have fattened on public money."[22]

Fehl's subsequent good behavior made him eligible for parole in early 1936. Codding pleaded with state authorities not to release Fehl, claiming he was "fundamentally a criminal and according to his own statements intends to return [to Jackson County] and avenge what his twisted brain considers injustices."23

George Putnam, Salem newspaper editor and former owner of the Medford *Tribune*, warned Ruhl that Fehl was "as crazy as Banks. . . . He's done nothing but brood and plan revenge against his 'persecutors' since in prison." Putnam pointed out that Fehl's plea for release was being supported by state treasurer Republican Rufus Holman, a wealthy Portland businessman who had been an active Klan leader in the 1920s. (In 1938, Holman won election to the US Senate as an extreme isolationist; in early 1941 he earned notoriety for making anti-Jewish statements on the Senate floor.) Governor Martin attempted a compromise by paroling Fehl on condition that he stay out of Jackson County. Fehl adamantly refused these terms and brought suit against the governor's action. Fehl's legal action delayed parole for a number of other inmates as well, provoking a prison riot in which one prisoner died.

Fehl accepted a conditional parole to Multnomah County in late 1936. He and Electa, forced to "live in their car" for the first several weeks in Portland, obtained low-paying, part-time jobs and received some financial support from family members and from Rufus Holman. While in Portland, Fehl initiated another suit against Governor Martin as a "conspirator" in preventing Fehl's return to southern Oregon.24 According to the parole's conditions, Fehl was eligible to return to Jackson County on August 16, 1937. Irrepressible, he arrived back in Medford early that very morning. Fehl, assuring authorities that he had returned "unarmed," demanded the sheriff's protection from would-be assailants and immediately filed suit to regain official recognition as county judge.25 Fehl circulated in the outlying districts, renewing old ties with GGC supporters. He wrote to his parole officer in Salem that Governor Martin's conditional parole, forbidding Fehl's return to southern Oregon, had been an illegal document "sealed in 'BLOOD OF REVENGE' to the EVERLASTING DISGRACE of a Great State, Oregon."

Within two months Fehl had initiated a flurry of lawsuits against various private parties and government officials, including a third proceeding against Governor Martin that asked $548,000 in damages. Relentless, the Fehls printed more inflammatory broadsides, including one (attributed to the "Citizen's Committee for Civil Liberties in Jackson County") that alleged that a trio of county officers, George Codding, George Neilson, and Clerk George Carter—whom Fehl dubbed "the three Georges"—had illegally conspired to have him declared insane. Indeed, the county filed a notice of insanity for Fehl in November. Neilson's brief presented medical evidence of Fehl's "paranoia and litigious dementia." It also referred to Fehl's attempt to purchase a high-powered rifle from a secondhand store, as well as his "meetings in the outlying hill districts ... in a second attempt to arouse the rabble of the county in his support."[26]

In late December 1937, after a lengthy and acrimonious trial, circuit court judge H. D. Norton judged Fehl to be insane. Shortly after Christmas, authorities returned Fehl to Salem, where he entered the Oregon State Hospital. Ariel Pomeroy, writing to the Salem *Capitol Journal*, observed there was "no place more effective than an insane asylum in which to place a politically inconvenient person, not unless the grave itself be employed." She warned of possible "civil war" if Fehl were placed "with the insane for an indefinite period of political cold storage." Pomeroy's predicted uprising did not occur. Fehl probably appeared as an isolated and bizarre personality to all but a dwindling number of committed loyalists. He remained in the Salem hospital until late in 1941. Upon release, Fehl returned again to his Oakdale Avenue home in Medford, where he initiated another round of suits to recover the back salary he felt was due him as county judge. By 1942, with Jackson County now hosting a huge army training base east of Medford, news of Fehl's ongoing and consistently unsuccessful legal proceedings faded from the pages of the press.[27]

LEGACY OF REBELLION

By the mid-1930s, the *Mail Tribune* had recovered sufficient financial ground for Ruhl to put it "in the black." Robert and Mabel Ruhl spent much of their time away from Medford on extended trips, particularly to southern California. Ruhl also made regular visits to Eugene as a member of the State Board of Higher Education. The search for a new president of the University of Oregon in 1937 entailed Ruhl's ongoing participation. Evaluating one applicant as "too nice for a tough job," he expressed particular interest in another candidate, "Dr. Erb from Stanford," who, although "young and inexperienced," impressed Ruhl "from the first." Erb got the job. Ruhl's willingness to focus more of his attention beyond the Rogue River Valley may have stemmed in part from his stated belief that "locally, peace and quiet ... reigned ever since" the end of the Good Government Congress.[28]

An influx of Dust Bowl migrants in the mid-1930s caused some resentment in southern Oregon, but economic improvement and federal and state resettlement programs lessened the social burden of supporting these impoverished newcomers. Although Jackson County's affairs lost their intense rancor of 1932–1933 during the New Deal, local passion for populist politics did not disappear. Upton Sinclair, the muckraking journalist whose 1934 Golden State gubernatorial campaign ran on a socialist platform of "End Poverty in

California" (EPIC) had some EPIC sympathizers in Jackson County. Jane Smack of Rogue River wrote Ruhl of her admiration for Sinclair's "fearlessness and hatred of hypocrisy" and, by inference, her disappointment in his defeated campaign.[29]

Of more political significance was the rising tide of anger among the region's elderly citizens. A southern California physician, Francis E. Townsend, had begun promoting his concept of an "old age revolving pension fund" plan in 1933. Townsend Plan clubs proliferated throughout the country, particularly in the far West, during the next two years. The Townsend Club movement took on important political strength in Oregon in 1935, where its evangelistic fervor held strong appeal among the elderly, especially in rural areas.[30]

More than 15,000 Townsend Plan supporters met in Portland's Jantzen Beach Park for an August rally that featured the quiet but forceful sixty-eight-year-old Dr. Townsend. Another major speaker at the three-day rally was Townsend Plan board member Judge John A. Jeffrey, the former Jackson County Populist and Klan attorney, who spoke in his vigorous stump-speech style.[31] Ruhl received numerous letters advocating or condemning the Townsend Plan. The Upper Rogue Townsend Club, one of many such organizations in southern Oregon, built a Townsend Hall near Prospect, where the group held regular meetings and other community events.[32] Townsendites' political muscle in southern Oregon became such that the district's Republican congressman James Mott served as "Townsend bloc" floor leader in the House of Representatives.[33]

In the presidential election of 1936, followers of Dr. Townsend, as well as those of the late Senator Huey Long (who had been assassinated the previous year) and Father Charles Coughlin, formed a potential bloc of dissatisfied voters who could challenge the New Deal. Townsend, Coughlin, and others founded the Union Party and urged their followers to vote for its presidential candidate, Congressman William Lemke, a veteran of agrarian protest movements in North Dakota. The Lemke candidacy, which faltered badly during the national campaign, received 5 percent of the Oregon vote. Southern Oregon, however, proved a relative stronghold for the Union Party. Jackson and Josephine Counties, with their active Townsendites, gave Lemke more than 10 percent and 18 percent of their vote, respectively. Although Franklin Roosevelt received a commanding majority in Jackson County, the same rural Populist holdout communities of the late 1890s and the "GGC hotbed" precincts of the 1932 election gave Lemke his largest margin of support. Out of three hundred votes cast in the perpetually disgruntled town of Rogue River, Lemke missed beating Roosevelt by only three votes. Republican candidate Alf Landon trailed, a distant third.[34]

* * *

In the 1936 senatorial campaign, McNary ran against a comparatively unknown maverick Democrat from the southern part of Oregon, Willis E. Mahoney. A young attorney from Washington State who came to Klamath County in the 1920s, Mahoney astounded the city of Klamath Falls when he won the crowded 1932 mayoralty race as a write-in candidate, having been previously ruled off the ballot on legal technicalities.[35] A strong Townsend Plan advocate and a professed enemy of privately owned utilities, Mahoney was later described by one political observer as a "Huey Long-type" demagogue.[36] The veteran McNary squeaked to a narrow victory over the aggressive newcomer in both the state and Jackson County returns. As with the Lemke vote, Mahoney's strongest Jackson County support came from rural communities.

Although they could be fierce and unforgiving of opposition, southern Oregon's Townsendites were benign in comparison to adherents of some other Depression-era political movements in the Pacific Northwest. In the states of Washington and Oregon, some lower-middle-class citizens (among them, former Klansmen) became active in William Dudley Pelley's fascistic, anti-Semitic Silver Shirts (or Silver Legion) during the late 1930s. The Silver Shirts may have had a (perhaps quite small) chapter in Medford, but they do not appear to have had a significant organized presence in Jackson County (although traditional, economically focused anti-Semitism had been part of many rural citizens' outlook since the early Populist movement.[37]

Some residents shared Pelley's virulent anti-Jewish sentiments. Protestant minister Edwin Deacon of Talent combined anti-Semitic conspiracy theory with anti–New Deal rhetoric in his letters to Ruhl. Deacon revealed himself as part of what historian Leo Ribuffo has called the "Old Christian Right" of fundamentalist, intensely anti-Semitic and anti-Catholic Protestantism. Deacon wrote in 1937 that the *Mail Tribune*'s editor had erroneously assumed "that we oppose the New Deal because we fear the personal ambition of F.D.R. to become a dictator." Deacon called Ruhl's attention to the Roman Catholic Church "that already has ... Mexico and France quite safely within its tentacles." Spain, in its second year of civil war, was also "struggling like Laocoon to free herself from its deadly coils" and Italy had been saved "only by the rise of Mussolini and a determined show of force." As for Jews, wrote Deacon, in Germany after the "Great War," "it was amazing how quickly the positions of influence and power fell into the hands of Jews." Deacon observed that "Hitler stepped forward ... and said 'This country shall be German, not Jewish.'" Seeing the New Deal as part of an international Jewish conspiracy, Deacon alerted readers that he and other knowledgeable Christians "look past the speech and message" of President Roosevelt and toward "the minds [apparently the Jews on the president's staff] that dictate them . . . at the hidden empire."[38]

After Llewellyn Banks's charismatic but skewed leadership four years previously, conspiracy-theory politics lost ground in southern Oregon. The Reverend Deacon, who may or may not have been a Banks supporter (or a Silver Shirt), evidently persuaded relatively few people to openly share his beliefs. Although ethnic and religious tolerance did not blossom in the Rogue River Valley during the late 1930s, steady improvement in agricultural and lumber markets deflected attention from traditional political scapegoats such as Jews, Catholics, or foreign immigrants.

With American military spending increasing by 1940–1941, the region's natural resource-based economy began to hum. The army's sixty-seven-square-mile Camp White training cantonment took shape on the Agate Desert near Medford in 1941. That same year, some Jackson County boosters joined with colleagues in adjacent counties in southwestern Oregon and northwestern California to form the State of Jefferson movement. Perceived lack of attention from Salem and Sacramento to the region's needs lay at the heart of this highly publicized "secessionist" campaign.[39]

Intended to spur infrastructure spending in the contiguous "forgotten corners" of the two states, the State of Jefferson movement was a short-lived and somewhat tongue-in-cheek publicity stunt launched by local establishments, and not a serious political insurgency. But the movement stemmed in part from—and helped to reinforce—the region's populist, sectional self-image as a place abused by distant elites.[40]

10
"It Can't Happen Here" . . . But Did It?

By 1940, portrayal of the Good Government Congress episode as an authoritarian movement—and Llewellyn A. Banks as its dictator—was embedded in the Jackson County establishment's interpretation of the event. This explanation doubtless received encouragement from the national success of Sinclair Lewis's *It Can't Happen Here.* The novel—which traces the rise of a charismatic, all-American fuehrer, Buzz Windrip, from out of the small-town West—appeared at the same time as Jackson County leaders defeated the campaign to pardon Banks and Fehl. The Lewis book's object lesson, as well as the emerging liberal interpretation of mass politics of which it soon became a part, warned of populist demagogues and their ability to lead the nation down a fascist road during economic upheavals.[1]

Announcing the Pulitzer Prizes for 1933, the *New York Times* had portrayed Banks as a "dictator" and his Good Government Congress as a demagogic, authoritarian outbreak. Writing to Harvard classmates in 1938, Ruhl mentioned the Pulitzer award for his newspaper's part in defeating "a gang of would-be Fascists." During the 1930s, as German fascism came to dominate the fears of many American commentators, Banks's original role as a native-born would-be Mussolini changed. By 1940, state policeman James O'Brien's first-person account of the Jackson County turmoil appeared under the title, "The Man Who Tried to Be Hitler in the U.S." Written for a popular audience, the magazine article cast Banks as a fascist demagogue who made his "bid for power by molding a solid organization from the masses."[2]

The core concept underlying the catchphrase "it can't happen here" was, of course, that "it"—a fascist takeover—indeed could (would?) happen here in America. Sinclair Lewis's intentional irony in choosing an anxious statement of American exceptionalism for the book's title served to amplify the sound of his warning. The desperate 1932–1933 period had generated widespread calls for an American man on horseback, and, by 1935, rising dissatisfaction with the New Deal again threatened to unite populist and reactionary elements into what observers like Lewis viewed as an incipient fascism.[3]

Lewis's protagonist, small-town newspaper editor Doremus Jessup, voices that warning to neighbors when one of them claims that fascism "couldn't

possibly happen here in America." Jessup responds, "The hell it can't"! . . .
There's no country in the world that can get more hysterical . . . than America.
. . . Why, where in all history has there ever been a people so ripe for dictatorship as ours?" Jessup reminds his listeners of Huey Long's "absolute dictatorship" in Louisiana, of anti-Semite "radio priest" Father Coughlin as "divine
oracle to millions," and of the 1920s Ku Klux Klan rise to power. [4]

But was the Jackson County Rebellion truly an incipient fascist movement? Despite Banks's alleged intention to expand his movement to state
and national levels, was the Good Government Congress aiming toward an
authoritarian solution to economic chaos? Or, was the Jackson County establishment's Lewis-like interpretation of the Jackson County Rebellion actually
an overblown reaction more akin to what one historian of the 1930s–1940s
period termed an anti-fascist "Brown Scare"? [5]

FASCISM, POPULISM, AND DEMAGOGUERY IN SOUTHERN OREGON

For believers in the "it can't happen here" view of American mass politics
during the Depression, Senator Huey Long and Father Charles Coughlin represented the fascist threat. Despite the rise of other demagogic leaders during
the 1930s, these two figures were seen as the most potent political messiahs.

Undeniably, Jackson County's Good Government Congress, like Long's
and Coughlin's far larger movements, developed in substantial part out of
the economic conditions of the Great Depression. Can one then consider
Llewellyn Banks as the Huey Long of southern Oregon? Or the GGC as a Pacific Northwest version of Coughlin's National Union for Social Justice, or his
more extreme Christian Front? Certain of the Good Government Congress's
broader complaints of unfairness had some legitimacy, but the organization
can be characterized accurately as the result of Depression-era demagoguery.
Created by two leaders who constantly agitated political discontents, the
Good Government Congress thrived on deep-seated populist sentiments.
Banks and Fehl accomplished their movement-building through newspaper
campaigns that appealed to local resentments and focused blame on identifiable local targets. Upon achieving political power, the two leaders attempted
to formalize their movement in order to consolidate control and to deflect the
effort of political enemies.

The Good Government Congress exhibited certain traits similar to those
of some strains of European fascism, ranging from nativist and anti-Semitic
appeals to the ultranationalist, anti-Communist rhetoric of various fascist
leaders. To some Medford observers, the cult of personality that centered on
Banks as the movement's champion and martyr underscores another fascistic

aspect of the GGC—a spellbinding persona ready-made for his portrayal as an American fuehrer.

However, the Good Government Congress's supposed fascistic traits were surface phenomena, and the fascist analogy unravels upon deeper examination. For that matter, so too does the traditional, 1930s liberal imputation of fascist tendencies to the better-known contemporary political movements led by Long and Coughlin. Alan Brinkley, an influential historian of right-wing American political movements, differentiates between the basic nature of the Long and Coughlin demagogies and those of European fascist leaders.[6]

In contrast to the collectivist and statist goals of fascism, Long's and Coughlin's "voices of protest" appealed to Americans' traditional independence and "opposition to centralized authority," and to the age-old belief in conspiracies of wicked elites. According to Brinkley, the lower-middle-class populism of Long and Coughlin had its strongest ideological roots in the Populist Revolt and in previous American agrarian/working-class insurgencies. Long and Coughlin were "manifestations of one of the most powerful [American] impulses . . . the urge to defend the autonomy of the individual" against the relentless expansion of the modern industrial state—and against the inordinate power of those few who controlled it. Although they castigated the concentration of wealth in the hands of the few, Long and Coughlin firmly believed—as did their People's Party predecessors—in the American free-enterprise system. Their followers yearned, not for submersion in a mass corporatist state, but for survival of individualistic capitalism.[7]

This same objective guided most members of the Good Government Congress, including Llewellyn Banks. The GGC preamble stressed that the organization had formed to confront an emergency situation wherein "the existing order of things have passed out of individual control." The GGC's stated aim was to wrest power from a selfish, corrupt elite and restore political control to the common people. Llewellyn Banks, the intellectual leader of the GGC, personified this traditional American populist objective. His unremitting fight—dating, according to him, to a childhood vow—against the fruit-consignment firms, as well as against large cooperatives such as the California Fruit Growers Exchange, against the Agricultural Marketing Act of 1929, and against other forms of centralized control over farm production, stemmed from Banks's intense individualism.[8] He spoke, like an old People's Party man, of Medford's packinghouses, many of them controlled by out-of-state investors, as "foreign-owned" and of the Traffic Association as holding punishing chattel mortgages on small orchards. Banks's defense attorney told the jury that Banks's ideas were that "the man that was entitled to the fruits of his toil was the man who took from the earth," and that this man "was the grower, not the banker and other big interests who happened to sit in their offices."[9]

Banks's prison essays were a mixture of nostalgia for an idealized American agrarian past and antimodernist anger at the present situation: "If our sons have widespreading fields, look to see them despoiled; the most despised creature . . . the American farmer's son." In terms of Banks's traditionalist, Populist ideology, one of his severest critics correctly claimed that "L. A. Banks . . . lived in an age long gone."[10]

It is time to retire the idea of the Jackson County Rebellion and similar movements as "fascistic." But how, when fascism has proven itself to be such a protean concept? Alan Brinkley remarked that a major problem with any examination of a movement's fascistic character is that there is no single agreed-upon definition of fascism. The definitions are many and often contradictory. In *The Anatomy of Fascism*, Robert O. Paxton, America's preeminent historian of fascism as a global phenomenon, has provided a judicious look at fascism, probing well beneath its surface traits that were made so familiar in old newsreel films. He presents nine "mobilizing passions" that drive fascist mass movements. For example, included as two of the nine are a sense of overwhelming crisis and the group's desire for closer integration of a purer community (by consent, if possible, by exclusionary violence, if necessary). Of the nine, the Good Government Congress exhibited two, at most three. Most of Paxton's nine "passions" emphasize mass group identity and are anti-individualistic in nature.[11]

Historian Michael Roberto's *The Coming of the American Behemoth* has resurrected and amplified a Marxist analysis of what an American fascism would/did look like. His critique dismisses the centrality of such traits as a charismatic leader or exclusionary ultranationalism as being necessary to fascism. Roberto sees the United States, because of tightening hegemony of large corporations and influence of the country's financial elite in politics, as uniquely prone to a fascistic capitalist dictatorship. The state and its power steadily become the servant of the corporate ruling class, which includes "plutocrats" and, more significantly, an ever-widening web of cooperating corporate-interest groups. If one accepts the validity of Roberto's view of American fascism, then Llewellyn Banks, with his extreme individualism and his anticorporate/anti-statist outlook, was actually an anti-fascist![12]

In addition to his hyper-individualism, Banks's focus on conspiracy and corruption lay deep within the American political tradition, what historian Richard Hofstadter in 1964 famously called "the paranoid style in American politics." Stoking outrage against the local elite, Banks possessed superb talents as a demagogue. However, neither this trait nor his personal magnetism and messianic appeal made Banks into an authoritarian duce. From colonial times into the twenty-first century, American political insurgencies' dynamic figures have been leaders who mobilized the masses with anti-elitist oratory that repeatedly expressed a few, key, simple ideas. Howard Mumford Jones, historian of colonial America, stated decades ago that colonial mobs and rebels were often "amenable to cunning leadership, sometimes disguised, sometimes demagogic."[13]

CONTINUITIES AND COMMONALITIES: FOUR DECADES OF PROTEST

A strong thread of agrarian discontent, dyed in the long tradition of what American historians have termed "backcountry rebellion," runs through southern Oregon's history. The Good Government Congress featured many of the same themes and patterns that had characterized the region's Populist movement, and the manifestation of the Ku Klux Klan. In effect, ongoing insurgency marks the four-decade period of discontent from the early 1890s to the early 1930s.

Undeniably, some major differences also marked the three episodes in Jackson County's forty-year period of insurgency. Southern Oregon's People Party and Ku Klux Klan were part of national phenomena, their local character determined in significant part by those organizations' national policies and goals. This fact differentiates them from the sui generis Good Government Congress, and it explains deep ideological distinctions between them. The local People's Party, although primarily an agrarian-based political reform movement, had a nativist component that owed less to the party's formal program than to the innate prejudices of its members. Farm families made up most of its membership in Jackson County. The Klan was overtly nativist in its goal, and it featured aspects of moral and political reform as well. Lower-middle-class residents of Jackson County's larger towns and rural people living near those towns formed its core. The GGC was popular in working-class neighborhoods of the valley's main towns, as well as among owners of small orchard holdings and dairy farms. Its popularity extended far into the county's most remote rural settlements, the area of the GGC's most rock-solid support. One could list other ways in which the three episodes were dissimilar. However, in terms of broader themes and patterns in local politics, their similarities are more important than the disparities.

This concept of a Jackson County or southern Oregon insurgent tradition lasting forty years displays persistent themes, and in the specific patterns of political action. The three major insurgencies, in the early 1890s, early 1920s, and early 1930s, coincided with periods of deep economic stress. Anxiety stoked resentments that regularly were expressed in several interrelated themes of focused conflict: agrarian/rural versus commercial/urban interests; producers versus managers/distributors; lower middle class/working class versus middle class/upper class; extremely localist outlooks versus relatively cosmopolitan viewpoints; and culturally "populist" versus culturally "elitist" outlooks.

Each of the outbreaks also had similar patterns of development. The insurgencies' overall pattern—although each factor varied in relative importance during the different episodes—consisted of several key factors: a solid base of support among economically threatened rural citizens; a powerful anti-elite sentiment expressed in the form of corruption/conspiracy accusations; a crucial organizational and propagandizing role played by local newspapers (including crusades against opposing newspapers as the voice of the elite); the early appearance of opportunistic and demagogic leaders; and the rhetorical use of both ethnic/religious nativism and moralistic reform to foster movement solidarity. The steadily growing importance of women as public participants in the local insurgent tradition was another significant factor. Additional aspects of the pattern throughout the four decades were the continuing dominance of particular rural communities as centers of discontent and the ongoing presence of certain individuals, either as leaders or as active members, during the different episodes.

The local People's Party was quintessentially a movement of, by, and for disgruntled farmers. Jackson County's Ku Klux Klan seems to have held some focused appeal for Rogue River Valley orchardists who were deeply frustrated by the post-boom decline, anxious over the effects of the postwar agricultural depression, and especially worried about the cost and supply of irrigation water. In other parts of the far West, the Klan opportunistically found other local anxieties to fasten on. The Good Government Congress united many rural people throughout the county in the same fashion and with the same general intentions as had the People's Party during a previous national depression.

Anger at perceived corruption by the local establishment, as well as establishment members' alleged political intrigues that, in effect, deflected the popular will, marked all three phases of the insurgent tradition. From the Jacksonville ring through the Medford gang, the county's commercial and professional elite remained the central target of the various insurgents' ire. A lively and pugnacious press effectively carried the message to all corners of the county throughout the four decades. Dissident-oriented newspapers, which included the Populists' reform journals and local weeklies, continued through the Medford *Clarion* and the *Pacific Record Herald*, and culminated with the daily inflammatory sensationalism of Bank's Medford *News*.

Political opportunists, skilled in oratorical or journalistic demagoguery, eagerly joined during the early phases of each episode, and they worked to make the insurgency their own. Although both men believed in the Good Government Congress cause, Earl Fehl and Llewellyn Banks, who so thoroughly mixed their own political and financial affairs with the broader cause, clearly operated as opportunistic demagogues. The same might be said for anti-Catholic John Jeffrey, who cannily hitched his own political wagon to the Populist crusade and later served the Jackson County night riders of the 1920s. William Phipps, although less successful in politics following his own Populist moment, helped fan the anti-elitist sentiments of the Klan episode into a temporary bonanza for his newspaper.

Nativist rhetoric, fueled in differing degrees and aimed at differing targets, by Jeffrey, Phipps, and Banks, remained a potent (if not always overt) force in southern Oregon throughout the period. Some local Populists, both leaders and supporters, subscribed to the anti-Catholic program of the American Protective Association (APA). Although the APA did not dominate the local People's Party, it evidently proved an important sub-rosa factor by the mid-1890s. Religious and ethnic bigotry, which continued as a strong if latent political force in southern Oregon during the first two decades of the twentieth century, found its loudest public expression with the Klan. William Phipps's references to stereotypical images of "opulent Jews" and the bejeweled ring-finger of a rich, "corrupt Pope" transformed prejudice into populist wrath. Although the bizarre anti-Semitic theories of Banks and the xenophobic themes of other GGC speakers did not overtly dominate the GGC, such sentiments probably gave the movement greater cohesion and additional support.

Moralistic-reform rhetoric, although not so dominant as with the Klan, definitely was present in both the People's Party and the Good Government Congress. The Good Government Congress's moral outrage at the "gang's" allegedly devious and corrupt actions echoed the Populist leaders' appeal, like that of the Grangers before them, for farmers to improve both their fields and their minds, in short, to "wake up" and unite into an intelligent and righteous force. Moralistic alarm obviously dominated much of the Klan's rhetoric, and this moralism proved far more specific, central, and pervasive in the Klan movement than in the insurgencies of the 1890s and 1930s. The Klan's national organization provided the major push for the emphasis on personal morality, the condemnation of licentiousness and drinking. Although many Jackson County Klansmen doubtless approved of this moralistic emphasis, the local Klan's populist appeal held at least equal or greater importance for most supporters in the main valley. Indeed, its obsession with Prohibition enforcement proved to be the Klan's Achilles' heel as a rural-based insurgency in Jackson County's hinterland. There, anti-Prohibition sentiments (or at least financially motivated violations of the Prohibition law) reduced the Klan's overall attraction in many outlying communities. Embarking on a far less divisive moral crusade, the GGC focused on purportedly corrupt and murderous aspects of Prohibition enforcement, thereby earning the loyalty of many hinterland residents, serving to unite residents from all rural sections.

Over the course of this four-decades-long insurgent tradition, women gained an increasingly public role as important participants. Southern Oregon's Farmers Alliance chapters and People's Party clubs, building on a foundation put in place by the Grange, encouraged public activity by farm women. Although the issue of suffrage was secondary to the goals of most Populists, women evidently acted as significant, if not full, partners in organizing conventions, rallies, and other public events. Women rarely gained mention in the local press as overt Klan supporters during the early 1920s, but the still-powerful Women's Christian Temperance Union prominently pushed much of the Klan agenda among the county's townsfolk. Given the substantial, if behind-the-scenes, activities of female Klan members documented in other parts of the country, Jackson County's Ladies of the Invisible Empire doubtless increased the local Klan's political and economic power through campaigns of boycott and personal acrimony against unwanted fellow citizens. During the tradition's 1930s episode, women formed a major portion (probably over one-third) of the GGC's membership, and some of them held positions of leadership during the organization's short lifespan. Henrietta Martin's very public role as the GGC's president demonstrated the political maturity of women during this last phase. In outlying areas, female organizers seem to have been key in forming local chapters, and women remained among Banks's most vocal and loyal supporters after the rebellion was crushed.

During the 1890s, the entire county—outside of the only two towns of any size, Jacksonville and Ashland—went solidly with the People's Party. After the pear boom of 1905 to 1912, the rural area had split into two zones: the main valley became more densely settled and increasingly dependent on large-scale irrigation, while the outlying zone retained the old hinterland pattern of individualistic agriculture, such as raising small herds of beef cattle, supplemented by seasonal work in the woods, hunting (whether in or out of season), and trapping. This divergence accounts, in part, for the very different levels of support that the two zones gave to the Klan. The Great Depression brought serious economic hardship to both zones, and it united them during the GGC phase.

The neighboring communities of Rogue River (Woodville/Evans Creek Valley), Gold Hill, and Sams Valley—all located on the north side of the river, and thus well outside of the Bear Creek Valley and quite distant from Medford—formed the most heavily and persistently insurgent area of Jackson

County. Residents of the county's northwestern quarter remained Populist through 1898, delivered Socialist presidential candidate Debs his strongest regional showing in 1912, even supported the Klan's slate and the compulsory School Bill in 1922, and gave enthusiastic support to the Good Government Congress. Although other outlying communities strongly supported various phases of the forty-year insurgency, citizens living on the north side of the river appear to have been in a state of near permanent disgruntlement.[14]

Finally, this long insurgent period had continuity in terms of certain individuals involved in its three main episodes. A number of vocal Ku Klux Klan sympathizers went on to become committed supporters of the GGC ten years later. Little information is available that would help answer the parallel question of possible continuity between the rank-and-file of the People's Party and that of the Klan. Nevertheless, two prominent Populist figures, Jeffrey and Phipps, later became closely identified with the local Invisible Empire. Jeffrey left Jackson County before the 1920s, but the one-time APA supporter served as the attorney for the Jackson County night-rider defendants. Remaining a political provocateur at heart, during the 1930s an aging John Jeffrey became one of Oregon's leading proponents of the Townsend Old-Age Pension Plan. Of all the personalities who were prominent during the forty-year span, William Phipps appears to have been among the most cynical and opportunistic. The one-time Populist candidate, former Klan mouthpiece, and legal counsel to the GGC's leader was an articulate and intelligent man. But Phipps, who spent most of his public career on an unsuccessful lookout for the main chance, seems to have been one who continually wet his finger and held it up to see which direction the next political breeze would blow.[15]

Jackson County's insurgent tradition owes much to the long American tradition of rural discontent. Furthermore, occurring in the far West during that region's transformation from frontier status to political maturity, it also can be seen as an especially western phenomenon of that period. Focusing on the conflict in the Kansas cattle-drive towns of the 1870s, historian Robert Dykstra goes beyond those towns' notorious history of brawling cowboys. Dykstra emphasizes that the cattle towns' pattern of internecine conflict owed more to local feuds between competing elite factions, between local farmers and Main Street, and between old-timers and newcomers.[16]

The West of the 1890s to the 1930s retained a legacy of political instability from the westward trek and early settlement. Compared to political patterns of older parts of the country, as political historian Paul Kleppner has explained, western politics of the period show the effects of increased mobility, including reduced partisan discipline and allegiance, with a resulting emphasis on voting for the person, not the party. This resulted in greater volatility from one election to the next, as well as a persistent tendency to view the region as an exploited, subservient colony of eastern capital and its local representatives. Western voters had a higher susceptibility than those of other areas to short-term political issues and a consequent predilection for impractical panaceas.[17]

The West's culture of Eden-seeking and boosterism also added to its pro-clivity for political cure-alls. Southern Oregon, Jackson County in particular, had been heavily boosted by promoters from the 1890s through the 1910s. The excessively high expectation of some longtime residents and many relative newcomers probably added a potent emotional component—that is, dashed hopes and an embittered search for scapegoats—to their political discontent during periods of economic difficulty.

And finally, Jackson County's weak, faction-ridden party system, typical of the West in the early twentieth century, provided an environment condu-cive to episodes of political instability. Local political-party organizations in the West, more so than in other regions of the country (which retained stron-ger, older partisan allegiances across the full spectrum of economic classes), tended to reflect the narrow interests of local elites. They also often neglected voters of lower economic, social, and educational levels. Because parties in the West did not penetrate nearly as far down into the grassroots level as in the East and South, lower-income groups "had no way to play a role in defining . . . problems, let alone in developing solutions to them."[18]

This exclusionary situation contributed directly to insurgent outbreaks. In periods of severe economic stress, such as occurred during the episodes in southern Oregon, the pressure evidently built up to such a degree that not only third-party but also "nonpartisan" antiestablishment movements took hold. Although tumultuous political developments during the 1890s, 1920s, and 1930s were certainly brought about by external economic and social fac-tors, they also played out in the way that they did thanks in some measure to political conditions endemic to the West.

THE JACKSON COUNTY REBELLION AND AMERICA'S LEGACY OF BACKCOUNTRY PROTEST

Returning attention to the Jackson County Rebellion, referring to the Good Government Congress of the 1930s, it is clear that the episode itself was not only part of a lengthy local insurgent tradition that became more violent over the years; it also sprang from the nation's tradition of backcountry rebellion.

In his speeches, Banks compared his Jackson County movement to the Boston Tea Party. His allusions to this and similar historic events, as well as his portrayal of GGC members as the spiritual descendants of New Eng-land "minutemen," were not cynical rhetorical flourishes used to legitimize intimidation and violence. Banks sincerely envisioned himself in the role of a patriot general fighting against a distant imperialist force—as well as against its local Tory lackeys.[19]

In contrast to the accusations of its fascistic nature, Banks saw himself and his followers as part of a long-standing American tradition of popular uprisings. In this, of course, he was correct. Given the Jackson County movement's causes and circumstances, Banks's perspective on the GGC has greater historical validity than does that of some of his critics. Historian John Shover's study of the radical 1930s Farmers Holiday Association movement explicitly depicts western Iowa's Cornbelt Rebellion as a final chapter in an American story that begins with Shays's Rebellion and ends with the agrarian unrest of the Great Depression. Southern Oregon's Good Government Congress episode can better be explained as part of this long national tradition of agrarian, backcountry rebellion.[20]

Americans' penchant for armed rebellion against authority began long before Daniel Shays and other armed regulators marched on the arsenal at Springfield, Massachusetts, in 1787. The term "regulator," as opposed to "rebel," for the Shaysites of 1786–1787, as well as for other such outbreaks, denotes that participants saw themselves not as rebelling against lawful authority but as confining—regulating—those in positions of authority when they overstepped their rightful bounds. Groups of colonial Americans, taking to the streets and the back roads as "the People out-of-doors," developed a tradition of direct action—"action" that "more often than not [took] the form of mob violence and crowd disturbance." Both urban riots and rural rebellions had punctuated the colonial years, particularly after 1700. Historians Howard Mumford Jones and Clarence Ver Steeg long ago pointed to the numerous backcountry revolts as symptomatic of the growing colonies' social and political instability during the eighteenth century. Many of these disorders, from minor disturbances in places such as Dedham, Massachusetts, during the 1720s or the larger North Carolina Regulation movement of 1766–1771 were rural, professedly democratic responses to the perceived selfishness or corruption of not-so-distant elites. In this sense, the American War for Independence can be seen as a backcountry rebellion, writ large.[21]

Shays's Rebellion of 1786–1787 continued the tradition of insurgency in dramatic fashion, contributing to the call for a constitutional convention—and thereby to the birth of the republic. It contained strong elements of localist resentment, class and cultural conflict, and agrarian protest, all exacerbated by serious economic distress. Shays's Rebellion was a movement of central and western Massachusetts farmers against the seaboard's commercial establishment, debtors against creditors, of rural "common people" against an "arrogant, urban" elite. Subsequent episodes, ranging from western Pennsylvania's Whiskey Rebellion of the 1790s and the Maine frontier's White Indian/Liberty Men uprisings of the 1790s–1810s through upstate New York's Antirent War of the 1830s–1840s, possessed similar attributes.[22]

Although each disturbance sprang from different local causes, the insurrections continued the tradition of rural uprisings. Responding to the nation's massive economic and social transformation after the Civil War, the old pattern of local, direct action by farmers evolved into more widespread, yet centralized and acceptable, forms of agrarian protest. Even so, the farmer-dominated, third-party movements of the Gilded Age, which culminated in the People's Party of the 1890s, retained much of the essential sound and fury of earlier protests. Although not characterized by personal violence, the Populist Revolt's embattled defense of local community and self-determination against the rising threat of Wall Street monopoly echoed protests that had been voiced by past rural insurgencies.[23]

Although Shover claimed the 1930s Cornbelt Rebellion of the Farmers' Holiday Association in the upper Midwest to be a final chapter in the tradition of American backcountry rebellion, historians have rightly challenged his assertion. While giving broad context to various historic episodes of backcountry rebellion such as Shays's Rebellion, Catherine McNicol Stock, Robert H. Churchill, and other more recent historians of late-twentieth-century rural-based protests point out that an especially radical form of agrarian-based unrest spread with a vengeance from the 1970s to the 1990s, not only in the Midwest but to other parts of the country, especially sections of the far West. And that, although not yet a mass movement, this trend—after having become deeply curdled out on America's extreme Far Right fringes with such attributes as violent vigilantism and a particularly vicious form of anti-Semitism—continues into the present day.[24]

The Jackson County Rebellion, or at least the ideology of its leader Llewellyn Banks, provided a forecast of this unfortunate trend. So too did the subsequent spread of William Pelley's Silver Shirts in the 1930s West. To be sure, this does not deny that the Good Government Congress owed its existence to the unsettled conditions of the Great Depression. The economic collapse and rising demagogic politics specific to that period were essential ingredients to the peculiar manifestation of the Jackson County movement.

It is a perilous, if understandable, temptation for a historian to interpret their own subject as somehow epitomizing a much larger historical theme. Yet, Jackson County during the early years of the Depression can be seen as something of a microcosm of the nation at large. A superficially booming 1920s decade gave way to pervasive economic distress. Financial speculators suffered major reversals in fortune. Production of a once-healthy industrial sector ground to a near-halt, and the ranks of the jobless grew. Farmers' discontent rose as prices fell and foreclosures spread through rural districts. And demagogues, who pointed at an elitist conspiracy to quash rightful populist democracy, inflamed antagonisms between social classes, economic interests, and even geographic sections.

After the rebellion had been subdued, emphasis on the movement's alleged fascistic demagoguery tended to slight its real historical roots and economic causes. Nevertheless, the authoritarian theme should not be dismissed. Llewellyn Banks, far more so than Earl Fehl, added a crucial dimension to the rebellion that otherwise would have been absent. Articulate and exhibiting wealth, Banks was a champion of the downtrodden who could combat the "gang" on its own ground. His personal magnetism, absolute certitude, and persuasiveness channeled mass discontent in a particular direction. Without him, the events of 1932–1933 would have been far different in character and result.

* * *

Writing in the late 1930s, some fifteen years before gaining a seat in the US Senate, Oregon journalist Richard Neuberger remarked that the Pacific Northwest's recent political history had been "almost without the individuals who occasionally make politics so ominous in other sections" of the country. Neuberger claimed that the "vast domain . . . [of the Northwest had] escaped the Huey Longs" and other demagogues who tried to usurp responsible government elsewhere in the nation during the Depression.[25]

Neuberger's inclusion of the qualifier "*almost* without" may have been a nod to the Jackson County episode. Although interpretation of the Good Government Congress as simply a fascistic movement is far wide of the mark, its emphasis on Banks's power to command intense loyalty and audacious action on the part of his followers is well placed. In that limited sense, it is clear that, in Jackson County, Oregon, it did happen here.

Epilogue

Following defeat of his 1935 pardon campaign and the departure of Ariel Pomeroy from southern Oregon, news of Llewellyn Banks faded from the pages of the local press. After Banks's wife and daughter left Salem in the mid-1930s, their contacts with the imprisoned Banks steadily dwindled and ended. Banks's siblings also abandoned their effort to have him freed. Llewellyn Banks spent all but the last few months of his life in the Oregon penitentiary, where he continued to work in the prison library for some years. With Banks coming up for possible parole in 1942, the prison doctor's report urged that Banks not be released, describing him as "an incurable psychotic ... [who] would harm someone if he should be let out into society." Seriously ill with cancer by the summer of 1945, the seventy-five-year-old Banks was taken to the state mental hospital in Salem, where he died on September 21. The *Tribune's* obituary article marked the death as the close of the "most violent period of Jackson County history."[1]

Earl Fehl remained in Jackson County after his release from the state mental hospital. Although his final years were relatively quiet ones, Judge Fehl continued his litigious battle to the end. In a final victory a few months before his death, Fehl obtained an injunction against the City of Medford regarding the fate of a large tree next to the Electa Fehl Building, a commercial structure and the last of his once-extensive real estate holdings. It had served as the site of numerous rummage sales during the 1950s. Fehl died, aged seventy-seven, at his Oakdale Avenue home on January 29, 1962. The Reverend Jouette Bray, one of the night-rider defendants of the 1922–1923 KKK episode and a GGC stalwart of the 1930s, officiated at the funeral. Among the pallbearers were several old friends from the foothills east of Medford. Fehl sustained his crusade against the "gang" even from the grave. His estate established the Electa H. Fehl Memorial Trust as a legal fund established for Jackson County defendants "wrongfully accused" of crimes or otherwise involved in severe legal conflict with local government.[2]

Robert Ruhl, who had begun his career with the *Mail Tribune* in 1911, remained its editor for twenty years following the Good Government Congress episode. In the early 1950s, Ruhl was one of the first mainstream journalists in the West (and one of the very few in Oregon) to criticize the methods of Senator Joseph McCarthy. The Pulitzer Prize remained the capstone to Ruhl's reputation. A former county commissioner, who had been one of the targets of the Good Government Congress, wrote to Ruhl in 1936 with gratitude that "it would have been impossible to have hung on without your support in those days." Although gratified at having received the Pulitzer, Ruhl wrote later in his life that the Ku Klux Klan fight of the early 1920s had required more courage and sacrifice on his part than did his anti-GGC stand. The anti-Klan crusade remained the episode in his career of which he felt most proud. Ruhl retired from the *Tribune* in the mid-1950s. He and his wife lived for several years in San Francisco for health reasons. Ruhl returned to Medford and died at age eighty-seven, on August 21, 1967.[3]

* * *

World War II and the nation's postwar boom changed forever the economic and social complexion of southern Oregon. The huge US Army training base at Camp White north of Medford infused Jackson County with cash. Numerous wood-products mills sprang up after the war to supply the American housing industry's seemingly insatiable appetite for lumber and plywood. Medford continued its dominance as the population throughout the Rogue River Valley soared during the 1960s to 1980s. Fruit orchards remained important, but the number of small orchardists steadily declined as a few large corporations came to dominate the scene.[4]

Since the 1990s, vineyards of varietal grapes and high-quality wineries have proliferated, and, even more recently, pasture acreages have been plowed to grow commercial marijuana and hemp. During the postwar years, residential subdivisions replaced many of the Bear Creek Valley's orchards and farms. The county's hinterland also changed drastically during the postwar years, submerging its old families with an influx of newcomers. Improved transportation, as well as the decline of small-scale agriculture and the increasing availability of relatively well-paying jobs in the wood-products industry during the postwar period, ensured that the area was no longer a remote backwater. By the 1990s, Jackson County's hinterland areas began to undergo noticeable gentrification, with construction of numerous expensive homes built on large-acreage properties.

Throughout the last seventy years, echoes of southern Oregon's old populist voice, although somewhat distorted by postwar social and political change, continued to be heard. The region gave 1968 presidential candidate George Wallace and subsequent third-party candidates substantially more votes than did the statewide returns. Jackson County politics also retained its traditional flavor of internal conflict during the period. Bitter recall campaigns have targeted a variety of local officials, from school board and city council members to county commissioners, again drawing the attention of upstaters to the belligerent tenor of southern Oregon's politics.

Far Right "citizens" organizations have found strong adherents among some local residents since the 1960s and 1970s. These include the Posse Comitatus (founded in Portland, Oregon, in 1969, by a former member of Pelley's Silver Shirts) as well as various extremist tax-protest groups. Even if their adherents in southern Oregon were few relative to the area's total popu- lation, their number in the region may have far exceeded the percentage of such people found in most other portions of the state. Some Jackson County residents of this kind have often been quite vocal in the form of regular opin- ion letters to the Tribune's editor. The ideology of some of these organizations contained strong components of anti-Semitic (and, for some, anti-Catholic) conspiracy theories, and all of them exhibited deep racism and thinly veiled threats of "patriotic" violence, trends that have only grown apace across the nation in the years since. Distrust and hatred of the federal government became another prominent component. Based on Jackson County elections since 1980, results for specific ballot measures or candidates for office permit some measure of support for the "populist New Right" agenda. Such support, including for presidential candidate Donald Trump in 2016 and 2020, appears proportionally strongest in the county's outlying areas.

In its recent fights over such questions as timber management on federal lands or moralistic would-be amendments to the state constitution prohibit- ing abortion and abridging civil rights for same-sex couples, Jackson County's experience really has not been significantly different from that of many other places in the West, or in the increasingly pluralistic, fractious, and polarized nation at large. Some aspects of the nation's intense political turmoil during the twenty-first century—the relentless, often crude anti-elitism and nativ- ism fanned by skilled demagogues in both the news media and the political arena—mirror southern Oregon's experience during the depths of the Great Depression.

America's legacy of backcountry rebellions and their tumultuously divi- sive politics gives the country's recent political battles a distinctive historical resonance. These national conflicts often resonate with rural passions and prejudices from decades before. Figuratively then, they echo the sound of shouts from a crowd of angry people massed on a courthouse lawn.

* * *

During the early 1990s, two elderly residents of Jackson County, each of whom recalled the events of 1932 and 1933, still held deeply divided opinions on Llewellyn Banks and his movement. One person, an orchardist's son interviewed in 1990, remembered Banks as an honest, courageous figure. He concluded, "I think they done him wrong, myself." Another longtime resident paused a moment when asked about the Good Government Congress episode, then shook his head and remarked, "It was all just so stupid, so very foolish."[5]

One can surmise that, in his final years, Llewellyn Banks's own opinion on the episode remained unchanged from his "Vision in the Mountains"—the final dream that Banks recounts in his 1934 prison memoir, *Weighed in the Balance.* This enigmatic scene, from a dream that had occurred in 1932, is Banks's allegory for the Jackson County Rebellion. A steely-eyed leader and his loyal troops of the mountainous hinterland stand ready to meet their oncoming foes in battle. Ever the grandiose narcissist, Banks wrote of an army of men, "marvelous men," and of their "Commander," who stood "looking off toward the valley below" where he saw thousands of other men, marching from the valley toward the mountain. "I dreamed no more," wrote Banks, but he pondered the meaning and saw one outstanding point to his dream: "The commander of the mountain hosts was viewing with PERFECT COMPOSURE the approach of the marchers from the valley. I know not when this vision will come to pass. But I cannot doubt its fulfillment."[6]

Appendix
List of Cited Items from Jackson County Archives

To reduce the length of the endnotes, the following archival documents have been assigned identifying item numbers 1 through 109. These documents—held in the Jackson County Archives (JCA) and cited in the narrative—are cited in the endnotes by their item numbers (1–109). (Note that these numbers are not archival, but have been generated by the author.) All these documents are held in the Jackson County Archives, Office of Jackson County District Attorney records (Record Group 8, #79A40 and #79A49). Photocopies of many of these JCA items, made by the author during his research, are also held in the collection of the Southern Oregon Historical Society in Medford, Oregon, under SOHS accession number #2006.50.1 (M52, shelf E, box 3).

Item 1:   "'A True Bill' (24 March 1933) and exhibit tag: 'Whip taken from Henrietta Martin'/'State v. H.B. Martin 71 et al.,'" DA/RG8/#79A40 (box 3/14), JCA.

Item 2:   "F. Wahl statement/'Oregon v. Henrietta Martin et al.,'" DA/RG8/#79A40 (box 3/14), JCA.

Item 3:   "Oregon v. C.H. Brown: Complaint/'Oregon v. H. Martin et al.,'" DA/ RG8/#79A40 (box 3/14), JCA.

Item 4:   "Mrs. J.B. Johnston, letter to Judge Coleman (16 August 1933)/unnamed file," DA\RG8\#79A40 (box 4/14), JCA.

Item 5:   "Amer. Legion Post No. 15, letter to Gov. C. H. Martin (18 July 1935)," DA/ RG8/#79A40 (box 4/14), JCA.

Item 6:   "I.E. Foy (American Legion post commander), letter to Gov. Martin (22 July 1935)/unnamed file," DA/RG8/#79A40 (box 4/14), JCA.

Item 7:   "GGC minutes and Resolution of 4 February 1933/'GGC, etc.' files," DA/ RG8/#79A40 (box 7/14), JCA.

Item 9:   "Transcript of E. Fehl's speech, 4 February 1933/GGC, etc. file," DA/ RG8/#79A40 (box 7/14), JCA.

Item 10: "Notes of GGC meeting, 18 February 1933/'Earl Fehl insanity hearing' file," DA/RG8/#79A40 (box 7/14), JCA.

Item 11: "S.A. Hopkins et al., letter to C. L. Brown [GGC sec'y] (14 March 1933)/'Copies of Statements,'" DA/RG8/#79A40 (box 7/14), JCA.

Item 12: "W.L. Stewart et al., letter to G. Codding (15 March 1933)/'Copies of Statements,'" DA/RG8/#79A40 (box 7/14), JCA.

Item 13:   "Janet Guches statement (24 March 1933)/'Copies of Statements' file," DA/RG8/#79A40 (box 7/14), JCA.

Item 14:   "G.A. Codding, letter to W.L. Stewart (28 March 1933)/'Copies of Statements' file," DA/RG8/#79A40 (box 7/14), JCA.

Item 15:   "Ted Dole, letter to district attorney (8 April 1933)/'Copies of statements' file," DA/RG8/#79A40 (box 7/14), JCA.

Item 16:   "Report from G.B. (14 May 1933)/'Copies of Statements,'" DA/RG8/#79A40 (box 7/14), JCA.

Item 17:   "D. H. Ferry, letters to Ralph Moody (17 and 29 July 1933), in 'State v. Fehl' file," DA/RG8/#79A40 (box 7/14), JCA.

Item 18:   "G. Codding, memo to G.W. Neilson (7 August 1933)/'State v. Fehl,'" DA/RG8/#79A40 (box 7/14), JCA.

Item 19:   "R.E. Moody, letter to G.A. Codding (17 December 1934)/'Invest. Material: B-F Affair,'" DA/RG8/#79A40 (box 8/14), JCA.

Item 20:   "Dr. R. Steiner, letter to Gov. Martin (11 April 1935)/'Copies of Statements,'" DA/RG8/#79A40 (box 7/14), JCA.

Item 21:   "W.L. Gosslin, 31 July 1935 memo to State Board of Control/'Paper on some of suits Fehl brought,'" DA/RG8/#79A40 (box 7/14), JCA.

Item 22:   "A Person Not Safe Behind Bars" (Burns) Harney County *Free Press*, 2 August 1935, 1; copy in DA/RG8/#79A40 (box 7/14), JCA.

Item 23:   "Respondent's Brief (October 1937)/'Earl Fehl Insanity Hearing,'" DA/RG8/#79A40 (box 7/14), JCA.

Item 24:   "A.B. Pomeroy, letter to the editor (24 November 1937)/'Earl Fehl Insanity Hearing,'" DA/RG8/#79A40 (box 7/14), JCA.

Item 25:   "E.B. Day, letter to G. Neilson (7 July 1941), and G. Neilson statement (24 February 1943)/'Earl Fehl Insanity Hearing,'" DA/RG8/#79A40 (box 7/14), JCA.

Item 26:   "Notes of E. H. Fehl speech/'GGC, etc. file,'" DA/RG8/#79A40 (box 7/14), JCA.

Item 27:   "E. Fehl speech excerpts/'GGC, etc.' file," JCA.

Item 28:   "Transcript of Fehl speech/'GGC, etc.' file," DA/RG8/#79A40 (box 7/14), JCA.

Item 29:   "E. Fehl speech transcript [by D.A. stenographer Walter Looker]/'GGC, etc.,'" DA/RG8/#79A40 (box 7/14), JCA.

Item 30:   "Closing argument/'Earl Fehl Insanity hearing' file," DA/RG8/#79A40 (box 7/14), JCA.

Item 31:   "In the Matter of . . . E. Fehl, charged as insane/'Earl Fehl Insanity Hearing,'" DA/RG8/#79A40 (box 7/14), JCA.

Item 32:   "E. Fehl affidavit/'Papers on some suits Fehl brought,'" DA/RG8/#79A40 (box 7/14), JCA.

Item 33:   "Re: Earl Fehl/'Earl Fehl Insanity Hearing file,'" DA/RG8/#79A40 (box 7/14), JCA.

Item 34:   "Judge E. Fehl v. Chas. H. Martin/'Papers on some suits brought by Fehl,'" DA/RG8/#79A40 (box 7/14), JCA.

Item 35:   Copies of Ariel Pomeroy letters, held in various files: DA/RG8, #79A40, JCA.

Item 36:   "Legal 10 Commandments as read by Mrs. Deacon [*sic*]/ 'GGC, etc.,'" DA/RG8/#79A40 (box 7/14), JCA.

Item 37:   "P[hil] Lowd statement/'GGC, etc. file,'" DA/RG879A40 (box 7/14), JCA.

Item 38: Affidavit of Chas. Troutfether, 22 July 1932, in "Good Government Congress, etc." file, District Attorney files, Record Group 8, Accession #79A40 (box 7/14), JCA.

Item 39: "Bates, Lively, and Pearson, letter to T.L. Breechen/'Copies of Statements,'" DA/RG8/#79A40 (box 7/14), JCA.

Item 40: "Copies of Statements file," DA/RG8/#79A40 (box 7/14), JCA.

Item 41: "'Why?' (broadside by 'Citizen's Committee for Civil Liberties of Jackson County')/'GGC, etc. file,'" DA/RG8/#79A40 (box 7/14), JCA.

Item 42: "Jail-cell conversation transcripts," DA/RG8/#79A49 (box 7/14 and 1/3), JCA.

Item 43: "Transcript of GGC speeches, 6 March 1933/'Invest. Material/Banks-Fehl Affair,'" DA/RG8/#79A40 (box 8/14), JCA.

Item 44: "Report of GGC Speeches (16 March 1933)/'Invest. Material, B-F Affair,'" DA/RG8/#79A40 (box 8/14), JCA.

Item 45: "Transcript of GGC speeches, 6 March 1933/'Invest. Material/Banks-Fehl Affair,'" DA/RG8/#79A40 (box 8/14), JCA.

Item 46: "Sgt. J. O'Brien statement and Sgt. E.B. Houston statement (19 March 1933) and 'Invest. Material: B-F Affair,'" DA/RG8/#79A40 (box 8/14), JCA.

Item 47: "D.H. F[erry], letter to G.W. Neilson (2 May 1933)/'L.A. Banks Trial papers,'" DA/RG8/#79A40 (box 8/14), JCA.

Item 48: "R.E. Moody, letter to G.A. Codding (17 December 1934)/'Invest. Material: B-F Affair,'" DA/RG8/#79A40 (box 8/14), JCA.

Item 49: "R.E. Pritchett statement, re: Joe Croft/'Invest. Material: B-F Affair,'" DA/RG8/#79A40 (box 8/14), JCA.

Item 50: "Virgil Edington statements/Invest. Material: Banks-Fehl Affair," DA/RG8/#79A40 (box 8/14), JCA.

Item 51: "History of dealings and connection with Banks [Virgil Edington]/'L.A. Banks Trial Papers,'" DA/RG8/#79A40 (box 8/14), JCA.

Item 52: "C.J. Connor affidavit/'Invest. Material: B-F Affair,'" DA/RG8/#79A40 (box 8/14), JCA.

Item 53: "Opening statement for the Defense by Joe Hammersly/'L.A. Banks Trial Papers,'" DA/RG8/#79A40 (8/14), JCA.

Item 54: "Codding notes/'L.A. Banks Trial papers,'" DA/RG8/#79A40 (box 8/14), JCA.

Item 55: "L.A. Banks expenses sheet/'Invest. Material: B-F Affair,'" DA/RG/#79A40 (box 8/14), JCA.

Item 56: "A.L. Coggins, letter to L.A. Banks (9 February 1933)/'Codding file,'" DA/RG8/#79A49 (box 1/3), JCA.

Item 57: "Milton Sexton statement (23 February 1933)," DA/RG8/#79A49 (box 1/3), JCA.

Item 58: "M.O. Wilkins statement (7 March 1933)/'Codding file,'" DA/RG8/#79A49 (box 1/3), JCA.

Item 59: "R.C. Cummings affidavit (11 March 1933)/'Codding file,'" DA/RG8/#79A49 (box 1/3), JCA.

Item 60: "Mason Sexton statement (11 March 1933)/'Codding file,'" DA/RG8/#79A49 (box 1/3), JCA.

Item 61: "Governor J.L. Meier, letter to Oregon Attorney General Van Winkle (18 March 1933)/'Codding file,'" DA/RG8/#79A49 (box 1/3), JCA.

Item 62:   "M[iles] Randall statement (22 March 1933)/'Codding file,'" DA/RG8/#79A49 (box 1/3), JCA.

Item 63:   "Louis F. Swanson affidavit (22 March 1933)/'Codding file,'" DA/RG8/#79A49 (box 1/3), JCA.

Item 64:   "L.A. Banks statement/'Codding file,'" DA/RG8/#79A49 (box 1/3), JCA.

Item 65:   "S.P. MacDonald, letter to district attorney (13 June 1933)/'Codding file,'" DA/RG8/#79A49 (box 1/3), JCA.

Item 66:   "H.R. Bower, letter to Oregon Deputy Attorney General R. Moody (18 July 1933)/'Codding file,'" DA/RG8/#79A49 (box 1/3), JCA.

Item 67:   "Glen Shelf statement (20 July 1933)/'Codding file,'" DA/RG8/#79A49 (box 1/3), JCA.

Item 68:   "A.R. Hoelting, letter to G. Codding (nd)/'Codding file,'" DA/RG8/#79A49 (box 1/3), JCA.

Item 69:   "S. P. MacDonald statement/'Codding file,'" DA/RG8/#79A49 (box 1/3), JCA.

Item 70:   "Mason Burl Sexton affidavit/'Codding file,'" DA/RGF8/#79A49 (box 1/3), JCA.

Item 71:   "Sam Carey statement/'Codding file,'" DA/RGF8/#79A49 (box 1/3), JCA.

Item 72:   "O.O. Clancy statement and Joe Daniels statement/'Codding file,'" DA/RG8/#79A49 (box 1/3), JCA.

Item 73:   "John Brock statement/'Codding file,'" DA/RG8/#79A49 (box 1/3), JCA.

Item 74:   "C.J. Connor affidavit, 'Codding file,'" DA/RG8/#79A49 (box 1/3), JCA.

Item 75:   "Milton Sexton affidavit/'Codding file,'" DA/RG8/#790A49 (box 1/3), JCA.

Item 76:   "Transcript of Davis/Sexton conversation while held in city-jail cell/'Codding file,'" DA/RG8/#79A49 (box 1/3), JCA.

Item 77:   "G. Shelf statement/'Codding file,'" DA/RG8/#79A49 (box 1/3), JCA.

Item 78:   "E.A. Fleming statement/'Codding file,'" DA/RG8/#79A49 (box 1/3), JCA.

Item 79:   Broadside ("Black Political Plot"); "Miles Randall affidavit/'Codding file,'" DA/RG8/#79A49 (box 1/3), JCA.

Item 80:   "Prospective juror lists (and informants' notes)/'Schermerhorn file,'" DA/RG8/#79A49 (box 1/3), JCA.

Item 81:   "Prospective jurors list/'Jury List for 1933' file," DA/RG8/#79A49 (box 1/3), JCA.

Item 82:   "Johnson notes/'Jury List for 1933,'" DA/RG9/#79A49 (box 1/3), JCA.

Item 83:   "T. Coleman, letter to G. Codding (26 February 1933)/unnamed file," DA/RG8/#79A49 (box 4/27), JCA.

Item 84:   "H. B. Martin, letter to G. A. Codding (14 February 1933)," DA/RG8/#79A49 (box 4/27), JCA.

Item 85:   "Daily Reports of 'G.B.,' 'D.,' or 'B.H.' (April 1933)/'State v. Mason B. Sexton,'" DA/RG8/#79A49 (box 4/27), JCA.

Item 86:   "Daily Reports by G.B. (20 April 1933)/'State v. M.B. Sexton' file," DA/RG8/#79A49 (box 4/27), JCA.

Item 87:   "Note on Flora Becknell/'State v. M. Sexton,'" DA/RG8/#79A49 (box 4/27), JCA.

Item 88:   "Transcript of overheard jail-cell conversation of E. Fehl (May 1933)/'Cuffel file,'" DA/RG8/#79A49 (box 4/27), JCA.

Item 89:   "Transcriptions of conversations in Medford City Jail overheard by D.A. stenographers Looker and Cuffel, 'Cuffle file,'" DA/RG8/#79A49 (box 4/27), JCA.

Item 90:   "Telephone memos/Cuffel file," DA/RG8/#79A49 (box 4/27), JCA.

Item 91:   "Summary of jury lists/'State v. Mason B. Sexton,'" DA/RG8/#79A49 (box 4/27), JCA.

Item 92:   "L. Hall; statement/unnamed file," DA/RG8/#79A49 (box 4/27), JCA.

Item 93:   "'Please Take Notice' to R.W. Ruhl/unnamed file," DA/RG9/#79A49 (box 4/27), JCA.

Item 94:   "A.R. Hoelting, letters to Gov. Julius Meier (13 February and 15 February 1933)," DA/RG8/#79A49 (box 5/27), JCA.

Item 95:   "Sen. H.P. Long (copy of) letter to L.A. Banks (30 March 1933)/unnamed file," DA/RG8/#79A49 (box 5/27), JCA.

Item 96:   "G.A. Codding, letter to state parole officer E.M. Duffy (2 April 1936)/'Perjury Cases file,'" DA/RG8/#79A49 (box 5/27), JCA.

Item 97:   "W.A. Banks, letter to A. Pomeroy (3 April 1933)/unnamed file," DA/ RG8/#79A49 (box 5/27), JCA.

Item 98:   "Petition to Hon. Charles H. Martin (1 June 1935) and T.A. Schollenberg statement (25 July 1935)/'Codding file,'" DA/RG8/#79A49 (box 5/27), JCA.

Item 99:   "Appellant's Reply Brief (Oct. 1944)/'Earl Fehl file,'" DA/RG8/#79A49 (box 5/27), JCA.

Item 100:   "'The Jackson County War' [by O. H. Goss; 16-page typescript]," DA/ RG8/#79A49 (box 5/27), JCA.

Item 101:   "Wesley McKitrick statement/Walter Jones file," DA/RG8/#79A49 (box 5/27), JCA.

Item 102:   "Miss Johnson's comments on Ed Gyger/Jury Panel notes/'Misc. GGC files and Art LaDieu file,'" DA/RG8/#79A49 (box 5/27), JCA.

Item 103:   "Oregon, Ex Rel G.A. Codding v. E. Fehl: Action for forfeiture of office/'Earl Fehl File,'" DA/RG8/#79A49 (box 5/27), JCA.

Item 104:   "F. Kelly: Daily Charts on L.A. Banks Mental Condition/unnamed file," DA/ RG8/#79A49 (box 5/27), JCA.

Item 105:   "Portions of opening statement: R.E. Moody/'Misc. GGC, Art Ladieu file,'" DA/RG8/#79A49 (box 5/27), JCA.

Item 106:   "Jury panel comments/'Art LaDieu file,'" DA/RG8/#79A49 (box 5/27), JCA.

Item 107:   "DA staff note: Argumentative Reasons . . . for Acquittal of John Glenn/'John Glenn file,'" DA/RG8/#79A49 (box 5/27), JCA.

Item 108:   "Perjury Cases file," DA/RG8/#79A449 (box 5/27), JCA.

Item 109:   "Notes of County Court and Misc. Notes, in 'Perjury Cases file,'" DA/ RG8/#79A449 (box 5/27), JCA.

Notes

CHAPTER 1

1 Williams, *Huey Long*, 630–631. For more on Long, see Hair, *Kingfish and His Realm* (Hair's biography of Long does not mention this particular radio broadcast); White, *Kingfish*.

2 "'Law and Order' Champion," *New York Herald Tribune*, 17 March 1933, p. 13; "Editor Kills Officer after Ballot Theft," *New York Times*, 17 March 1933, p. 22-L.

3 Schorer, *Sinclair Lewis*, 608. Lewis's whereabouts and interests during the 1933–1935 period are documented in Schorer's biography of Lewis, pages 446–454, 573–574, 593–599, 608–614, and 623–625.

4 "Pulitzer Awards Made for 1933," and "Newspaper Fought Rise of Dictator," *New York Times*, 8 May 1934, pp. 1 and 20.

5 Lewis's papers, held in the Beinecke Library at Yale University, were reviewed for items (e.g., newspaper clippings about the 1933 shooting or the 1934 Pulitzer award) that might provide clear evidence of the novelist's familiarity with the Jackson County episode. No newspaper clippings, other than reviews of Lewis's own works, were found in the collection for the late 1920s–1930s, however, and Lewis's 1933–1934 correspondence does not allude to the affair. Although Lewis's knowledge of the Oregon occurrence may remain problematic, given his presence in New York City during the period of the news coverage, it would seem quite likely that he did read about the events. Whether or not Sinclair Lewis actually read the brief newspaper accounts of the "Jackson County Rebellion" is not an important question when turning to an account of the episode itself.

6 Sternsher, *Hitting Home*; Garraty, *Great Depression*, 166.

7 The terms "Populist/Populism" and "populist/populism," which are used often in this work, are not interchangeable. The former, upper-case, term refers to the Populist or Peoples' Party of the 1890s; the latter term (following the *American Heritage Dictionary*, 3rd ed.) is more broadly used to describe the political beliefs or rhetoric that support the rights and power of the "common people" in their struggle against the privileged elite. Lower-case populism, then, subsumes the historic American political movement known as Populism.

CHAPTER 2

1 See "Rogue River" and "Oregon Donation Land Law" entries in the online *Oregon Encyclopedia of History and Culture* (hereinafter OEHC), www.oregonencyclopedia.org. The Applegate Trail, or Applegate Cut-Off, was Oregon's Southern Emigrant Road—an alternate route of the Oregon Trail that was first used in 1846 by Willamette Valley-bound settlers; it branched off from the California Trail in northwestern Nevada. Many who traveled it after 1852 stopped in Southern Oregon to settle.

2 For comprehensive narrative accounts of the Indian War period in southern Oregon, see Beckham, *Requiem for a People*. For Joel Palmer's opinions on the activities of settler militias in southern Oregon, see O'Donnell, *Arrow in the Earth*. Useful if dated overviews

of Jackson County's history include Tucker, "History of Jackson County," and Gilmore, "A History of the Rogue River Valley." Also see Southern Oregon Historical Society, *Land in Common.*

3 This chapter's narrative on the region's events during the Civil War period draws from LaLande, "Dixie of the Pacific Northwest."

    Regarding the sectional makeup of the area's "pioneer settlers," a circa 1881 list of 105 living members of the Southern Oregon Pioneers Association (who arrived in the region during the 1850s as adults) provides county or town birthplaces for most (but not all) of these members. Of the 105 members listed, a total of seventy-two were or had been engaged in farming. Of the seventy-two farmers, at least forty-three originally came from the American South (largely the Upper South), the border states, or the southern one-third of Ohio, Indiana, and Illinois; that is, the so-called Butternut areas of the Ohio River Valley that had been largely settled by southerners from Virginia (including West Virginia) and Kentucky. Of the twenty-three nonfarmers listed (who included merchants, physicians, attorneys, a banker, a cabinetmaker, and a surveyor), all but two of them either came from north of the Mason-Dixon Line (and the northern portion of the midwestern states) or were foreign-born emigrants.

4 For Oregon's history of official Black exclusion, see "Black Exclusion Laws in Oregon," *OEHC*; for the Beaver State's long history of White supremacy in general, see Thompson, "Expectation and Exclusion."

5 LaLande, "Dixie of the Pacific Northwest," 42.

6 Portland *Oregonian* (hereinafter *Oreg.*), 19 October 1861; *Oreg.*, 12 October 1861.

7 See LaLande, "Dixie of the Pacific Northwest," 65–66, for a discussion of Douglas County's Champagne Riot of 1866, southern Oregon's most notable episode of actual violence resulting from tensions of the Civil War; see also the "Champagne Riot" entry, *OEHC*.

8 For example, see Jacksonville *Democratic Times* (hereinafter *DT*), 5 September 1890, p. 1; *Ashland Tidings* (hereinafter *AT*), 30 October 1891, p. 1; *AT*, 12 February 1892, p. 2. Acreage and production figures from county assessor's report, as given in "Jackson County Census," *DT*, 10 October 1895, p. 2; *DT*, 17 January 1895, p. 2.

    This chapter's narrative on the region during the Populist Revolt draws heavily from LaLande, "Little Kansas in Southern Oregon," 149–176. Unless otherwise indicated, population figures given in this and succeeding chapters are from Bureau of Municipal Research and Service, *Population of Oregon Cities*. Also, "Population of First Judicial District," *DT*, 8 January 1892, p. 2.

9 Both Phoenix and Talent are situated on the railroad, as are Central Point, Gold Hill, and Woodville. Phoenix served the Eden Precinct, a farming neighborhood located between Phoenix and Medford; Talent served the Wagner Creek Valley area; Eagle Point was the hub of the Little Butte Creek ranching area; Gold Hill, on the north side of the Rogue River, was one of the main trading centers of the large Table Rock or Sam's Valley district; Woodville (later renamed Rogue River), also on the north bank of the river, served the scattered population of the Evans Creek Valley, near the Josephine County line; and Central Point's rural population extended from Medford north to the Rogue River. The Applegate Valley, located in the Siskiyous west of the Bear Creek Valley, contained about five hundred to six hundred people in 1890, most of them farmers and miners (*DT*, 8 January 1892, p. 2).

10 Throughout this work, unless otherwise indicated, all national, state, and county election results for southern *Oreg*on, from the Civil War period through the Great Depression, are from Onstine, *Oregon Votes*. Precinct tallies are from the "Official Vote of Jackson

County" tables that appear in post-election issues of the Jacksonville, Ashland, or Medford newspapers.

11 The shelves of university libraries groan under the weight of the many volumes written about the Populists. For one of the first comprehensive histories, and still a very useful narrative, see Hicks, *The Populist Revolt*. A highly influential interpretive work, very critical of the Populists as primitive and paranoid reactionaries, is Hofstadter, *Age of Reform*. Among the many post-Hofstadter works rehabilitating the Populists, perhaps the most influential (but also creating its own controversies) is Goodwyn, *Democratic Promise*. (Debate over the nature of the Populist movement, and whether it was a significantly ethnic-identarian movement and not simply a farmer-laborer reform movement, continues. For example, see Jason Frank "The Uses of Populist History," *Boston Review*, 2020, https://bostonreview.net/forum_responsejason-frank-uses-populisms-diverse-histories/. An excellent survey of the extensive literature is the bibliographic essay in Miller, *Oklahoma Populism*. To date, the only comprehensive treatments of the People's Party in Oregon are Harrington's 1935 MA thesis, "The Populist Movement in Oregon, 1890–1896," and Griffiths's PhD dissertation, "Populism in the Far West, 1890–1900." Both works concentrate on the Portland-area reformist intelligentsia and give little discussion on southern Oregon. (In addition, both Harrington and Griffiths erroneously attribute Jackson County's strong Populist sympathies to its mining industry; however, southern Oregon's by-then modest mining economy was based on gold, not silver, and the region's Populist strength clearly derived from agrarian discontent.)

12 *DT*, 15 May 1891, p. 2; *MM*, 28 January 1892, p. 2. The Farnham, or Eagle, Flouring Mill of Ashland published an 1892 contract milling charge of ten cents per bushel (*DT*, 4 March 1892, p. 3); other mills were in Jacksonville, Medford, Central Point, and Eagle Point. The county's flouring mills were separate, locally owned operations, not part of a syndicate; the accusation of a "milling trust" may have reflected more fear than reality, although informal collusion between mill owners cannot be discounted.

13 *DT*, 25 March 1892, p. 1; *AT*, 1 April 1892, p. 2; *Southern Oregon Mail* (hereinafter *SOM*), 26 August 1892, p. 2; *SOM*, 13 May 1892, p. 2. Oregon's state and local elections were held on the first Monday in June until after 1900, when Progressive Era legislation resulted in conformity with the date of national elections in November.

14 Goodwyn, *Populist Moment*, 67; *AT*, 11 September 1891, p. 3; *DT*, 24 April 1891, p. 3; *DT*, 29 May 1891, p. 3; *DT*, 12 June 1891, p. 3. Both Holt and Breese had been active in the local branch of Oregon's short-lived Union Party. See Harrington, "Populist Movement in Oregon," 19–24; *DT*, 24 April 1890, p. 2; *DT*, 23 May 1890, p. 2; *DT*, 6 June 1890, p. 2. Jessie Beeson, seventeen years old in 1891, belonged to a prominent pioneer family of the Wagner Creek/Talent area. Stella Duclose (or Duclos), a Nebraska emigrant, was twenty-two years old in 1891; the 1900 census lists her as a single woman, working as a servant in a Medford household.

For a detailed treatment of the important public role of women in the Alliance and early Populist movements of the Great Plains, see Wagner, "Farms, Families, and Reform." The Populists' attention to farm women as a key political (albeit disenfranchised) component in the agrarian movement had solid precedent in southern Oregon. The region's rural women had been subordinate yet active participants in local political endeavors as members of the Patrons of Husbandry, or Grange, since the 1870s to the 1880s. The Grange sponsored education and self-improvement efforts on behalf of farm wives and daughters, it gave women equal membership status within the organization, and it often publicly supported greater political rights for women in the larger society. See Nordin, *Rich Harvest*; and Marti, *Women of the Grange*.

15 *DT*, 15 January 1892, p. 2. In regard to the anti-Semitic overtone of the term "heartless Shylocks," see the discussion in the text on the issue of anti-Jewish sentiment in Jackson County of the 1890s.

16 *DT*, 18 December 1891, p. 3; *AT*, 4 March 1892, p. 2; *AT*, 11 March 1892, p. 3; *DT*, 11 March 1892, p. 3; *AT* and *DT*, March–May 1892.

17 *AT*, 4 March 1892, p. 3; *DT*, 7 May 1896, p. 2; *DT*, 11 May 1896, p. 2; *DT*, 14 May 1896, p. 2; *SOM*, August–November 1892. Breese had been active in the Greenbacker movement prior to his arrival in Oregon. Wakefield, who did not serve as a full-time minister, was associated with the Methodist Episcopal Church.

18 *SOM*, 22 April 1892, p. 2; *SOM*, 28 October 1892, p. 2; *SOM*, 20 May 1892, p. 4; *Medford Mail* (hereinafter *MM*), 30 June 1893, p. 3. For a discussion of Populists' "movement culture," see Goodwyn, *Populist Moment*, 20–35.

19 *DT*, 11 December 1891, p. 3; *AT*, 27 November 1891, p. 2; *AT*, 11 December 1891, p. 2; *AT*, 26 February 1892, p. 3; *SOM*, 22 April 1892, p. 2; *MM*, 15 December 1893, p. 2. The cooperative proposals seem to have been victims of internal disputes, intercommunity rivalries, and defensive price-cutting by the commercial mills. Kertson sold his Populist *Southern Oregon Mail* to Republican A. S. Blinton in early 1893; Blinton, wishing to cast off the Populist mantle, quickly returned the paper to its original name and changed its motto to the more fitting "Man Was Born to Hustle."

20 *SOM*, 13 May 1892, p. 2; *AT*, 10 June 1892, p. 3; *SOM*, 20 May 1892, p. 2; *MM*, 10 January 1896, p. 7.

21 *SOM*, 17 June 1892, p. 2; *AT*, 22 January 1894, p. 2; *AT*, 8 March 1894, p. 3; *AT*, 12 March 1894, p. 3; *MM*, 25 May 1894, p. 2. An Eagle Point correspondent (*AT*, 12 February 1894, p. 2) wrote of one ranch's foreclosure sale that brought out "about 100 men and boys ... representing all the cash on Butte creek."

22 *AT*, 15 March 1894, p. 2; *AT*, 7 June 1894, p. 2.

23 "enjoyed little influence": Harrington, "Populist Movement in Oregon," 54; for a brief discussion of this phenomenon in the Northwest's other agrarian Populist stronghold, see Riddle, "Populism in the Palouse," 109. *AT*, 26 October 1896, p. 2; *DT*, 9 May 1890, p. 2; *AT*, 26 October 1896, p. 2; *DT*, 14 March 1898, p. 2.

24 *DT*, 7 May 1896, p. 2; *AT*, 14 May 1894, p. 2.

25 For the classic charge of Populist anti-Semitism, see Hostadter, *Age of Reform*, 70–93. Focusing on western Populists, Larson finds the accusation to be weak; see *Populism in the Mountain West*, 156. The Populists' anti-Jewish remarks were not without important precedent in rural America. The Grangers 1874 "Ten Commandments" featured one that forbid members from having "Jewish middlemen between thy farm and [the great wheat market of] Liverpool to fatten on thy honest toil"; see Nordin, *Rich Harvest*, 240.

   As an example of anti-Chinese bias during the 1890s, one Medford laundry, advertising in Republican Blinton's *Medford Mail*, urged customers to "beat the Chinaman ... get your laundry work done by white people"; *MM*, 2 March 1894, p. 3. The APA had spread from the middle west to Oregon by 1894, creating much controversy during Portland's school board election that year; see "The APA," *AT*, 2 April 1894, p. 2. For an overview, see Higham, *Strangers in the Land*, 74–84. Griffiths ("Populism in the Far West," 406–411) cites evidence that links a few prominent Populists with the APA, and he admits it had some influence among the party ranks in certain areas of the West.

26 Mention of APA activities and candidates are found in numerous articles, *DT*, December 1895 through May 1896.

27 *MM*, 17 April 1896, p. 2; *AT*, 12 November 1896, p. 3. The notable exception to Ashland's stalwart Republicanism occurred with the 1892 presidential race, when the North Ashland precinct gave a plurality to Populist Weaver. This precinct included the town's

lower economic class neighborhoods, including the new Railroad Addition, where many Southern Pacific Railroad employees lived. In 1896, however, North Ashland returned a narrow majority for McKinley, while the town's more affluent neighborhoods gave the Republican solid support.

28 *VR*, 8 July 1897, p. 2; *VR*, 15 July 1897, p. 2; *DT*, 2 May 1898, p. 2; *DT*, 14 March 1898, p. 2. Aside from the four years after Woodrow Wilson's 1912 presidential victory, Republicans held most county and state elective positions in Jackson County throughout the 1900s–1920s. By the mid-1920s, registered Republicans outnumbered Democrats in the former "Bourbon [Democratic] stronghold" by more than two to one; see Secretary of State, *State of Oregon Blue Book*, 101.

CHAPTER 3

1 For historical overviews of the local orchard industry, see Cordy, "History of the Rogue River Valley"; Atwood, *Blossoms and Branches*.

2 *MM*, 7 June 1901, p. 2; *MM*, 2 May 1902, p. 1; *Medford Daily Tribune* (hereinafter *MDT*), 8 June 1908, p. 2; *MDT*, 22 January 1908, p. 1; *MDT*, 19 February 1909, p. 1; *MM*, 29 August 1902, p. 2; Cordy, "History of the Rogue River Valley," 17–18; Whistler and Lewis, *Rogue River Valley Project*, 34–35.

3 *MM*, 22 March 1901, p. 2; *MM*, 11 November 1904, p. 1; *DT*, 20 April 1908, p. 1; Cordy, "History of the Rogue River Valley," 8; *MDT*, 18 December 1907, p. 1; *MDT*, 21 March 1908, p. 1; *DT*, 20 April 1908, p. 1; *MDT*, 7 December 1907, p. 1.

4 Based on the club's 1911 membership list, most of the University Club's members were alumni of private eastern schools, particularly Harvard, Yale, and Williams, but also Columbia, Union, Georgetown, and others. For personal recollections of the social aspects of the pear boom, see Atwood, *Blossoms and Branches*, 30–77 (the boom's "Chicago connection" is discussed on pages 53–54); Otto Frohnmayer, personal interview with author, 21 February 1991.

5 Whistler and Lewis, *Rogue River Valley Project*, 15; Backes, "Ashland Area," 67–84.

6 *MDT*, 24 April 1908, p. 1; Cordy, "History of the Rogue River Valley," 9–12; Backes, "Ashland Area," 33–34; Medford *Mail Tribune* (hereinafter *MMT*), 2 June 1914, p. 4.

7 "The Merry . . . Minstrels" (editorial cartoon), *MDT*, 22 May 1908, p. 1; *MDT*, 10 April 1912, p. 1; *MMT*, 25 October 1912, p. 1; *MM*, 1 June 1900, p. 2; *MM*, 15 November 1901, p. 2. Jackson County from the 1890s through the 1930s exhibited the factional, volatile electoral character described as distinctively "Western" by Paul Kleppner, "Politics without Parties," in *The Twentieth Century West*, 295–338. For a brief but comprehensive discussion of the West's "distinctive pattern" of state and local politics during the Progressive Era, see White, *"It's Your Misfortune,"* 377–384.

8 Turnbull, *History of Oregon Newspapers*, 252. The date of Ruhl's first employment with the *Mail Tribune* is uncertain; available records are incomplete and contradictory. By Ruhl's own accounts, written in the 1930s and 1940s, he joined the *Tribune* in 1911; other records and personal sources suggest that he may have been referring to his association with the Medford *Sun* at that date, and that he did not join the *Tribune* until immediately after World War I.

9 *MDT*, 17 January 1908, p. 1. The valley's short-lived colony of Greek immigrants, most of them single, male railroad workers, also caused concern during this period; see *MMT*, 28 October 1912, p. 1. From the 1850s through the 1880s, Jackson County contained a sizable and often-harassed minority of Chinese laborers, many of them employed in the mines or on railroad construction, but by 1900 most of the very few Chinese remaining were scattered laundry and store owners. Despite the campaign to exclude them, a few Japanese did move to Medford and environs, including at least one family that owned a

small orchard; these residents were removed in 1942 as a result of Executive Order 9066. Ashland Commercial Club publicity flier, printed on reverse side of the club's official stationery (Ashland, 1915; author's personal collection).

10 *MMT*, 20 February 1914, pp. 1 and 3; *MMT*, 19 March 1914, p. 4.

11 *MM*, 11 November 1904, p. 2; *MDT*, 18 December 1907, p. 1; *MDT*, 29 April 1908, p. 1; *MDT*, 27 May 1908, p. 1; *MDT*, 30 May 1908, p. 1; *MDT*, 21 September 1908, p. 2. For discussion of newly enfranchised women as key to passage of prohibition in western states, see Cott, *Grounding of Modern Feminism*, 105.

12 *MMT*, 7 November 1912, p. 2.

13 *MDT*, 5 December 1907, p. 1; *MDT*, 11 December 1907, p. 1; *MDT*, 6 November 1908, p. 2; *MMT*, 9 April 1912, p. 4; *MMT*, 13 May 1918, p. 4.

14 *MMT*, 12 March 1914, p. 2; *MM*, 21 June 1901, p. 2; *MMT*, 5 November 1920, p. 3; *MMT*, 30 October 1922, p. 3.

15 *MMT*, 27 July 1921, p. 4; *MMT*, 14 July 1921, p. 4. Much of the Klan portion of this chapter draws from LaLande, "Beneath the Hooded Robe," 42–52. For an overview of the 1920s KKK in Oregon, see "Ku Klux Klan" entry, *OEHC*.

16 Ruhl attended Phillips Academy in Andover, Massachusetts, before entering Harvard; although a member of the class of 1903, he officially graduated in 1904. Ruhl and Roosevelt do not seem to have been close personal friends during college, but Ruhl's subsequent strong support of the New Deal later caused him to chastise some fellow alumni as hidebound reactionaries. Biographical material on Ruhl comes from a variety of sources, including the collection of his personal papers (cited below) and his obituary, *MMT*, 22 August 1967, p. 1. Except where otherwise indicated, biographical material on other principals in this and succeeding chapters obtained from these sources: *Who's Who in Oregon, Vol. 1, 1929–1930; Who's Who for Oregon, 1936–1937; Who's Who for Oregon, 1942–1944.*

   MMT, 6 November 1922, p. 6. There remains some question about when the Medford Klan was established. January 1921 is the date given by Rothwell, "Ku Klux Klan in the State of Oregon," 117; indirect evidence in the *Tribune* strongly suggests that same date. In any case, the Medford Klan, organized by a Kleagle (recruiter) traveling from California to Portland, seems to have been the first in Oregon, simply owing to the city's location as the first major northbound stop on both the main railroad and the highway route from California.

17 Medford *Sun* (hereinafter *Sun*), 26 February 1922; *MMT*, 27 August 1921. The "bootlegger war" is covered in the *MMT* between mid-August 1921 and March 1922; particularly articles for 18–22 August, 24 February, and 13 March. Jackson County's prohibition raids must be viewed in a regional, and even national, context (i.e., such episodes were on the rise throughout the Pacific Northwest during this time); see Murray, "Issues and Personalities," 213–233 (esp. p. 228).

18 *Sun*, 16 July 1922, p. 8.

19 The "water politics" issue is not unique; the KKK fastened onto various local grievances in other communities, from the competition of chain stores faced by small-town businesses to Salt Lake City Protestants' frustration over the political dominance by Mormon civic leaders.

20 The 1921 water crisis is reported in numerous editions of the *MMT* between mid-July and mid-September; in particular, see various articles of 20–29 July; political reaction to the shut-off of water to Medford's orchards is featured in articles for 11–24 August and 8 September. The TID's water-rights dispute involved the Sterling Mine, a large hydraulic gold mine near Jacksonville that dated to the 1870s; see *MMT*, 24 October 1922, p. 8.

21 Rothwell, "The KKK in Oregon," 120. The characterization of Klan members as men who possessed little "wealth, education, or professional position" was made some years ago by Jackson, *Ku Klux Klan in the City*, 18-19 and 246-247. But see, for example, MacLean, *Behind the Mask of Chivalry*, and Gordon, *Second Coming of the Ku Klux Klan*. For comparative purposes (including revelations on the social and economic prominence of local Klan leaders in one Oregon community), see Toy, "Robe and Gown," in Lay, *Invisible Empire in the West*, 153-184.

22 *MMT*, 4 August 1922, p. 3.

23 Interestingly, according to county records, Phipps's marriage to Clara Rader, member of an Eagle Point farming family, in 1909, had been officiated by a priest. (Biographical data on W. E. Phipps compiled from various official records compiled by historian Sue Waldron.)

24 Medford *Clarion* (hereinafter *Clarion*), 16 July 1922; *Clarion*, 6 August 1922, p. 6; *Clarion*, 11 August 1922, p. 6; Turnbull, *History of Oregon Newspapers*, 253.

25 For a discussion of Oregon's compulsory school bill, see Tyack, "Perils of Pluralism," 74-98; and Bryant, "Ku Klux Klan." *MMT*, 15 May 1922, p. 2; *AT*, 24 May 1922, p. 1; Saalfeld, *Forces of Prejudice in Oregon*, 5.

26 For a thorough examination of women's roles and goals in the Klan movement, see Blee, *Women of the Klan*. Blee's study focuses on Indiana but generalizes on the Klanswoman phenomenon nationwide; the book includes a photo of Klanswomen marching in the Josephine County seat of Grants Pass, Oregon.

27 *Sun*, 2 April 1922, p. 1; Roberts, "The Ku-Kluxing of Oregon," 490; *Clarion*, 1 September 1922, p. 6. For discussions of Speaker Kubli's prominent role in Oregon during the Klan period, see Clark, "The Bigot Disclosed," 180; and Toy, "Ku Klux Klan in Oregon," in *Experiences in a Promised Land*, 280.

28 *Clarion*, 23 June 1922, p. 1; Sheriff C. E. Terrill, letter to Gov. B. Olcott, 14 May 1922, TS, vol. 5, Ben Olcott Papers, Special Collections, University of Oregon Library, Eugene, np.

29 *Clarion*, 21 July 1922, p. 1; 17 August 1923, p. 4; 15 September 1922, p. 6.

30 *Clarion*, 11 August 1922, p. 6; 18 August 1922, p. 8; 25 August 1922, p. 8. For two examples of Ruhl's anti-Klan editorials, see "Law or Lawlessness," *MMT*, 3 April 1922, p. 4; "End the Farce," *MMT*, 17 May 1922, p. 4.

31 Until the 1960s, most historians of the 1920s Klan emphasized the organization's nativist philosophy as its core appeal; for Oregon, Saalfeld's *Forces of Prejudice* is an example of this interpretation. Following Jackson's *Ku Klux Klan in the City*, a number of historians stressed the Klan's strength as due to its self-proclaimed position as an agent of "moral reform"; essays that employ this approach for the Oregon Klan include Toy, "Ku Klux Klan in Oregon"; Toll, "Progress and Piety," 75-85; and Horowitz, "Social Mobility and Personal Revitalization," 365-384, as well as Horowitz's *Inside the Klavern*, which presents the meeting minutes of a Klan in LaGrande, Oregon. Most recently, a "populist interpretation" of the Klan has come to the fore. Focusing on the West, an excellent exposition of this approach (which includes broad interpretive essays by Leonard J. Moore and Shawn Lay as well as new pieces on the Oregon Klan by Toy and Horowitz) is Lay, *Invisible Empire in the West*.

32 Turnbull, *An Oregon Crusader*, 75. O. Frohnmayer interview. *Sun*, 30 July 1922, p. 1. George Codding, Medford attorney and an apparent Klan supporter, was up for election as the Legion's state commander that year; the Jackson County controversy evidently contributed to his defeat. Helen Colvig Cook, letter to Mrs. Donald L. [Star] Colvig, 15 August 1922, in Colvig family correspondence (collection privately held by Timothy Colvig).

33 *MMT*, 26 October 1922; *MMT*, 24 October 1922, p. 3; *Clarion*, 18 August 1922, p. 1; Helen Colvig Cook, 15 August 1922. Phipps's "Non-partisan league" mention for the IAVL story may have been a cunning double entendre, intended to tar the group by association with the Non-Partisan League (NPL) of the northern Great Plains, the radical agrarian organization that many had considered as unpatriotic, even disloyal, during the war, and that was still very much in the national news—hardly a fitting description for the prominent business interests of Jackson County's IAVL. Ironically, in 1922 the anti-NPL North Dakota business establishment organized the similarly named Independent Voter's Association (IVA) to combat the growth of the NPL (see Stock, *Main Street in Crisis*, 72–73; *Clarion*, 1 September 1922, p. 6).

34 *MMT*, 25 October 1922, p. 3; 28 October 1922, p. 6; 27 October 1922, p. 4. Cowgill, who had formerly been an engineer for the Copco-owned Rogue River Valley Canal Company, battled the RRVCC after joining MID. He called the private canal company's allegedly slipshod construction work at Fish Lake dam "criminal" and was run out of the company's work camp in 1923. With Thomas, Cowgill, and Phipps acting as political allies in 1922, the MID began using the *Clarion* for all official notices in preference to the *Tribune*; see Medford Irrigation District, Board of Directors' "Minute Book #4," 1 February 1922 to 2 September 1924, MID offices, Medford.

   Opponents' military records, or the absence thereof, became an issue during the campaign when E. E. Kelly criticized Thomas's and Cowgill's lack of service overseas. Supporting Kelly, the *Tribune*'s social section featured a large 1918 photograph, taken in the trenches of the Western Front, of a helmeted, grim-faced Colonel Kelly; see "Col. E. E. Kelly in the Front Line Trenches," *MMT*, 27 October 1922, p. 2 (sec. 2). Thomas had not been in the military, but Cowgill served stateside in the National Guard during the war; later, in 1942–1943, Col. Cowgill, an American Legionnaire, commanded the paramilitary State Guard, composed of volunteer units of "coastal guerrillas" that patrolled Oregon beaches; see Eugene *Register-Guard*, 23 January 1992, p. 4A.

35 Interestingly, Republican Ashland voted overwhelmingly for Klan-backed Democratic gubernatorial candidate Walter Pierce (whose Republican opponent, Ben Olcott, was anti-Klan); the only Ashland precinct to give Pierce less than a 67 percent majority was the working-class Railroad District, location of Holy Rosary Roman Catholic Church. Regarding the School Bill, before it went into effect, the US Supreme Court declared it unconstitutional.

36 *AT*, 21 November 1923, p. 3.

37 *AT*, 7 March 1923, p. 1; *Sun*, 11 March 1923, p. 1. (Bray's first name is spelled variously in the press as Jewett and Jouette.) *Clarion*, 23 March 1923, p. 8.

38 *Clarion*, 23 June 1923, p. 1.

39 *AT*, 10 September 1924, p. 3.

40 Turnbull, *History of Oregon Newspapers*, 253–254. The Robert W. Ruhl papers (privately held; Medford, Oregon) contain the following supportive correspondence to Ruhl: Letter from L. R. Wheeler (V.P., Portland Telegram), 13 March 1923; letter from Harry L. Kuck (publisher, Pendleton Tribune), 9 February 1923; letters from Gov. Ben W. Olcott, 16 May and 18 November 1922; letter from Reginald Parsons (Seattle-based Jackson County orchardist), 5 May 1922; letter from Rev. John Powers, 13 November 1922.

41 Edward C. Kelly, letters to Mary Greiner (3 and 6 August 1928), in Edward E. Kelly Family Papers, MSS 1434 and 1434-1, Oregon Historical Society manuscript collections, Portland.

42 *MMT*, 28 October 1928, p. 5; *MMT*, 16 May 1927, p. 1. Two of the several detailed accounts of the DeAutremont case are Sturholm and Howard, *All For Nothing*, and Chipman, *Tunnel 13*.

43 *MMT*, 6 November 1924, p. 6.

CHAPTER 4

1 "Once In A While" (title of Banks's regular editorial column, hereinafter OIAW), Medford *Daily News* (hereinafter *News*), 8 October 1929, p. 1.
(Author's note: Other than my 1993 doctoral dissertation and subsequent article in *Oregon Historical Quarterly* (OHQ), the only other previously published work on the Jackson County Rebellion episode is *Rebellion, Murder, and a Pulitzer Prize*, by Joe R. Blakely; self-published in 2015, the narrative portion relies very heavily on the 1993 dissertation and *OHQ* article; the remainder of Blakely's publication consists of a transcript of L. A. Banks's murder trial in Eugene.)

2 E. C. Kelly, letters to Mary Greiner (8, 13, 19, and 21 June 1928), Kelly Family Papers.

3 *News*, 17 September 1929, p. 1; 8 October 1929, p. 1; 8 October 1929, p. 1 (sec. 2). Banks's remodeling of the *News*'s new office at 117 West Main included a large curved counter made of Philippine mahogany, indirect lighting, and murals of forest scenes. The *News* had been owned and edited by Lee Tuttle from 1924 until Banks's purchase; Turnbull, *History of Oregon Newspapers*, 253.

4 First used during Calvin Coolidge's administration as a promise of prosperity, the Republican Party's pro-"big business" slogan persisted into Herbert Hoover's presidency.

5 *News*, 20 October 1929, p. 1; *News*, 26 September 1929, p. 1. Under the Chamberlin-Ferris Act of 1916, which implemented a US Supreme Court decision, nineteenth-century railroad-grant lands in western Oregon that were still owned by the Southern Pacific Railroad (successor of the original Oregon & California Railroad Company) were "revested" to the federal government, with a portion of the funds then generated from timber harvest on these lands going to the respective counties (in lieu of property taxes lost because of federal ownership). In 1937, the Oregon and California Land Act and subsequent measures would provide for an even more generous share of timber-sale funds to the counties; see entry on O-and-C Land Act, *OEHC*. When timber prices were high, the O-and-C Lands arrangement was a major boon to county coffers.

6 Agnes C. Kelly, letter to Mary Greiner, 16 June 1928, Kelly Family Papers. E. C. Kelly, letters to Mary Greiner (6 and 30 July 1928; 11 and 12 August 1928), Kelly Family Papers. Kelly considered Ruhl to be a moderate "Hamiltonian"; he admired Ruhl's "sincerity," although, in the late 1920s, Kelly stated that he did "not agree with him on most of his editorials or views" (30 July 1928), Kelly Family Papers.

7 E. C. Kelly, letters to Mary Greiner (6 and 30 July 1928; 11 and 12 [August?] 1928), Kelly Family Papers.

8 LaLande, *Medford Corporation*, 71–75. For discussion of important structural changes occurring in the American lumber market during the period, changes that deepened the already severe lumber depression, see Bernstein, *The Great Depression*, 83–87, as well as Robbins, "Western Lumber Industry," in *The Twentieth Century West*, 233–256. In addition to the large Owen-Oregon operation and one medium-sized mill (Timber Products of Medford), Jackson County contained approximately twenty small lumber mills; see Jackson County Commissioners' Journal, vol. 23, p. 313, JCA.

9 On the 1920s modernization of agriculture, see Fitzgerald, "Accounting for Change," in *The Countryside in the Age of the Modern State*; W. H. Joyce (Sec'y, Rogue River Co.), letter to Robert Ruhl, 18 August 1931, Ruhl Papers; *MMT*, 7 August 1932, p. 1; Cordy, "History of the Rogue River Valley," 28; Backes, "Ashland Area," 66; Van Hoevenberg

testimony, "State of Oregon vs. Llewellyn A. Banks" (trial transcript, p. 1155), Supreme
Court file #7853, State of Oregon Archives (hereinafter "State v. Banks," SOA). Fruit
Growers League members tended to be the larger orchardists of the valley. Providing
a global view of the impacts of agricultural overproduction during the late 1920s and
on into the early Depression is Garraty, *Great Depression;* Cordy, "History of the Rogue
River Valley," 20–21.

10 *MMT*, 28 October 1928, p. 3; *News*, 19 July 1929, p. 3; *News*, 5 July 1931, p. 1.

11 Cordy, "History of the Rogue River Valley," 21; *MMT*, 19 November 1930, p. 1.

12 *News*, 15 November 1929, 1. The above review of the county's relief problems is drawn
from various front-page articles, *MMT*, June 1931 through August 1932. Brief assessment
of the incapacity of most pre–New Deal local relief efforts to match the actual relief needs
is given in McElvaine, *Great Depression*, 79–81, and Romasco, *Poverty of Abundance*,
142–172.

13 R. Ruhl, "Thirtieth Anniversary Report" and letter to Mabel Ruhl, 15 September
1930, Ruhl Papers. *Pacific Record Herald* (hereinafter *PRH*), 16 July 1931, p. 3; and 24
December 1932, p. 3; *MMT*, 3 November 1932; *MMT*, 3 August 1932, p. 1; *MMT*, 4
August 1932, p. 1; *News*, 1 October 1931, p. 4.

14 Oral history interviews with Arthur Jeldness, Jack Hollenbeak, and Bill and Zelda
Edmondson, in Rogue River National Forest, *Recollections*. The Jacksonville *Miner* for the
1932–1934 period contains many references to Jacksonville's mining-related "population
boom," the result of renewed small-scale placer mining in the nearby Applegate Valley
as well as the resettlement of "relief" families in Jacksonville houses that had been
abandoned for unpaid taxes. For examples of incidents in the renewed "bootlegger war,"
see *MMT*, 5 November 1930, p. 4; *MMT*, 20 October 1932, p. 2; *MMT*, 3 November
1932, p. 4.

15 Recent decades have brought a resurgence of historical studies of rural America's
confrontation with the profound socioeconomic transformations of the late nineteenth
and early twentieth centuries. Termed by some the "new rural history," these include
Hahn and Prude, *Countryside in the Age of Capitalist Transformation* (1985); Stock, *Main
Street in Crisis* (1992); and Stock and Johnston, *Countryside in the Age of the Modern State.*

16 "Exhibit 3" (undated 1932 *MMT* article by Eva Hamilton) in Affidavit of Prejudice, "State
v. Banks," SOA; 1933 photographs of Banks home in same file. Banks had purchased
the house, built circa 1912, from orchardist John L. Root (George Kramer, personal
communication, 1993).

17 Except where otherwise cited, all biographical/autobiographical material on Banks
is taken from his own testimony, "State v. Banks," 660–788, SOA. A name search in
California newspapers, 1910–1930, indicates that soon after his arrival in Los Angeles,
Llewellyn Banks became manager (and likely also the owner) of the Pacific Coast Citrus
Fruit Auction Company. He almost immediately set about challenging the dominance
of the California Fruit Growers Exchange (CFGE, better known as the "Sunkist"
cooperative), urging small citrus growers to sell their fruit for cash, not by consignment
through middlemen. Banks (described by one Riverside newspaper in 1922 as "the well-
known Los Angeles citrus man") and his first wife, Florence, are regularly mentioned
in the society pages of the Los Angeles press as entertaining friends at their Hollywood
home. In the early 1920s Banks moved to Riverside County, where he had already begun
buying up numerous orange- and lemon-orchard properties. Banks also brought suit
against the CFGE for "restraint of trade," accusing the cooperative of conspiring against
him.

18 Banks testimony, "State v. Banks," 667, SOA. Information on Banks's wife and daughter is
included in several pieces of correspondence, Ruhl Papers.

19 Glenn Higinbotham, oral history interviews with Janet Werren, 15 June 1990; adding additional first-person evidence of pro-Banks attitudes among small orchardists is George Obenchain testimony, "State v. Banks," 975, SOA. Banks's apparent wealth and generosity led to the legend among supporters that he regularly carried on his person "a large sum of money in a money-belt"; see "Ex. 4," Affidavit of Prejudice, "State v. Banks," SOA.

20 "Pipes For Mayor" (adv.), *MMT*, 30 October 1928, p. 3.

21 Biographical material from E. H. Fehl testimony, "State v. Banks," 940–946, SOA; Henry Fehl obit., Fehl Papers (uncatalogued collection), Southern Oregon Historical Society, Medford.

22 *PRH*, 19 May 1932, p. 1.

23 *MMT*, 27 October 1927, p. 2; *MMT*, 3 November 1924; see also Fehl's unsigned/undated typescripts of draft editorials or letters to R.W. Ruhl, Fehl Papers.

24 *MMT*, 1 November 1924, p. 6; *MMT*, 2 November 1926, p. 3; *MMT*, 7 November 1928, p. 1.

25 *PRH*, 25 September 1930, p. 1; *PRH*, 10 December 1931, p. 4.

26 For examples of Banks's anti-USDA editorials, see the following *News* OIAW columns: "Quarantine Crusaders," 22 April 1931, p. 1; untitled, 19 November 1929, p. 1; "Patience Exhausted," 16 April 1931, p. 1. For a brief treatment of the Cow War, see DiLeva, "Frantic Farmers Fight Law," in *Hitting Home*, 126–147, as well as Stock, *Rural Radicals*, 81–86.

27 Dan Hull (retired Medford cooperative packing-house manager), personal interview with the author, 9 March 1993.

28 For examples of Banks's anti-cooperative editorials, see these OIAW columns in the *News*: "Why Prosperity?," 21 November 1929, p. 4; "Why Co-ops Not Wanted," 23 November 1929, p. 1; "Compulsory Co-op," 5 December 1929, p. 1; "They Shall Not Pass," 2 May 1931, p. 1; "Need There Be Bloodshed?," 3 May 1931, pp. 1 and 2; "Murder Will Out?," 27 May 1931, p. 1. For background on the 1920s cooperative movement and the 1929 act, see Soule, *Prosperity Decade*, 242–246; Hicks, *Republican Ascendancy*, 193–214; and especially Saloutos and Hicks, *Agricultural Discontent*, 286–289. On Lubin, see Agresti, *David Lubin*. Lubin arrived in the United States as a child; he and his parents were Jewish immigrants from Poland.

 The history of the Ford-Sapiro dispute, along with a useful discussion of problems of cooperative marketing in the 1920s, is given in Wik, *Henry Ford and Grass-Roots America*, 126–141. Like Lubin, Sapiro was also Jewish. For more on agricultural cooperatives during the early twentieth century, see Woeste, *Farmer's Benevolent Trust*, and Moses, "G. Harold Powell."

29 See the following OIAW columns in the *News*: 19 June 1931, p. 1; "Hoover Dictatorship," 28 July 1932, p. 1; "Impeach Hoover," 2 July 1931, p. 1; "The Mellon Family," 9 April 1932, p. 1; "Fear Not," 27 June 1932, p. 4; "Bureaucracy," 29 October 1931, p. 1.

30 *News*, 11 March 1932, p. 1; *News*, 21 May 1931, p. 1 (unless indicated otherwise, all emphasis is as in the original quotations).

31 See following OIAW columns in the *News*: "Betrayal," 13 June 1931, p. 1; "Nicaragua," 23 April 1931, p. 1; "The Feast," 27 October 1931, p. 1; "The Master Mind," 19 June 1931, p. 1; "America's Mortal Enemy," 24 April 1932, p. 1.

32 See following OIAW columns in the *News*: "A Jew for President," 9 September 1931, p. 1; "The Jews," 5 October 1932; "When a Jew," 10 April 1932, p. 1. The brothers Harry and David Rosenberg were major Rogue River Valley growers, packers, and owners of Bear Creek Orchards; their support of cooperative marketing and other ventures was anathema to Banks; nevertheless, he did not personally target them, as Jews, in his newspaper. (The brothers changed their surname to Holmes in the late 1930s, supposedly to circumvent

a boycott of their fruit label by German purchasers.) Oregon elected Portland's Jewish department-store owner Julius Meier as governor in 1930. Banks supported Meier's independent candidacy; however, even in 1932–1933, when Banks had become highly critical of Meier's policies, he did not use anti-Semitism in his attacks on the governor.

33 See following *News* OIAW columns: untitled, 24 June 1932, p. 4; "Pershing and Butler," 21 July 1932, p. 4. Butler was familiar to *Ore*gonians for having helped to establish Governor Meier's new Oregon State Police.

34 OIAW. "The Khaki Shirts," *News*, 12 October 1932, p. 4. Brief discussions of the Khaki Shirts are Schlesinger, *Age of Roosevelt*, 79–80, as well as Brinkley, *Voices of Protest*, 275–276.

35 See following *News* OIAW columns: "Senator Huey P. Long," 1 May 1932, pp. 1 and 4; "Dishonored Pygmies," 21 April 1932, p. 1; "Senator Huey Long," 5 May 1932, p. 1. Long's activities and national popularity during this period are detailed in Williams, *Huey Long*, as well as in Hair, *Kingfish and His Realm*. All upper-case emphases, in this quotation and in others throughout the book, are original.

36 *News*, 26 July 1932, p. 1.

37 *News*, 28 June 1931, p. 2.

38 R.W. Ruhl, letter to Mabel Ruhl, 19 June 1931, Ruhl Papers.

39 Gerald Latham, personal interview with author, November 1989.

40 *PRH*, 11 December 1930, p. 1.

41 *PRH*, 30 July 1931, p. 4. In addition to new legal controls, the county's dairymen were hard hit by the "disastrous" effects of their own 1932–1933 milk war; see Jackson County Commissioners' Journal, vol. 23, p. 313, JCA.

42 *PRH*, 12 March 1931, p. 1. For an example of Fehl's anti-Prohibition sentiments, see "The Eighteenth Amendment," *PRH*, 9 July 1931, p. 4.

43 Numerous articles in *PRH*, 4 July–5 November 1930; *News*, 10 July–4 November 1930; *MMT*, 22 October 1930, p. 1; *MMT*, 23 October 1930, p. 1; *MMT*, 24 October 1930, p. 1; R.W.R., letter to Mabel Ruhl, 15 September 1930, Ruhl Papers. McNary was one of the few Republican senatorial incumbents returned to office that year, another indication of his popularity among Oregon farmers; see Neal, *McNary of Oregon*, 126–127 (Neal's book does not mention Banks's 1930 independent candidacy). McNary's endorsement of the Agricultural Marketing Act, which proved to be unpopular in the Pacific Northwest—due to perceived discrimination against the region's produce because of the act's resulting stabilization corporation—had come after his seven-year, unsuccessful battle for parity; see Johnson, "Charles L. McNary," 138–140.

44 *MMT*, 5 November 1930, p. 8; PHR, 25 September 1930, p. 4. Although all Republican candidates were at great risk in 1930, McNary's poor showing in Jackson County is surprising, given his strong victory in the rest of Oregon. Jackson County had been McNary's weakest county in 1918, but by 1924 it had become his fifth strongest. McNary, who detested speech-making, did not campaign hard in southern Oregon during 1930; this may have contributed to the senator's vulnerability to an aggressive and charismatic "hometown" rival, Banks. See DeWitt, "Charles L. McNary," 85.

45 *PRH*, 6 November 1930, p. 1; *PRH*, 13 November 1930, p. 1.

46 For examples, see following *News* OIAW columns: 31 August 1932, p. 1; 11 September 1932, p. 1; 12 May 1931, p. 1; 16 December 1932, p. 1; 4 November 1931, p. 1.

47 Emil Zimmerlee, personal interview with author, 13 May 1992; Jack Hollenbeak, in Rogue River National Forest, *Recollections*, vol. 3, 51–53. *MMT*, 15 November 1930; *MMT*, 16 November 1930, p. 1; *PRH*, 17 November 1930, p. 1; *PRH*, 28 November 1930,

p. 1; *PRH*, 28 October 1932, p. 3. Fehl returned to the Dahack case regularly throughout 1931–1932.

48 *News*, 11 March 1932, p. 1; *MMT*, 11 August 1932, p. 1; *MMT*, 28 August 1932, p. 1; *MMT*, 2 August 1932, p. 1; D. H. Ferry, letter to R. W. Ruhl, 24 September 1932, Ruhl Papers.

49 L. A. Banks testimony, "State v. Banks," 727–729, SOA; Affidavit of Chas. Troutfether, 22 July 1932, in "Good Government Congress, etc." file, District Attorney files, Record Group 8, Accession #79A40, Jackson County Archives (hereinafter cited as "item/file name," DA/RG8/#79A40 (box 7/14), JCA). *News*, 31 March 1932, p. 1. Banks reported spending more than $9,000 on his 1930 Senate race; see *MMT*, 15 November 1930, p. 8. The following sources indicate that Banks used the threat of blackmail to gain advertisers: Erwin, "Crusades of the Past," 54; Latham interview; George M. Payne (wire service agent, Cincinnati, OH), letter to R. W. Ruhl, 19 May 1932, Ruhl Papers.

Note that the Troutfether affidavit cited above is designated as Item 38 in the list of cited documents obtained from the District Attorney records held in the Jackson County Archives (JCA). To reduce the length of the endnotes, all subsequent citations of specific JCA documents refer to the enumerated item in the list of these 109 documents, provided as an appendix.

50 Llewellyn A. Banks, letter to Earl H. Fehl, 4 January 1932, Earl H. Fehl Papers, Southern Oregon Historical Society.

51 *News*, 22 March 1932, p. 1; *AT*, 12 January 1933, p. 1; *MMT*, 3 August 1932, p. 1; *MMT*, 4 August 1932, pp. 1 and 7; *MMT*, 5 August 1932, p. 2; *MMT*, 32 August 1932, p. 1; LaLande, *Medford Corporation*, 76.

CHAPTER 5

1 For the country's "dazed" reaction, see Leuchtenberg, *Franklin D. Roosevelt*, 18–27. For a history of the farmers' revolt in Iowa, which included several episodes of violence, see Shover, *Cornbelt Rebellion*; FHA leader Milo Reno, a fiery former preacher and Populist, shared many of Llewellyn Banks's opinions on farmers' marketing solidarity, currency inflation, the Federal Reserve Bank "conspiracy," and the Jews.

2 *MMT* and *News*, 22 March–19 May 1932; *News*, 15 May 1932, p. 4; *News*, 22 May 1932, p. 1. The county judge acted as juvenile judge, ruled on insanity hearings, and held direct control over various county agencies.

3 E. Zimmerlee interview.

4 For "excerpts" from March 1932 speeches by Fehl, see JCA Item 27.

5 *News*, 21 April 1932, p. 1; *News*, 24 April 1932, p. 1. Longtime congressional representative Willis Hawley, thought by many at the time to be Oregon's "permanent fixture" in Congress, lost his 1932 primary race to a much younger man who emphasized the ruinous impact of "Hawley's tariff."

6 *MMT*, May–August 1932; *News*, 2 June 1932, p. 1. The phrase "Banks-Fehl" is simply a fortuitous, but unintentional, pun on the American banking system during this period; although it was not commonly used until after the 1932–1933 Jackson County episode, the Jackson County district attorney's archival records do call the episode the "Banks-Fehl Affair." I employ it here to describe their political movement before the formal founding of the Good Government Congress in January 1933.

7 *MMT*, 8 August 1932, pp. 1 and 5; *MMT*, 11 August 1932, p. 1; Atwood, *Blossoms and Branches*, 55 and 225; G. Latham interview; *MMT*, 14 August 1932, p. 4.

8 Ruhl typically did not arrive at the *Tribune* office until late mornings, particularly during the summer, when he played golf in the cool of the early hours. "1932 notes to Harvard alumni report, thirtieth anniversary," 2, Ruhl Papers; see also Ernest [Gilstrap], letter to

R. W. Ruhl, 14 September 1932, as well as R. W. Ruhl, letter to Mabel Ruhl, 30 June 1931, Ruhl Papers.

9 Reginald H. Parsons, letter to R. W. Ruhl, 16 October 1933, Ruhl Papers.
10 E. Zimmerlee interview; J. Hollenbeak, in Rogue River National Forest, *Recollections*, 52.
11 G. Latham interview.
12 D. H. F[erry], letter to R. W. Ruhl, 18 September [1932], Ruhl Papers. According to Ruhl, the *Tribune's* circulation declined during the 1932–1933 unrest from close to five thousand to well under four thousand subscribers; see R. W. Ruhl, letter to Ralph Norman (Journalism Department, Indiana University), 1 November 1933, Ruhl Papers.
13 *MMT*, 7 November 1932, p. 6; *MMT*, 7 November 1932, p. 1.
14 *PRH*, 15 September 1932, p. 1.
15 *MMT*, 7 November 1932, p. 4. All three candidates ran as Independents.
16 Socialist Party presidential candidate Norman Thomas accounted for most of the remaining 5 percent.
17 *MMT*, 7 November 1932.
18 *MMT*, 10 November 1932, p. 4.
19 *Courier* quoted in *MMT*, 11 August 1932, p. 6; *Oregonian* quoted in *AT*, 6 February 1933, p. 3; *AT*, 21 January 1933, p. 3; *MMT*, 13 October 1932, p. 8.
20 A. Schoeni, telephone interview with the author, 24 April 1992; *PRH*, 17 March 1932, p. 1 (L. A. Banks later emphasized that the jury that found against Fehl included persons employed by the California-Oregon Power Company and the "milk trust," two targets of Fehl's anticorruption crusades); *MMT*, 17 November 1932, p. 1; *MMT*, 18 November 1932, p. 1; Jacksonville *Miner* (hereinafter *Miner*), 1 January 1933–17 March 1933. Harlan Clark (former Jacksonville resident), personal interview with author (Eugene, Oregon), 3 June 1991. Mr. Clark, a personal friend of Leonard Hall's, recalls that Hall received secret refuge at Clark's home one evening when the threats seemed especially serious.
21 JCA Item 58. John Billings, personal interview with the author, 18 February 1991; JCA Item 6; Ruhl, letter to R. Norman, Ruhl Papers; G. Latham interview; Alicia Ruhl MacArthur, transcribed oral history interview/tape 142 (7 March 1980), Southern Oregon Historical Society, Medford; *MMT* 11 November 1996, pp. 8–9.
22 Appellant's Brief, March 1934, "State v. Banks," SOA; JCA Items 101, 50, and 52.
23 *AT*, 29 December 1932, p. 1; *News*, 1 January 1933, p. 1; *AT*, 5 January 1933, p. 1. Although Fehl castigated the "midnight" appointment of Nealon, the commissioners' record indicates that his appointment took place during regular business hours at 1:00 p.m.; see Jackson County Commissioners' Journal, vol. 23, p. 207, JCA.
24 *AT*, 6 January 1933, p. 1; *AT*, 7 January 1933, p. 1; *AT*, 10 January 1933, p. 1; Jackson County Commissioners' Journal, vol. 23, p. 332, JCA; *AT*, 29 December 1933, pp. 1 and 3.
25 "at no less than": JCA Item 100 (which is a brief, personal recounting of the 1932–1933 tumult, titled "The Jackson County War," by a local observer, O. H. Goss, written in 1933; see also JCA Item 65; "frequent and heavy feeders": JCA Item 94; "a couple of commissioners": JCA Item 26; *Miner*, 20 January 1933, p. 1; JCA Item 100.
26 "Nine attorneys!"; L. A. Banks testimony, 697–705, "State v. Banks," SOA; JCA Item 56; JCA Item 57.
27 *MMT*, 26 October 1932, p. 1; JCA Item 17.
28 Gordon Stanley, personal interview with the author, August 1990. JCA Item 94.
29 *Miner*, 20 January 1933, p. 1; L. A. Banks testimony, 687–688, "State v. Banks," SOA.
30 The Declaration," *News*, 8 January 1933, p. 1; JCA Item 52; *News*, 25 January 1933, p. 1; *News*, 29 January 1933, p. 4.

31 *News*, 20 January 1933, p. 4; *News*, 24 January 1933, p. 1; JCA Item 100.

32 *AT*, 4 February 1933, p. 1; JCA Item 100, p. 15.

33 JCA Item 27.

34 JCA Item 27; JCA Item 7.

35 *AT*, 4 February 1933, p. 1; JCA Item 58.

36 JCA Items 84 and 9; *News*, 1 February 1933, p. 1.

CHAPTER 6

1 GGC membership card [Defense Ex. 4], "State v. Banks," SOA.

2 See Morris, *Forging of the Union*, 322.

3 JCA Item 5; JCA Item 94.

4 A.E. Reames, letter to R.W. Ruhl, 7 February 1933, Ruhl Papers; JCA Item 102; JCA Item 45. "Pink sheet" was probably a double entendre; Hall occasionally published the *Miner* on pink or green newsprint as a publicity gimmick. *News*, 31 January 1933, p. 1. The "Communists" that Banks referred to probably included O. H. Goss, leader of the county's Unemployed Council, who broke with Banks over the GGC's "dictatorial" direction; there is no evidence that Goss (who wrote "The Jackson County War," JCA Item 100) was anything more "sinister" than an aggressive spokesman for the rights of the area's jobless.

5 *Oreg.*, 6 March 1933, p. 1; Fitzgerald, "Accounting for Change," 202.

6 JCA Item 88; R.W. Ruhl, letter to R. Ingliss, 19 December 1934, Ruhl Papers; J. Billings interview; County Commissioners' Journal, vol. 23, p. 232, JCA.

7 JCA Items 15 and 17; JCA Item 56.

8 Ohrt, *The Rogue I Remember*, 46.

9 J. Hollenbeak, in Rogue River National Forest, *Recollections*, 52; JCA Item 17; Peter Sage, telephone interview with the author, 3 February 1993.

10 The district attorney's GGC investigatory files, held in the county archives, contains one file folder titled "List of Some Members of the Good [Government] Congress," but the folder was empty at the time of the author's examination of the county DA files in 1992 (DA/RG8/#79A49 [box 5/27], JCA); its contents evidently have either been mislaid or purposely purged.

11 JCA Items 17 and 80; D.H. F[erry], letter to R.W. Ruhl, 17 August 1932, Ruhl Papers.

12 For an extended discussion of women's political participation during this period, see Cott, *Grounding of Modern Feminism*, especially pages 97–114, 209–211, 224–225, and 277–280.

13 JCA Items 65 and 59. Reddy's and Gore's support included appearances as character witnesses at Banks's trial. One of Banks's bodyguards recalled Reddy saying during the height of the GGC crisis that "he would like to hear of something happening . . . that he would like to hear of a 'hanging tree'" for Banks's opponents; see JCA Item 51. JCA Item 56; Jackson County Commissioners' Journal, vol. 23, p. 231, JCA.

14 *Oreg.*, 6 March 1933, p. 1.

15 *AT*, 10 March 1933, p. 4.

16 JCA Item 100 (Mr. Goss's personal narrative, "The Jackson County War," includes a doubtless self-serving account of his challenge to Banks; however, much of the brief narrative is substantiated by other JCA Items); see also JCA Items 13, 58, and 62.

17 JCA Item 7. Letter from Andy Simpson to L.A. Banks; *News*, 1 February 1933, p. 4.

18 "old folks . . . the churchy people," D.H. F[erry], letter to R.W. Ruhl, 13 September 1932, Ruhl Papers; "which brought," JCA Item 67; "a constant barrage," JCA Item 100; "the foreign population," JCA Item 70.

19 JCA Item 81; "State v. Banks," 692, SOA; G. Latham interview; J. Bray testimony, "State v. Banks," 880, SOA (Bray almost certainly perjured himself in Banks's defense). D. M. Lowe's GGC support in indicated by mention in district attorney files of several unnamed GGC supporters who were members of D. M. Lowe's family.
20 Election results, *MMT*, 8 November 1924, p. 6.
21 Letter from L. M. Sweet, Beagle, Oregon, 26 March 1922, in *MMT*, 28 October 1922, p. 4.
22 JCA Item 63.
23 W. J. Jones testimony, "State v. Banks," 833-837, SOA.
24 JCA Item 85.
25 G. Obenchain testimony, "State v. Banks," 973-974, SOA; *MMT*, 30 March 1934, p. 1.
26 A. Cox testimony, "State v. Fehl," 924-926, SOA.
27 M. Murray testimony, "State v. Banks," 892-909, JCA.
28 JCA Item 87.
29 M. Powell testimony, "State v. Banks," 863-873, SOA. Several handwritten notes in the DA's GGC investigatory files allude to a romantic liaison between Mrs. Powell and L. A. Banks, but there is nothing else to corroborate this.
30 A. Pomeroy testimony, "State v. Banks," 997-998, SOA; see also copies of Pomeroy letters in Ruhl Papers and in various files in the Jackson County Archives, DA Office/ Record Group 8, #79A40.
31 A. Pomeroy testimony, "State v. Banks," 997-998, SOA; see also copies of Pomeroy letters in Ruhl Papers and in various files in the JCA: DA Office/Record Group 8, #79A40.
32 O. Allenderfer testimony, "State v. Banks," 1147-1151, SOA.
33 H. Van Hoevenberg testimony, "State v. Banks," 1155-1159, SOA; Atwood, *Blossoms and Branches*, 55. R. Seaman testimony, "State v. Banks," 1094-1100, SOA.

CHAPTER 7
1 JCA Item 29.
2 JCA Items 10 and 58; R.W. Ruhl, letter to Rev. E.H. Malkemus, 12 May 1933, Ruhl Papers.
3 JCA Item 36.
4 JCA Items 51 and 9; L.A. Banks testimony, "State v. Banks," 758-759, SOA.
5 JCA Item 58; G. Latham interview with author; JCA Item 69.
6 *News*, 3 February 1933, p. 1; *News*, 27 January 1933, p. 1; *News*, 9 February 1933, p. 1.
7 JCA Items 67 and 68. JCA Items 78 and 70. (Connor's talk may have dealt with the Filipinos and Mexican immigrants who were then the subject of much negative publicity—as foreign-born, low-paid "job stealers"—in central California's cropland and orchard areas.)
8 JCA Items 92 and 68.
9 *Tidings*, 21 February 1933, pp. 1 and 4. The records vault, which was meant to store trial evidence, ballots, and other important materials, had thick concrete walls reportedly embedded with steel bars; if the room had by then been fitted with the intended steel bars over the windows, the burglary would have been virtually impossible.
10 Unless otherwise cited, the ballot theft narrative draws on the following sources in various sub-files of the District Attorney records, RG8, #79A40 and #79A49 of the JCA: JCA Items 70, 57, 73, 74, 101, 78, 71, 62, 50, 51, and 37, as well as transcriptions of conversations in Medford City Jail overheard by DA stenographers Looker and Cuffel: JCA Items 88 and 89; JCA Items 58 and 66.
11 JCA Item 72.

12 D.H. F[erry], letter to C.C. Chapman, 10 September 1932, Ruhl Papers; R.G. Parsons, letter to H.D. Norton, 16 October 1933, Ruhl Papers; H. Clark interview.

13 JCA Item 70.

14 *Tidings*, 27 February 1933, pp. 1 and 3.

15 All jail conversation transcripts in DA/RG8/#79A49 [box 7/14 OR 1/3], JCA.

16 JCA Item 76. (During World War II, Fluher flew US Army transport planes in South America; he perished in 1948 when his Beechcraft Bonanza failed and plummeted into Lake of the Woods.)

17 *Tidings*, 28 February 1933, p. 1; JCA Item 37; *Tidings*, 27 February 1933, p. 1.

18 JCA Items 103, 37, 2, 3, 51; O'Brien, "The Man Who Tried to Be Hitler," 42–47. (This pulp-magazine article likely was at least partially ghostwritten; however, virtually all of its statements are corroborated by other accounts in the district attorney's investigative files); Erwin, "Crusades of the Past," 54.

19 Sen. H.P. Long's letter to Banks, JCA Item 95.

20 JCA Item 44; G. Latham interview (Latham recalls watching this rally from near the library).

21 JCA Item 44. The 6 March event was filmed by California-Oregon Power Company newsreel cameraman Horace Bromley (video in possession of Southern Oregon Historical Society).

22 JCA Item 44.

23 Robert Ruhl, letter to Richard (Dick) Ingliss, 19 December 1934, Ruhl Papers; L.A. Banks testimony, "State v. Banks," 720, SOA; "Appellant's brief, State v. Banks," 6, SOA; JCA Item 53.

24 JCA Items 13, 37, 50, 49, 62. Forty-four years old in 1933, District Attorney George A. Codding grew up in North Dakota and moved to Oregon in about 1910; he obtained a law degree from Willamette University in 1912 and relocated to Medford, marrying into a local family. Codding, having served overseas in an aero squadron during World War I, was a prominent American Legionnaire and member of various fraternal lodges.

25 Warrant for arrest of L.A. Banks, "State v. Banks," SOA (this blood-stained warrant served as a State's exhibit; the form's usual arresting authority, granted to "any sheriff or deputy," had been crossed out and replaced with Prescott's name); E. E. Kelly testimony, "State v. Banks," 198–199, SOA; May Powell, "State v. Banks," 866–868, SOA.

26 JCA Item 46.

27 E. Fehl testimony, "State v. Banks," 960–961, SOA; L. A. Banks testimony, "State v. Banks," 720–722 and 760–764, SOA; Bill of Exceptions (17 October 1933), "State v. Banks," 13, SOA; P. Lowd testimony "State v. Banks," 441, SOA.

28 L.A. Banks, letter to Rev. L.F. Belknap (16 March 1933), State's Ex.; E. Banks, note to L.A. Banks (16 March 1933), State's Ex.; L.A. Banks testimony, 762; E.A. Fleming testimony, 78; all found in "State v. Banks," SOA.

29 JCA Items 46; Respondent's Brief (March 1934), "State v. Banks," 2–3, SOA; L.A. Banks testimony, "State v. Banks," 763, SOA; E.A. Fleming testimony, "State v. Banks," 85–86, SOA.

30 JCA Item 46; A.K. Lumsden testimony, "State v. Banks," 377–378, SOA; L. Bown testimony, "State v. Banks," 595–599, SOA.

The Associated Press story of the post-shooting events at the Banks residence, carried in the front section of the *New York Times*, incorrectly had the police "storming the barricades" of the house; the arrest was definitely accomplished peacefully; see "Editor Kills Officer," *New York Times*, 17 March 1933, 22-L.

31 JCA Item 36.

32 *Tidings*, 17 March 1933, p. 1; *Oreg.*, 17 March 1933, p. 1.

33 O'Brien, "The Man Who Tried to Be Hitler," 100.

34 JCA Item 61; R.W. Ruhl, letter to Gov. J. Meier, 19 March 1933, Ruhl Papers.

35 JCA Item 39; for example, see "Drive in Jackson County Continues," *Oreg.*, 18 March 1933, p. 8.

36 *Oreg.*, 20 March 1933, p. 3; JCA Item 104.

37 JCA Item 95.

CHAPTER 8

1 *Oreg.*, 27 April 1933, p. 1; 28 April 1933, p. 1; 7 May 1933.

2 *MMT*, 16 March 1933, p. 4.

3 *MMT*, 16 March 1933, p. 4.

4 *MMT*, 16 March 1933, p. 4; JCA Item 90; *MMT*, 16 March 1933, p. 1.

5 JCA Item 90; *MMT*, 17 March 1933, p. 8.

6 JCA Item 11.

7 JCA Item 12; JCA Item 14.

8 JCA Item 53; E.H. Malkemus, letter to R.W. Ruhl, 13 May 1933, Ruhl Papers.

9 *Oreg.*, 18 March 1933, p. 8; JCA Item 71; JCA Item 93; JCA Item 63.

10 JCA Item 86.

11 JCA Item 86; JCA Item 16. The informant "G.B." may have been Guy Bates (possibly related to miner F. A. Bates), an anti-GGC resident of the Rogue River area; although his information about GGC "guerrillas" and their planned violence may have been based only on rumor or incorrect inferences, the tenor of other local informants' reports certainly lends support to such fears; JCA Item 83.

12 *MMT*, 17 March 1933, pp. 1 and 5 (original emphasis).

13 *MMT*, 16 May 1933, p. 1; [no first initial] Slater, letter to R.W. Ruhl, 18 March 1933, Ruhl Papers.

14 JCA Item 104. During the pretrial and trial period, Banks's daughter, Ruth May Banks, stayed with family members who came to Medford for that purpose.

15 JCA Item 97. W. A. Banks lived in Tujunga, California, an affluent residential section in the mountains near Los Angeles. *JCA Item 104.*

16 JCA Items 104, 50, and 46.

17 Moody's legal expertise led to numerous special appointments; according to the 1942–1944 *Who's Who for* Oregon, Moody coordinated Gov. Charles Martin's anti-"labor racketeering" drive of 1937–1939.

18 Affidavit by L.A. Banks, 15 April 1933, "State v. Banks," SOA; *Oreg.*, 2 May 1933, pp. 1 and 3; Eugene *Register-Guard* (hereinafter *R-G*), 3 May 1933, p. 1; *Oreg.*, 3 May 1933, p. 1; *R-G*, 3 May 1933, p. 1.

19 *R-G*, 3 May 1933, p. 2; Donald Husband (retired Lane County attorney), telephone interview with the author, May 1991; JCA Item 53.

20 Except where otherwise cited, all material on the Banks trial is from the 1,300-page official transcript, "State v. Banks," SOA.

21 JCA Item 47; *Oreg.*, 13 May 1933, p. 1. Banks's pride in his colonial New England lineage earned a sneer from DA George Codding, who responded in his handwritten notes with the comment "Codfish Aristocracy," JCA Item 54.

22 *Oreg.*, 19 May 1933, p. 1.

23 *Oreg.*, 22 May 1933, pp. 1 and 2.

24 *Oreg.*, 22 May 1933, p. 6.

25 JCA Item 1.

26 *Oreg.*, 7 June 1933, p. 5; 23 June 1933, p. 1; 27 June 1933, p. 3; 28 June 1933, p. 3; 2 July 1933, p. 3; JCA Item 107.

27 *Oreg.*, 11 June 1933, p. 3; 12 July 1933, p. 6; 13 July 1933, p. 10; 14 July 1933, p. 5; 15 July 1933, p. 3; 16 July 1933, p. 1; 17 July 1933, p. 1.

28 *Oreg.*, 13 July 1933, p. 10; 16 July 1933, p. 1; 19 July 1933, p. 1.

29 *Oreg.*, 27 July 1933, p. 1; 28 July 1933, p. 5; 29 July 1933, p. 2; 1 August 1933, p. 4; 3 August 1933, p. 1; 5 August 1933, p. 1; Klamath Falls *Evening Herald* (hereinafter *KFH*), 29 July 1933, p. 1; 31 July 1933, p. 1; 2 August 1933, p. 1; 4 August 1933, p. 1; 5 August 1933, p. 1.

30 *Oreg.*, 8 August 1933, p. 1; 9 August 1933, p. 1; 10 August 1933, p. 1; 10 August 1933, p. 2.

31 *KFH*, 8 August 1933, pp. 1 and 8.

32 *Oreg.*, 6 August 1933, pp. 1 and 2; 7 August 1933, p. 4; *Oreg.*, 8 August 1933, p. 6. The grand jury, accepting Davis's contention that he was defending himself, refused to indict him; see R.W. Ruhl, letter to A.B. Pomeroy, 10 October 1933, Ruhl Papers.

33 JCA Item 4.

34 R.E. Moody, letter to R.W. Ruhl, 10 May 1933, Ruhl Papers.

35 JCA Item 91.

36 JCA Item 91; JCA Item 106.

37 JCA Item 82.

38 The typed jail-cell conversation transcripts are held in the "Codding file"/DA/ RG8/#79A49 (box 1/3), and the "Copies of Statements file," DA/RG8/#79A40 (box 7/14), JCA. Most of the courthouse conversations, transcribed verbatim in shorthand or longhand, and then by typewriter, are held in the "Cuffel file" and the "Perjury Cases file"/DARG8/#79A449 (boxes 4/27 and 5/27), JCA; see especially JCA Item 109, the lengthy transcript labeled "Notes of County Court and Misc. Notes."

39 JCA Item 18.

40 For the seminal statement of this concept of national "incorporation," see Trachtenberg, *Incorporation of America*. For a more geographically focused interpretation that uses the concept of incorporation, see Richard Maxwell Brown, "Western Violence: Structure, Values, Myth," *Western Historical Quarterly* 26. Brown's treatment of late-nineteenth and early-twentieth century western history explains many of the region's separate episodes of popular violence within the unifying concept of a prolonged "Western Civil War of Incorporation." It was a bitter and widespread war between the combined forces of incorporation—financial, political, extralegal—that were controlled by industrialists, railroad magnates, large landowners, and conservative businessmen of the West, on the one side, versus the numerous small producers (farmers, wage workers, etc.) who resented and resisted the loss of individual control that incorporation brought.

41 JCA Item 94.

42 F.H. Bartholomew, letter to R.W. Ruhl, 28 April 1933, Ruhl Papers.

43 "Pulitzer Awards Made for 1933," *New York Times*, 8 May 1934, pp. 1 and 20 (see also sidebar article, "Newspaper Fought Rise of 'Dictator,'" on p. 20).

44 *MMT*, 8 May 1934, pp. 1 and 6.

45 R.W. Ruhl, letter to Dean C.W. Ackerman, 26 September 1933, Ruhl Papers.

46 R.W. Ruhl, letter to C.W. Ackerman, 1 September 1933, and C.W. Ackerman, letter to R.W. Ruhl, 7 September 1933, Ruhl Papers. For discussion of Pulitzer recipients, see Rothmyer, *Winning Pulitzers*, 8; Bates, *Pulitzer Prize*, 104 and 248–249.

47 R.W. Ruhl, letter to C.W. Ackerman, 3 May 1934, Ruhl Papers.

48 Undated clippings, Ruhl Papers.

49 Undated clippings, Ruhl Papers.

50 S. Smith, letter to R.W. Ruhl, 24 May 1934, Ruhl Papers.

51 H. Clark interview. In addition to his Pulitzer editorial, see Ruhl's mention of Hall in his letter to Ralph Norman, 1 November 1935, Ruhl Papers.

52 A. Deakin, postcard to R.W. Ruhl, 26 July 1935, Ruhl Papers. H.B. Martin, letter to R.W. Ruhl, 4 June 1935, Ruhl Papers. A.B. Pomeroy, letter to R.W. Ruhl, 9 May 1934, and R.W. Ruhl, letter to A.B. Pomeroy, 15 May 1933, Ruhl Papers. Some anti-GGC spokesmen opportunistically seized on the fact that one of the insurgent organization's leaders was a woman. Leonard Hall in particular employed misogynous stereotypes, ridiculing Henrietta Martin as a hysterical, meddling female. Evan Reames dismissed her as "an excitable woman . . . who would readily lead a mob" (A.E. Reames, letter to R.W. Ruhl, 7 February 1933, Ruhl Papers). Ruhl did not express scornful sentiments toward Henrietta Martin as a woman, but he did address her treatment in the public arena. Responding to Ariel Pomeroy's call for "chivalry" toward Martin, Ruhl reminded her that "when a woman enters practical politics, as Mrs. Martin did, charges public officials with all sorts of . . . crimes, she can't expect—and should not expect—to hide behind her sex when those who are fought . . . fight back. She can't have her cake and eat it. She can't hope to give and never take. Women should not ask the protection of chivalry . . . when they enter a game in which chivalry never has and I fear never will have a place" (R.W. Ruhl, letter to A.B. Pomeroy, 10 October 1933, Ruhl Papers).

53 R.C. Notson, letter to R.W. Ruhl, 11 March 1933; P.R. Kelty, letter to R.W. Ruhl, 20 March 1933; R.W. Ruhl, letter to C.C. Chapman, 11 December 1934; Ruhl Papers; JCA Item 105.

    O. H. Goss coined the term "Jackson County War" for his brief, handwritten anti-Banks memoir; Ruhl's close personal friend Leonard Carpenter continued to use the phrase "revolution in the valley" as late as the 1970s; see Atwood, *Blossoms and Branches*, 56–57.

54 "Newspaper Expose to Be Dramatized in Pulitzer Playhouse" (undated/unattributed newspaper clipping), Ruhl Papers; Hohenberg, *Pulitzer Prize Story*, 50–51. Debunking of the Hohenberg "myth" is the main theme of a lively, if inadequately documented, sixteen-page undergraduate research paper by Jack Arends, "Robert W. Ruhl, the *Medford Mail Tribune* and the Good Government Congress."

CHAPTER 9

1 JCA Item 30.

2 Brown, *History of the Rogue River National Forest*, unpaginated (1933 section); Civilian Conservation Corps, *Official Annual: Medford District-Ninth Corps Area*.

3 LaLande, *Medford Corporation*, 81–83; MMT, 4 April 1934, p. 1; *Oreg.*, 9 July 1933, p. 2; MMT, 26 February 1934, p. 8. As documented in research by Jay Mullen, "Communist agitators" who attempted to organize the Rogue River Valley's pear pickers during the 1934 harvest were summarily arrested on charges of criminal syndicalism. The mid-1930s witnessed a tremendous upsurge in aggressive labor union recruitment throughout the nation and the Pacific Northwest; even though Jackson County was not immune to such efforts, the local establishment effectively inoculated the region from the more radical unionization drives. Mullen, "Oregon's Sacco and Vanzetti Case."

4 R.W. Ruhl's Harvard alumni "Thirty-Fifth Anniversary Report," Ruhl Papers. For an example of Ruhl's pro–New Deal stance, see his editorial, "Another Great F. D. Victory," MMT, 26 March 1934, p. 4; R.W. Ruhl, letter to Sen. C.L. McNary, 10 December 1934; C.H. Martin, letter to R.W. Ruhl, 9 November 1934; and E.C. Kelly, letter to R.W. Ruhl,

21 November 1934; Ruhl Papers. For Governor Martin, see Murrell, *Iron Pants:* Oregon's *Anti-New Deal Governor.*

5 W.A. White, letter to R.W. Ruhl, 8 February 1937, Ruhl Papers.

6 *MMT*, 19 February 1934; 22 March 1934, p. 6; 9 February 1934, p. 1; 30 March 1934, p. 1.

7 *MMT*, 4 April 1934, p. 1; R.W. Ruhl, letter to H. Martin, 12 April 1936, Ruhl Papers.

8 *MMT*, 30 March 1934, p. 1.

9 Banks, *Weighed in the Balance*, 38.

10 Banks, *Weighed in the Balance*, 44–45, 65.

11 Banks, *Weighed in the Balance*, 63. For a detailed history the English origins of British-Israelism, its eventual export to the United States, and its ultimate transformation into the viciously anti-Semitic Christian Identity movement of the present time, see Barkun, *Religion and the Racist Right.* A major American proponent of the British-Israel movement during the 1930s was William Cameron, the virulently anti-Semitic editor of Henry Ford's *Dearborn Independent.* However, Banks may have come under the influence of British Israelism during his years in southern California, where the movement became especially strong among certain evangelical and Pentecostal Protestant sects. It also proved popular among some Oregon residents during and after the Depression; see Burley and Ross, "From Nativism to White Power," 564–585.

12 Banks, *Weighed in the Balance*, 68–69; *Oreg.*, 6 August 1933, p. 10; *MMT*, 13 April 1934, p. 1. This autobiography either was never finished or has been lost.

13 R.E. Moody, letter to R.W. Ruhl, 17 December 1934, Ruhl Papers; JCA Item 48; R.W. Ruhl, letter to R. Ingliss, 19 December 1934, Ruhl Papers; G.F. Moran, letter to R.W. Ruhl, 17 December 1934; R. Ingliss, letter to R.W. Ruhl, 14 December 1934; Ruhl Papers; R.W. Ruhl, letters to Gov. Meier, 8 and 12 December 1934; R.W. Ruhl, letter to G.F. Skipworth, 9 December 1934; all found in Ruhl Papers.

14 R.W. Ruhl, letter to C.C. Chapman, 11 December 1934; F.D. Kellogg, letter to R.W. Ruhl, 7 January 1935; Ruhl Papers; A.B. Pomeroy, letter/petition to Gov. Martin, 24 July 1935, Ruhl Papers; A.B. Pomeroy, letter/compendium to Gov. Martin, 8 August 1935, Ruhl Papers; Dean W.L. Morse, letter to R.W. Ruhl, 24 July 1935, Ruhl Papers; W.L. Morse, letter to E.E. Kelly, 19 July 1935, Ruhl Papers; W.L. Morse, letter to Gov. Martin, 16 July 1935, Ruhl Papers; W.L. Morse, letter to A.B. Pomeroy, 19 July 1935, Ruhl Papers.

15 "Petition to Hon. Charles H. Martin (1 June 1935) and T.A. Schollenberg statement (25 July 1935)/'Codding file,'" DA/RG8/#79A49, JCA. According to the Eugene *Register-Guard* (as quoted in *AT*, 19 July 1935, p. 1), the signature of Neuberger and other Democratic liberals on the Banks petition was actually simply one part of their larger attempt to embarrass the increasingly conservative Governor Martin.

16 *AT*, 19 July 1935, p. 1; "A Person Not Safe Behind Bars" (Burns) Harney County *Free Press*, 2 August 1935, p. 1 (copy in JCA Item 22); *Southern* Oregon *Miner*, 19 July 1935, p. 1; Medford *News*, 17 July 1935, p. 1.

17 Salem Oregon *Statesman*, 3 August 1935, p. 1; *Oreg.*, 3 August 1935, p. 1; *MMT*, 7 August 1935, p. 1; *MMT*, 8 August 1935, p. 1. Kellaher was not convicted of the bribery charge.

18 JCA Items 21, 32, and 64.

19 JCA Item 20.

20 JCA Item 21. (Pomeroy's letter quoted in part and attached to original memo as Ex. H)/'Paper on some of suits Fehl brought,' JCA Item 32. (It is possible, even likely, that Banks himself composed this letter.)

21 *MMT*, 8 May 1934, p. 3; W.L. Gosslin, letter to R.W. Ruhl, 18 July 1935, Ruhl Papers; R.W. Ruhl, letter to W.L. Gosslin, 22 July 1935, Ruhl Papers; *MMT*, 8 April 1936, p. 1.

22 R.W. Ruhl, letter to Gov. Martin, 13 May 1935, Ruhl Papers; *MMT*, 20 May 1935, p. 1; *MMT*, 20 April 1934; *MMT*, 14 August 1935, p. 1; *MMT*, 21 August 1935, p. 3; JCA Item 79.

23 JCA Item 96.

24 G. Putnam, letter to R.W. Ruhl, 11 May 1935, Ruhl Papers; *AT*, 19 January 1937, p. 1; JCA Item 33. For background on Holman, see MacColl, *The Growth of a City*. See various letters, notes, and other items, Fehl Papers; also, JCA Item 34. Fehl brought suits against Jackson County almost immediately upon his release; see E.H. Fehl, letter to Mr. and Mrs. J.H. Young, 11 April 1937, Fehl Papers.

25 *MMT*, 16 August 1937, pp. 1 and 5; *MMT*, 7 September 1937, pp. 1 and 8.

26 E.H. Fehl, letter to E.M. Duffy, 26 August 1937, Fehl Papers; *MMT*, 5 October 1937, p. 1; JCA Items 41, 31, and 23.

27 *MMT*, 20 December 1937, p. 1; JCA Items 25 and 99.

28 R.W. Ruhl, letter to Mabel Ruhl, 7 November 1937, Ruhl Papers. Donald M. Erb served as president of the university from 1938 until his untimely death from pneumonia in 1943. Although his tenure at Eugene was brief, Erb compiled a solid record. He brought the sciences back to the campus, after budget-cutting and political pressure had moved them to rival Oregon State University in Corvallis, and he aggressively prepared the university for the expected postwar expansion in enrollment and programs (Keith Richards, University of Oregon archivist, personal communication). R.W. Ruhl, letter to Ralph Norman, 1 November 1935, Ruhl Papers.

29 J. Billings interview. Mr. Billings worked for one of the migrant resettlement programs, traveling between Jackson County and Coos County on the coast; he recalled in particular one family whose solution to broken plumbing was "to chop a hole in the bedroom floor for a privy." Overall, conflicts between local residents and "Okie" immigrants seems to have been minor. J. Smack, letter to R.W. Ruhl, 6 December 1934, Ruhl Papers.

30 Schlesinger, *Politics of Upheaval*, 34. For a comprehensive treatment of the movement, see Holtzman, *Townsend Movement*.

31 *Oreg.*, 3 August 1935, p. 1; *Oreg.*, 5 August 1935, p. 1.

32 P.J. Kirkpatrick, letter to R.W. Ruhl, 3 September 1935, Ruhl Papers; E. Deacon, letter to R.W. Ruhl, 31 December 1934, Ruhl Papers; J. Hollenbeak interview.

33 Holtzman, *Townsend Movement*, 90-94.

34 Holtzman stresses Townsendite support in Lemke's Oregon showing. Brief overviews of the Union Party debacle are given in Brinkley, *Voices of Protest*; Leuchtenberg, *Franklin D. Roosevelt*; and Schlesinger, *Politics of Upheaval*.

35 *KFH*, 10 November 1932, p. 1; *KFH*, 15 November 1932, p. 1.

36 Burton, *Democrats of Oregon*, 78.

37 Toy, "Silver Shirts in the Northwest," 139-146. Pelley's Silver Shirt Legion was a nationwide movement. The approximate number of members in the Silver Shirts' Medford chapter is unknown; see Burley and Ross, "From Nativism to White Power," 570.

38 E. Deacon, letter to R.W. Ruhl, 18 April 1937, Ruhl Papers. Deacon's particular brand of anti-Semitism may have been influenced by the ideas of the nationally known Reverend Gerald B. Winrod, a fundamentalist Protestant leader from Kansas. Winrod's magazine, *The Defender*, stoked belief in a Jewish conspiracy behind the threat of worldwide Communism; Winrod openly supported Hitler's anti-Jewish policies throughout the 1930s. See Ribuffo, *The Old Christian Right*; as well as the classic treatment by Lipset and Raab, *Politics of Unreason*.

In recent decades, the historiography of American Far Right movements, in particular those of the late twentieth and early twenty-first centuries, has expanded greatly. Two examples include Catherine Stock's previously cited *Rural Radicals* (1996) and Robert H. Churchill, *To Shake Their Guns in the Tyrant's Face* (2009). A more focused geographic scope is found in David A. Neiwert, *In God's Country: The Patriot Movement and the Pacific Northwest* (Pullman: Washington State University Press, 1999); and Elinor Langer, *A Hundred Little Hitlers: The Death of a Black Man, the Trial of a White Racist, and the Rise of the Neo-Nazi Movement in America* (New York: Henry Holt, 2003), which deals specifically with Portland, Oregon.

39 Kramer, *Camp White.*

40 In a heavily publicized ceremony, complete with newsreel cameras recording the event for a national audience, the "State of Jefferson" formally "seceded" from Oregon and California late in 1941. The effort initially generated much attention but was quickly abandoned after 7 December. See LaLande, "The State of Jefferson," as well as Peter Laufer, *The Elusive State of Jefferson: A Journey through the 51st State* (Guilford, CT: TwoDot, 2013).

CHAPTER 10

1 Sinclair Lewis, *It Can't Happen Here*, 33–34. Made into a theater production, the story enjoyed wide national popularity in 1936. Metro-Goldwyn-Mayer studio's planned film production but halted the project, evidently due largely to fear that the German and Italian governments would ban the showing of all MGM productions in reprisal. The stage version continued its run through the end of the decade. See Schorer, *Sinclair Lewis*, 614–625.

  Regarding the fundamental question, "What is a demagogue?," historian Reinhard H. Luthin uses a standard dictionary definition: a political leader "skilled in oratory and flattery and invective; appealing to the passions rather than to the reason of the public; and arousing racial, religious, [or] class prejudices." See Luthin, *American Demagogues*, 3.

2 *New York Times*, 8 May 1934, p. 20; Ruhl, "Thirty-Fifth Anniversary Report," Ruhl Papers. In a 1980 interview, Ruhl's daughter, Alicia, remarked on the episode's "fascistic" character: see oral history interview with Alicia Ruhl McArthur, Southern Oregon Historical Society, Medford.

  O'Brien, "Man Who Tried to Be Hitler," 45 (O'Brien's article may well have been ghostwritten); O. H. Goss's circa-1934 personal, handwritten account, "The Jackson County War" (pp. 1–2), hinted at a brownshirt-type insurrection, portraying the GGC "gunmen" who "stalked the streets openly" as "swaggering, vindictive, misanthropes, who would have killed with a word." The view of the GGC as fascistic evidently remained part of the lore of the *Mail Tribune*'s staff long after Ruhl's departure. Jack Arends, who worked for the *Tribune*, probably reflected the "It Can't Happen Here" interpretation of local journalists in a 1979 paper, which opens with a bit of hyperbole about "men march[ing] through the streets with guns . . . a mob [breaking] into the courthouse," and the proceeds to emphasize that the "town was not an alpine village in . . . early Nazi Germany . . . not a city in Fascist Italy, nor was it a Russian village enduring a Stalinist purge. The town was Medford, Oregon, U.S.A."

3 For two prominent liberal historians' echoing of this theme, see Leuchtenberg, *Franklin D. Roosevelt*, 38–39, and chapter 5, especially 96–103; and Schlesinger, *Politics of Upheaval*, chapter 2.

4 Lewis, *It Can't Happen Here*, 21–22. (As mentioned in chapter 1, it is possible that the novel's characterization of Doremus Jessup owes at least something to the Jackson

County insurrection. Lewis's initial villain, Windrip, is aided and then usurped by fascistic newspaperman Lee Sarasohn, who may contain a bit of Llewellyn Banks.)

5 Banks's hope to expand the GGC geographically was mentioned by Banks supporter Virgil Edington (JCA Item 50) and by Officer James O'Brien of the Oregon State Police in his 1941 published account of the episode. In *The Old Christian Right*, Ribuffo draws a parallel between the Red Scare of 1919–1920 and the subsequent use of a fascist bogeyman in the 1930s–1940s. His revisionist concept of a "Brown Scare" points to liberal commentators' tendency to portray as foreign and fascistic those movements that in reality were endemic, traditional "right-wing 'populism'" that merely resurfaced dramatically during the 1930s. Although not critical of their campaign to combat such forces, Ribuffo points out that the "extremist interpretation" of American liberals was not without its own self-interest and hypocrisy.

6 Brinkley, *Voices of Protest* (see especially pp. ix–xii, 143–168, 261–262, and 268–283).

7 Brinkley, *Voices of Protest*, 160–162, xi, 144–146. Brinkley and other post-liberal revisionists are certainly not the first to stress the distinction between Long's and Coughlin's movements, on the one hand, and fascism, on the other. Louis Hartz, in his seminal liberal "consensus" interpretation of American history, emphasized that the two men—with their nonhierarchical approach and "hardy pragmatism"—were not fascists at all but "Americanists to the hilt." See Hartz, *Liberal Tradition in America*, 276. Although Brinkley acknowledges that European fascism and American demagogic populism of the 1930s shared a number of ideas and anxieties, and that they "drew from similar political traditions" of populistic discontent, he states (p. 282) that neither Long nor Coughlin were "fascists in any meaningful sense of the term." Of particular value in tracing the long tradition of populism in the United States, with special emphasis on the twentieth-century rise of right-wing (and often elite-led) populism, is Kazin's *Populist Persuasion*.

8 For discussion of Herbert Hoover's 1929 Agricultural Marketing Act as an enlightened and benign effort toward "syndicalist/corporate-capitalist" control, see Williams, *Contours of American History*, 436–437.

9 "J. Hammersly opening statement/'L.A. Banks Trial Papers,'" DA/RG8/#79A40 (box 8/14), JCA. Hardly one to promote a formally fascist solution for America's social and economic ills, from prison Banks actually railed against the allegedly dark, foreign-tainted plot inherent in the US Mint's new Mercury dime, with its fasces symbol on the reverse face of the coin.

10 Banks, *Weighed in the Balance*, 44. "O. Goss/'The Jackson County War' (p. 15)," DA/RG8/#79A49 (box 5/27), JCA.

11 Paxton, *Anatomy of Fascism*, 219–220. The late Italian novelist and intellectual Umberto Eco proposed fourteen major characteristics of fascism in "Eternal Fascism: Fourteen Ways of Looking at a Blackshirt," *New York Review of Books* (22 June 1995). Yale philosopher Jason Stanley has recently offered a simpler (and perhaps simplistic) definition of fascism as "a cult of the leader who promises . . . restoration in the face of humiliation" brought on by Leftists, minorities, and immigrants, and who paints all his opponents as enemies and traitors.

12 Roberto, *Coming of the American Behemoth*.

13 Hofstadter, *Paranoid Style in American Politics*. Hofstadter, in his highly influential interpretation of the 1890s Populist movement, *The Age of Reform* (p. 22), took pains to caution readers that "Populism, for all its zany fringes, was not an unambiguous forerunner of modern authoritarian movements."

14 Even though spanned by a few bridges between the mouth of Evans Creek and Sam's Valley by the 1890s, the turbulent Rogue River may have served as a sufficient psychological barrier, long after it had ceased being a physical one, isolating north-side residents from

the rest of the county. Located either on or relatively close to the railroad, yet distant from the county's commercially powerful urban core, these communities north of the Rogue felt left out of political decision making. The town of Rogue River, situated close to the Josephine County line, and closer to its county seat of Grants Pass than to Jacksonville or Medford, seems to have perceived itself as especially neglected by Jackson County government.

15 The loss of the 1890 US Census data, as well as the secret nature of Klan membership, would be the main hurdles to such a study. In addition, the tremendous demographic change experienced between the two episodes make the tracing of such connections problematic.

16 Dykstra, *Cattle Towns*, 179-206.

17 For detailed discussions of the West's dominant political traits from the Populist Revolt through the Depression, see Kleppner, "Politics without Parties," and Rowley, "The West as Laboratory," in *The Twentieth Century West*, 339-357, as well as White's, *It's Your Misfortune*, 353-387.

18 Kleppner, "Politics without Parties," 327. Kleppner stresses how the West's nonpartisan, often "anti-party," politics contributed to its distinctive volatility.

19 JCA Item 100. Banks's public hatred of Herbert Hoover as "that Englishman in the White House" and tool of the Bank of England gives Banks's Revolutionary War–era sentiments more than a metaphorical reality. Allusions to the War for Independence as a means to legitimize popular violence has, of course, characterized many protest movements throughout subsequent American history; see Brown, *Strain of Violence*, 33 and 63.

20 Shover, *Cornbelt Rebellion*, 2. A more nuanced interpretation of the Farmers Holiday Association is given by Stock, in *Main Street in Crisis*, 128-142.

21 Wood, *Creation of the American Republic*, see 319-328. Although the frequency of urban riots, many of them ethnically or religiously based, increased during the early nineteenth century, the long-accepted practice in Atlantic Seaboard cities of occasional "mobbing" began to be systematically suppressed after 1800; see Gilje, *Rioting in America*. Rural rebellions, which persisted in traditional form much longer than did traditional urban riots, also antedated the city mob. Bacon's Rebellion, which convulsed seventeenth-century Chesapeake Bay society, was in some respects the original American backcountry rebellion. Although other factors (such as Virginia Governor Berkeley's Indian policy and intra-elite factional conflict) played key causal roles, the episode expressed many of the rural-based, populist/anti-(Tidewater) elite sentiments that would later become hallmarks of the tradition. See Washburn, *The Governor and the Rebel*; Bernard Bailyn, "Politics and Social Structure in Virginia," in *Seventeenth-Century America*, 90-115. See also Jones, *O Strange New World*, 275-285; and Ver Steeg, *The Formative Years*, 144-149; as well as Lockridge, *A New England Town*, 103-118; Kay, "The North Carolina Regulation," in Young, *The American Revolution*, 71-123. For an interpretive overview, see Brown, "Back Country Rebellions," in Brown and Fehrenbacher, *Tradition, Conflict, and Modernization*, 73-99.

22 For an interpretation that, in effect, places the Massachusetts episode within the tradition of backcountry rebellions, see Szatmary, *Shays's Rebellion*; see also Gross, *In Debt to Shays*. Additional histories of America's backcountry rebellions are plentiful. For example, see Richards, *Shays's Rebellion*; Slaughter, *The Whiskey Rebellion*; Taylor, *Liberty Men and Grand Proprietors*; Ellis, *Landlords and Farmers*; Kars, *Breaking Loose Together*; and Bouton, *Taming Democracy*.

23 See Robert Wiebe's concept of rural/small-town America's late nineteenth-century "island communities" as presented in *The Search for Order*.

24 See Stock, *Rural Radicals*, and Churchill, *To Shake Their Guns in the Tyrant's Face*.

25 Neuberger, *Our Promised Land*, 313. Neuberger, because of his tangential personal involvement in the attempts to gain a pardon for Banks, may have been either sincere or disingenuous in his omission of Llewellyn Banks's recent, sensational role in Oregon politics. As a youthful signer of the 1935 Banks-pardon petition, he may have wished to put that act behind him. Alternatively, Neuberger might have seen the Good Government Congress as too brief and too "local" to merit mention in a book addressed to a national audience.

EPILOGUE

1 Author's personal interview with Ruth Banks at her residence, Tacoma, Washington, 1995; Oregon State Penitentiary records, Banks, Llewellyn A., prisoner 12697.

2 *MMT*, 29 January 1962, p. 1; *MMT*, 31 January 1962, A-11; Sam Harbison (attorney for Fehl Memorial Trust), personal communication, 12 March 1993.

3 Billings, letter to R. W. Ruhl (undated: January–June) 1936, Ruhl Papers; R. W. Ruhl, "Fiftieth Anniversary Report to Harvard Alumni" (1952), Ruhl Papers; *MMT*, 22 August 1967, p. 1; *MMT*, 22 August 1967. The annual Ruhl Lecture series at the University of Oregon, sponsored by School of Journalism, memorializes Ruhl's journalistic career.

4 Between the 1930s and the 1970s, the number of orchardists declined from more than four hundred to about one hundred while the acreages remained relatively constant; see Cordy, "History of the Rogue River Valley," 28.

5 G. Higinbotham interview; Elton Petri, personal communication, 1992.

6 Banks, *Weighed in the Balance*, 70–71.

Bibliography

MANUSCRIPT SOURCES

California-Oregon Power Company. Captioned newsreel film footage of events in Southern Oregon, 1927–1933. Southern Oregon Historical Society, Medford.

E. E. Kelly Family Papers (correspondence and miscellaneous materials: E. E. Kelly and E. C. Kelly, ca. 1922–1940). Mss. 1434 and 1434–1, Manuscript Collections. Oregon Historical Society, Portland.

Fehl Family Papers (correspondence and miscellaneous materials: Earl H. Fehl and Delbert Fehl, ca. 1905–1950; uncatalogued collection). Southern Oregon Historical Society, Medford.

"Good Government Congress" investigatory records (correspondence, case files, and miscellaneous materials). Jackson County District Attorney's Office, Record Group 8, Accession #79A40 and #79A49. Jackson County Archives, Medford/White City.

"In The Circuit Court of the State of Oregon for the County of Jackson, State of Oregon, plaintiff, vs. Llewellyn A. Banks and Edith R. Banks, defendants," and same "for the County of Lane"; Oregon Supreme Court file #7853 (Accession #78A-23, folders 1–3). Oregon Supreme Court records. State of Oregon Archives, Salem.

"Jackson County Commissioners' Journal," volume 23 (May 1932–February 1934). Jackson County Archives, Medford/White City. (Titles and provenance of the 109 individual documents cited in the narrative are listed in the appendix).

"Medford Irrigation District–Board of Directors' Minutes." Medford Irrigation District, Medford.

Robert W. Ruhl Papers (correspondence and miscellaneous materials, ca. 1920–1967). University of Oregon Library, Special Collections, Eugene (papers privately held by Ruhl family, Medford, at the time of the author's research).

Rogue River National Forest. Recollections: People and the Forest. Vols. 2 and 3. Medford: Rogue River National Forest, 1990.

Rogue River National Forest Historical Records Collection. Seattle: National Archives.

NEWSPAPERS

Ashland Tidings, 1890–1935 (AT)
Central Point American, 1933
Democratic Times (Jacksonville), 1890–1900 (DT)
Eugene Register-Guard, 1933 and 1992 (R-G)
Jacksonville Miner, 1933 (Miner)
Klamath Falls Evening Herald, 1932–1933 (KFH)
Medford Clarion, 1921–1923 (Clarion)
Medford Daily News, 1927–1933 (News)
Medford Daily Tribune, 1907–1910 (MDT)
Medford Mail, 1892–1906 (MM)

Medford *Mail Tribune*, 1911–1967 (*MMT*)
Medford *Sun*, 1922–1923 (*Sun*)
New York *Herald Tribune*, 1933–1934
New York Times, 1933–1934
The (Portland) *Oregonian*, 1892–1896 and 1932–1935 (*Oreg.*)
Oregon Statesman (Salem), 1934–1935
Pacific Record Herald (Medford), 1922–1933 (*PRH*)
Salem *Capitol Journal*, 1933–1935
Southern Oregon Mail (Medford), 1892–1893 (*SOM*)
Southern Oregon Miner (Ashland), 1933
Valley Record (Ashland), 1896

OTHER PRIMARY SOURCES: ARTICLES, BOOKS, AND PAMPHLETS
Ashland Commercial Club. Publicity flier; official stationery. Ashland: Commercial Club, 1915.
Banks, Llewellyn A. *Weighed in the Balance: A Famine Foreseen*. Salem: np, 1934 (copy held in Oregon State Library, Salem).
Erwin, Ray. "Crusades of the Past: For Good Government." *Editor and Publisher*, December 1957, pp. 54–55.
Lewis, Sinclair. *It Can't Happen Here*. New York: P. F. Collier, 1935.
Neuberger, Richard L. *Our Promised Land*. New York: Macmillan, 1938.
O'Brien, James R. "The Man Who Tried to Be Hitler." *True Detective Mysteries*, February 1940, pp. 41–48 and 97–112.
Roberts, Waldo. "The Ku-Kluxing of Oregon." *Outlook*, March 14, 1923, pp. 490–491.
Secretary of State. *State of Oregon Blue Book and Official Directory, 1927–1928*. Salem: State Printing Department, 1927.
Walling, A. G. *History of Southern Oregon*. Portland: A. G. Walling Printing, 1884.
Whistler, John T., and John H. Lewis. *Rogue River Valley Project: Irrigation and Drainage*. Salem: US Department of the Interior/US Reclamation Service, in cooperation with the State of Oregon, 1916.
Who's Who in Oregon, 1929–1930. Vol. 1. Oregon City: Oregon City Enterprise, 1929.
Who's Who for Oregon, 1936–1937. Portland: Capitol Publishing Company, 1936.
Who's Who for Oregon, 1942–1944. Portland: Capitol Publishing Company, 1942.

SECONDARY SOURCES: BOOKS, ESSAYS IN EDITED VOLUMES, DISSERTATIONS, AND THESES
Agresti, Olivia Rossetti. *David Lubin: A Study in Practical Idealism*. Berkeley: University of California Press, 1941.
Atwood, Kay. *Blossoms and Branches: A Gathering of Rogue Valley Orchard Memories*. Medford: Gandee Printers, 1980.
Backes, G. Byron. The Ashland Area and Its Environs. MA thesis, University of Oregon, Eugene, 1959.
Bailyn, Bernard. "Politics and Social Structure in Virginia." In *Seventeenth-Century America: Essays in Colonial History*, edited by James Morton Smith. Chapel Hill: University of North Carolina Press, 1959.
Barber, William J. *From New Era to New Deal*. Cambridge, UK: Cambridge University Press, 1985.

Barkun, Michael. *Religion and the Racist Right: The Origins of the Christian Identity Movement.* Chapel Hill: University of North Carolina Press, 1994.

Bates, J. Douglas. *The Pulitzer Prize: The Inside Story of America's Most Prestigious Award.* New York: Birch Lane Press, 1991.

Beckham, Stephen Dow. *Requiem for a People: The Rogue Indians and the Frontiersmen.* Norman: University of Oklahoma Press, 1971.

Bernstein, Michael A. *The Great Depression: Delayed Recovery and Economic Change in America, 1929–39.* Cambridge, UK: Cambridge University Press, 1987.

Blee, Kathleen M. *Women of the Klan: Racism and Gender in the 1920s.* Berkeley: University of California Press, 1991.

Bouton, Terry. *Taming Democracy: "The People," the Founders, and the Troubled Ending of the American Revolution.* New York: Oxford University Press, 2007.

Brinkley, Alan. *Voices of Protest: Huey Long, Father Coughlin, and the Great Depression.* New York: Vintage Books, 1983.

Brown, Carroll A. *History of the Rogue River National Forest, 1933–1969.* Medford: Rogue River National Forest, nd.

Brown, Richard Maxwell. *Strain of Violence: Historical Studies of American Violence and Vigilantism.* New York: Oxford University Press, 1975.

———. "Back Country Rebellions and the Homestead Ethic in America, 1740–1799." In *Tradition, Conflict, and Modernization: Perspectives on the American Revolution,* edited by Richard Maxwell Brown and Don E. Fehrenbacher. New York: Academic Press, 1977.

Bryant, Janet W. The Ku Klux Klan and the Oregon Compulsory School Bill of 1922. MA thesis, Reed College, Portland, Oregon, 1970.

Bureau of Municipal Research and Service. *Population of Oregon Cities, Counties and Metropolitan Areas, 1850–1957: A Compilation of Census Counts and Estimates in Oregon.* Information Bulletin No. 106. Eugene: University of Oregon, 1958.

Burton, Robert E. *Democrats of Oregon: The Pattern of Minority Politics, 1900–1956.* Eugene: University of Oregon Books, 1970.

Chipman, Art. *Tunnel 13: The Story of the DeAutremont Brothers and the West's Last Great Train Hold-up.* Medford: Pine Cone Publishers, 1977.

Churchill, Robert H. *To Shake Their Guns in the Tyrant's Face: Libertarian Political Violence and the Origins of the Militia Movement.* Ann Arbor: University of Michigan Press, 2006.

Clanton, Gene O. *Populism: The Humane Preference in America, 1890–1900.* Boston: Twayne Publishers, 1991.

Cott, Nancy F. *The Grounding of Modern Feminism.* New Haven, CT: Yale University Press, 1987.

DeWitt, Howard A. Charles L. McNary: An Appraisal of His Early Political Career. MA thesis, University of Oregon, Eugene, 1967.

DiLeva, Frank D. "Frantic Farmers Fight Law." In *Hitting Home: The Great Depression in Town and Country,* edited by Bernard Sternsher. Chicago: Quadrangle Books, 1970.

Dykstra, Robert R. *The Cattle Towns.* New York: Atheneum, 1972.

Ellis, David M. *Landlords and Farmers in the Hudson Mohawk Region, 1790–1850.* Ithaca, NY: Cornell University Press, 1946.

Fitzgerald, Deborah. "Accounting for Change." In *The Countryside in the Age of the Modern State,* edited by Catherine McNicol Stock and Robert D. E. Johnston. Ithaca, NY: Cornell University Press, 2001.

Gaboury, William J. *Dissension in the Rockies: A History of Idaho Populism.* New York: Garland Publishing, 1988.

Garraty, John A. *The Great Depression.* Garden City, NY: Anchor Press/Doubleday, 1987.

Gilje, Paul A. *Rioting in America.* Bloomington: Indiana University Press, 1999.

Gilmore, Jesse Lee. A History of the Rogue River Valley Pioneer Period, 1850–1860. PhD diss., University of California, Berkeley, 1952.

Goodwyn, Lawrence. *Democratic Promise: The Populist Moment in America.* New York: Oxford University Press, 1976.

———. *The Populist Moment: A Short History of the Agrarian Revolt in America.* New York: Oxford University Press, 1978.

Gordon, Linda. *The Second Coming of the Ku Klux Klan: The Ku Klux Klan of the 1920s and the American Political Tradition.* New York: LiveRight Press, 2017.

Griffiths, David Burke. Populism in the Far West, 1890–1900. PhD diss., University of Washington, Seattle, 1967.

Gross, Robert A. *In Debt to Shays: The Bicentennial of an Agrarian Rebellion.* Charlottesville: University of Virginia Press, 1993.

Hahn, Steven, and Jonathan Prude, eds. *The Countryside in the Age of Capitalist Transformation: Essays in the Social History of Rural America.* Chapel Hill: University of North Carolina Press, 1985.

Hair, William Ivy. *The Kingfish and His Realm: The Life and Times of Huey P. Long.* Baton Rouge: Louisiana State University Press, 1991.

Harrington, Marion. The Populist Movement in Oregon, 1890–1896. MA thesis, University of Oregon, Eugene, 1935.

Hartz, Louis. *The Liberal Tradition in America: An Interpretation of American Political Thought since the Revolution.* New York: Harcourt, Brace, Jovanovich, 1955.

Hicks, John D. *The Populist Revolt: A History of the Farmer's Alliance and the People's Party.* Lincoln: University of Nebraska Press, 1931.

———. *Republican Ascendancy, 1921–1933.* New York: Harper and Row, 1963.

Higham, John. *Strangers in the Land: Patterns of American Nativism, 1860–1925.* New York: Atheneum, 1963.

Hofstadter, Richard. *The Age of Reform, From Bryan to F.D.R.* New York: Random House, 1955.

———. *The Paranoid Style in American Politics and Other Essays.* New York: Alfred A. Knopf, 1964.

Hohenberg, John. *The Pulitzer Prize Story.* New York: Columbia University Press, 1959.

Holtzman, Abraham. *The Townsend Movement: A Political Study.* New York: Bookman Associates, 1963.

Horowitz, David A. "Order, Solidarity, and Vigilance: The Ku Klux Klan in LaGrande, Oregon." In *The Invisible Empire in the West,* edited by Shawn Lay, 185–215. Urbana: University of Illinois Press, 1991.

———. *Inside the Klavern: The Secret History of a Ku Klux Klan of the 1920s.* Carbondale: Southern Illinois University Press, 1999.

Jackson, Kenneth T. *The Ku Klux Klan in the City, 1915–1930.* New York: Oxford University Press, 1967.

Johnson, Roger Taylor. Charles L. McNary and the Republican Party during Prosperity and Depression. PhD diss., University of Wisconsin, Madison, 1967.

Jones, Howard Mumford. *O Strange New World: American Culture, the Formative Years.* New York: Viking Press, 1952.

Kars, Marjoleine. *Breaking Loose Together: The Regulator Rebellion in Pre-Revolutionary North Carolina.* Chapel Hill: University of North Carolina Press, 2002.

Kay, Marvin L. Michael. "The North Carolina Regulation, 1766–1776." In *The American Revolution: Explorations in the History of American Radicalism*, edited by Alfred F. Young, 71–123. DeKalb: Northern Illinois University Press, 1976.

Kazin, Michael. *The Populist Persuasion: An American History*. Rev. ed. Ithaca, NY: Cornell University Press, 2017.

Kleppner, Paul. "Politics without Parties: The Western States, 1900–1984." In *The Twentieth Century West: Historical Interpretations*, edited by Gerald D. Nash and Richard W. Etulain, 295–338. Albuquerque: University of New Mexico Press, 1989.

Kramer, George. *Camp White: City in the Agate Desert*. White City: Camp White 50th Anniversary Committee, 1992.

LaLande, Jeffrey M. *Medford Corporation: A History of an Oregon Logging and Lumber Company*. Medford: Klocker Printery, 1979.

———. "It Can't Happen Here" in Oregon: The Jackson County Rebellion, 1932–1933, and Its 1890s–1920s Background. PhD diss., University of Oregon, Eugene, 1993.

Larson, Robert W. *Populism in the Mountain West*. Albuquerque: University of New Mexico Press, 1986.

Lay, Shawn, ed. *The Invisible Empire in the West: Toward a New Historical Appraisal of the Ku Klux Klan of the 1920s*. Urbana: University of Illinois Press, 1992.

Leuchtenberg, William E. *The Perils of Prosperity*. Chicago: University of Chicago Press, 1958.

———. *Franklin D. Roosevelt and the New Deal, 1932–1940*. New York: Harper and Row, 1963.

Lipset, Seymour Martin, and Earl Raab. *The Politics of Unreason: Right-Wing Extremism in America, 1790–1977*. 2nd ed. Chicago: University of Chicago Press, 1978.

Lockridge, Kenneth A. *A New England Town: The First Hundred Years: Deadham, Massachusetts, 1636–1736*. New York: W. W. Norton, 1985.

Lowitt, Richard. *The New Deal and the West*. Bloomington: Indiana University Press, 1984.

Luthin, Reinhard H. *American Demagogues: The Twentieth Century*. Boston: Beacon Press, 1954.

MacColl, E. Kimbark. *The Growth of a City: Power and Politics in Portland, Oregon, 1915 to 1950*. Portland: Georgian Press, 1979.

MacLean, Nancy. *Behind the Mask of Chivalry: The Making of the Second Ku Klux Klan*. New York: Oxford University Press, 1994.

Marti, Donald. *Women of the Grange: Mutuality and Sisterhood in Rural America, 1866–1920*. New York: Greenwood Press, 1991.

McElvaine, Robert S. *The Great Depression: America, 1929–1941*. New York: Times Books, 1984.

Miller, Worth Robert. *Oklahoma Populism: A History of the People's Party in the Oklahoma Territory*. Norman: University of Oklahoma Press, 1987.

Moore, John Hammond. "Communists and Fascists in a Southern City: Atlanta, 1930." In *Hitting Home: The Great Depression in Town and Country*, edited by Bernard Sternsher, 85–97. Chicago: Quadrangle Books, 1970.

Morris, Richard B. *The Forging of the Union: 1781–1789*. New York: Harper and Row, 1987.

Mowry, George E. *The California Progressives*. New York: Quadrangle/New York Times Books, 1951.

Murrell, Gary. *Iron Pants: Oregon's Anti-New Deal Governor, Charles Henry Martin*. Pullman: Washington State University Press, 2000.

Neal, Steve. *McNary of Oregon: A Political Biography*. Portland: Western Imprints/Oregon Historical Society, 1987.

Nordin, Sven D. *Rich Harvest: A History of the Grange, 1867–1900*. Jackson: University of Mississippi Press, 1974.

Nugent, Walter T. K. *The Tolerant Populists: Kansas, Populism, and Nativism*. Chicago: University of Chicago Press, 1963.

O'Donnell, Terrence. *An Arrow in the Earth: General Joel Palmer and the Indians of Oregon*. Portland: Oregon Historical Society Press, 1992.

Ohrt, Wallace. *The Rogue I Remember*. Seattle: The Mountaineers, 1979.

Onstine, Burton W. *Oregon Votes: 1858–1972*. Portland: Oregon Historical Society, 1973.

Paxton, Robert O. *The Anatomy of Fascism*. New York: Vintage Books, 2004.

Pollack, Norman. *The Populist Response to Industrial America: Midwestern Populist Thought*. Cambridge, MA: Harvard University Press, 1962.

Ribuffo, Leo P. *The Old Christian Right: The Protestant Far Right from the Great Depression to the Cold War*. Philadelphia: Temple University Press, 1983.

Richards, Leonard. *Shays's Rebellion: The American Revolution's Final Battle*. Philadelphia: University of Pennsylvania Press, 2002.

Robbins, William G. "The Western Lumber Industry." In *The Twentieth Century West: Historical Interpretations*, edited by Gerald D. Nash and Richard W. Etulain, 233–256. Albuquerque: University of New Mexico Press, 1989.

Roberto, Michael Joseph. *The Coming of the American Behemoth: The Origins of Fascism in the United States, 1920–1940*. New York: Monthly Review Press, 2018.

Romasco, Albert U. *The Poverty of Abundance: Hoover, the Nation, the Depression*. New York: Oxford University Press, 1965.

———. *The Politics of Recovery: Roosevelt's New Deal*. New York: Oxford University Press, 1983.

Rothmyer, Karen. *Winning Pulitzers: The Stories behind Some of the Best News Coverage of Our Time*. New York: Columbia University Press, 1991.

Rowley, William D. "The West as Laboratory and Mirror of Reform." In *The Twentieth Century West: Historical Interpretations*, edited by Gerald D. Nash and Richard W. Etulain. Albuquerque: University of New Mexico Press, 1989.

Saalfeld, Lawrence J. *Forces of Prejudice in Oregon, 1920–1925*. Portland: Archdiocesan Historical Commission, 1984.

Saloutos, Theodore, and John D. Hicks. *Agricultural Discontent in the Middle West, 1900–1939*. Madison: University of Wisconsin Press, 1951.

Schlesinger, Arthur M. Jr. *The Age of Roosevelt: The Crisis of the Old Order, 1919–1933*. Boston: Houghton-Mifflin, 1957.

———. *The Age of Roosevelt: The Politics of Upheaval*. Boston: Houghton-Mifflin, 1960.

Schorer, Mark. *Sinclair Lewis: An American Life*. New York: McGraw-Hill, 1961.

Schwantes, Carlos A. *Coxey's Army: An American Odyssey*. Lincoln: University of Nebraska Press, 1985.

Schwartz, E. A. *The Rogue River Indian War and Its Aftermath: 1850–1980*. Norman: University of Oklahoma Press, 2010.

Shover, John L. *Cornbelt Rebellion: The Farmers' Holiday Association*. Urbana: University of Illinois Press, 1965.

Slaughter, Thomas P. *The Whiskey Rebellion: Frontier Epilogue to the American Revolution*. New York: Oxford University Press, 1986.

Soule, George. *Prosperity Decade: From War to Depression: 1917–1929*. New York: Rinehart and Company, 1947.

Southern Oregon Historical Society. *Land in Common: An Illustrated History of Jackson County, Oregon*. Medford: Southern Oregon Historical Society, 1997.

Stanley, Jason. *How Fascism Works: The Politics of Us and Them*. New York: Random House, 2018.

Sternsher, Bernard, ed. *Hitting Home: The Great Depression in Town and Country*. Chicago: Quadrangle Books, 1970.

Stock, Catherine McNicol. *Main Street in Crisis: The Great Depression and the Old Middle Class in the Northern Plains*. Chapel Hill: University of North Carolina Press, 1992.

———. *Rural Radicals: Righteous Rage in the American Grain*. Ithaca, NY: Cornell University Press, 1996.

Stock, Catherine McNicol, and Robert D. Johnston, eds. *The Countryside in the Age of the Modern State*. Ithaca, NY: Cornell University Press, 2001.

Sturholm, Larry, and John Howard. *All for Nothing: The True Story of the Last Great Train Robbery*. Portland: BLS Publishing, 1976.

Szatmary, David P. *Shays's Rebellion: The Making of an Agrarian Insurrection*. Amherst: University of Massachusetts Press, 1980.

Taylor, Alan. *Liberty Men and Great Proprietors: The Revolutionary Settlement on the Maine Frontier, 1760–1820*. Chapel Hill: University of North Carolina Press, 1990.

Toy, Eckard V. Jr. "The Ku Klux Klan in Oregon." In *Experiences in a Promised Land: Essays in Pacific Northwest History*, edited by G. Thomas Edwards and Carlos A. Schwantes, 269–286. Seattle: University of Washington Press, 1986.

———. "Robe and Gown: The Ku Klux Klan in Eugene, Oregon." In *The Invisible Empire in the West*, edited by Shawn Lay, 153–184. Urbana: University of Illinois Press, 1991.

Trachtenberg, Alan. *The Incorporation of America: Culture and Society in the Gilded Age*. New York: Hill and Wang, 1982.

Tucker, William P. History of Jackson County, Oregon. MA thesis, University of Washington, Seattle, 1931.

Turnbull, George S. *History of Oregon Newspapers*. Portland: Binfords and Mort, 1939.

———. *An Oregon Crusader*. Portland: Binfords and Mort, 1955.

Ver Steeg, Clarence L. *The Formative Years, 1607–1763*. New York: Hill and Wang, 1964.

Wagner, MaryJo. Farms, Families, and Reform: Women in the Farmers' Alliance and Populist Party. PhD diss., University of Oregon, Eugene, 1986.

Washburn, Wilcomb C. *The Governor and the Rebel: A History of Bacon's Rebellion in Virginia*. Chapel Hill: University of North Carolina Press, 1957.

White, Richard. *"It's Your Misfortune and None of My Own": A New History of the American West*. Norman: University of Oklahoma Press, 1991.

White, Richard D. *Kingfish: The Reign of Huey P. Long*. New York: Random House, 2006.

Wiebe, Robert H. *The Search for Order, 1877–1920*. New York: Hill and Wang, 1967.

Wik, Reynold M. *Henry Ford and Grass-Roots America*. Ann Arbor: University of Michigan Press, 1972.

Williams, T. Harry. *Huey Long*. New York: Alfred A. Knopf, 1970.

Williams, William Appleman. *The Contours of American History*. Chicago: Quadrangle Books, 1961.

Woeste, Victoria Saker. *The Farmer's Benevolent Trust: Law and Agricultural Cooperation in Industrial America, 1865–1945*. Chapel Hill: University of North Carolina Press, 1998.

Wood, Gordon S. *The Creation of the American Republic, 1776–1787*. Chapel Hill: University of North Carolina Press, 1969.

JOURNAL AND NEWSPAPER ARTICLES; UNPUBLISHED SECONDARY
SOURCES

Arends, Jack. "Robert W. Ruhl, The Medford Mail Tribune and the Good Government Congress." Undergraduate research paper. Washington State University, 1979.

Burley, Shane, and Alexander Reid Ross. "From Nativism to White Power: Mid-Twentieth-Century White Supremacist Movements in Oregon." *Oregon Historical Quarterly* 120, no. 4 (2019): 564–585.

Clark, Malcolm Jr. "The Bigot Disclosed: 90 Years of Nativism." *Oregon Historical Quarterly* 75 (June 1974): 109–190.

Cordy, Clifford. "History of the Rogue River Valley Fruit Industry." Medford, copy of type-script on file at Southern Oregon Historical Society, 1977.

Garson, Robert A. "Political Fundamentalism and Popular Democracy in the 1920s." *South Atlantic Quarterly* 76 (Spring 1977): 219–233.

Gilje, Paul A. "The Baltimore Riots of 1812 and the Breakdown of the Anglo-American Mob Tradition." *Journal of Social History* 13 (Summer 1980): 547–564.

Horowitz, David A. "The Klansman as Outsider: Ethnocultural Solidarity and Antielitism in the Oregon Ku Klux Klan of the 1920s." *Pacific Northwest Quarterly* 80 (January 1989): 12–20.

———. "Social Mobility and Personal Revitalization: Oregon's Ku Klux Klan in the 1920s." *Oregon Historical Quarterly* 90 (Winter 1989): 365–384.

LaLande, Jeff. "Beneath the Hooded Robe: Newspapermen, Local Politics, and the Ku Klux Klan in Jackson County, Oregon, 1921–1923." *Pacific Northwest Quarterly* 83 (April 1992): 42–52.

———. "A Little Kansas in Southern Oregon: The Course and Character of Populism in Jackson County, 1890–1900." *Pacific Historical Review* 63 (May 1994): 149–176.

———. "The 'Jackson County Rebellion': Social Turmoil and Political Insurgence in Southern Oregon during the Great Depression." *Oregon Historical Quarterly* 95 (Winter 1994/95): 406–471.

———. "'Dixie of the Pacific Northwest': Southern Oregon's Civil War." *Oregon Historical Quarterly* 100 (Spring 1999): 32–81.

———. "'The State of Jefferson': A Disaffected Region's 160-Year Search for Identity." *Oregon Historical Quarterly* 118 (Spring 2017): 14–41.

McClintock, Thomas C. "Seth Lewelling, William S. U'Ren and the Birth of the Oregon Progressive Movement." *Oregon Historical Quarterly* 68 (September 1967): 197–220.

Moses, H. Vincent. "G. Harold Powell and the Corporate Consolidation of the Modern Citrus Enterprise, 1904–1922." *Business History Review* 69 (1995): 119–155.

Mullen, Jay. "The Party of Hicks and Hayseeds." *Table Rock Sentinel* 12 (September/October 1992): 15–22.

———. "A Local Perspective of Oregon Populism." Paper presented at the Forty-Fifth Pacific Northwest History Conference, Salem, 1992.

———. "Oregon's Sacco and Vanzetti Case: State v. Boloff." Paper presented at the Forty-Sixth Pacific Northwest Conference, Eugene, 1993.

Murray, Keith. "Issues and Personalities of Pacific Northwest Politics, 1889–1950." *Pacific Northwest Quarterly* 41 (July 1950): 213–233.

Ostler, Jeffrey. "Why the Populist Party Was Strong in Kansas and Nebraska but Weak in Iowa." *Western Historical Quarterly* 23 (November 1992): 451–474.

Phelps, Christopher. "The Posse Rides Again: Nazi Skinheads Make Headlines, but Christian Patriots May Be Greater Racist Threat to Oregon." *Portland Alliance* 10 (September 1990): 1, 6–8.

Riddle, Thomas W. "Populism in the Palouse: Old Ideas and New Realities." *Pacific Northwest Quarterly* 65 (July 1974): 97–109.

Rothwell, C. Easton. The Ku Klux Klan in the State of Oregon. BA thesis, Reed College, Portland, 1924.

Thompson, Carmen P. "Expectation and Exclusion: An Introduction of Whiteness, White Supremacy, and Resistance in Oregon History." *Oregon Historical Quarterly* 120 (Winter 2019): 358–367.

Toll, William. "Progress and Piety: The Ku Klux Klan and Social Change in Tillamook, Oregon." *Pacific Northwest Quarterly* 69 (April 1978): 75–85.

Toy, Eckard V. Jr. "Silver Shirts in the Northwest: Politics, Prophecies, and Personalities in the 1930s." *Pacific Northwest Quarterly* 80 (October 1989): 139–146.

Tyack, David B. "The Perils of Pluralism: The Background of the Pierce Case." *American Historical Review* 74 (October 1968): 74–98.

Voeltz, Herman C. "Coxey's Army in Oregon, 1894." *Oregon Historical Quarterly* 65 (September 1964): 263–295.

Index

Page numbers in *italics* indicate images

and Ruhl as target, 46, 58, 68, 91
support for after arrest, 104, 129, 131
trial, 110–111, 113
and violence, 92, 98–99
See also Good Government Congress;
Pacific Record Herald (Medford)
Fehl, Electa, 45, 65, 124, 129, 131
Ferry, D. H., 54, 59, 84–85, 105
Fisher, Eli, 15
Fish Lake, 29, 166n34
Fitch, L. E., 104
Fleming, E. A., 85, 95, 100, 101, 108
flouring mills, 11
Fluher, Henry "Heinie," 97
Ford, Henry, 30–31, 47, 48
foreclosures, 42, 44, 53, 55
Forest Service and Civilian Conservation
Corps, 123, 125
Fruit Growers' Bank, 97
Fruit Growers League, 25, 41

gambling, 27
gang language
and Banks, 51, 54
and class, 115
and Fehl, 45, 46, 51
Garraty, John, 3
Gates, Charles E. "Pop," 31, 60, 61, 80, 85
Geiger (GGC member), 100
George Prescott Park, 123
Glenn, John, 94, 96, 110, 113
Gold Hill
Good Government Congress support,
82, 105, 127
and Populist Revolt, 10
and tradition of rebellion in area,
142–143
gold mining, 5, 42, 54, 164n20
golf, 24–25
Good Government Congress
areas supporting, 81, 142–143
and class, 3, 68, 78–81, 83
creation of, 65–68
disbanding of, 125
goals of, 82–84, 137
impact of, 103
leadership by Banks and Fehl, 3, 91–92,
97–98
meetings and rallies, 66–68, 75–76, 91,
97–98
membership cards, 77, 104–105
name, 77

and 1934 election, 124
red-baiting by, 78, 84
renunciation of, 104–105
and Revolution imagery, 144–145
shooting aftermath, 104–106
and tradition of rebellion in area,
139–144
trials, 106–114, 123
and violence, 3, 91, 92, 96–97, 98–101,
105, 111–112
See also ballot theft by Good Government
Congress; Prescott shooting
Good Government Congress, membership
arrests, 96, 101–102
blacklist, 112–113
demographics, 68, 78–82
and KKK, 85–87
numbers, 80–81
profiles, 86–89
Gore, William, 83, 108
Goss, O. H., 84, 85, 173n4, 178n53, 181n2
Gould, Dave, 104
Grange, 82, 141, 142, 161n14, 162n25
Great Depression
and demagoguery, 1
and economics of area, 2–3
and employment, 40–43, 54, 123–124,
131–132
as factor in Jackson County Rebellion,
1–3
and New Deal, 123–124, 125, 131–134,
164n16
Greek immigrants, 163n9
Greensprings Mountain Boys, 63, 89
Guches, Janet, 100

Hall, Leonard
on ballot theft events, 93
and Committee of One Hundred, 89
on Martin, 178n52
and Pulitzer Prize to Ruhl, 116, 117
threats to, 62
whipping of, 82, 97, 110
See also *Miner* (Jacksonville)
Hammersly, Joseph L., 107, 108
Hanley, Alice, 34
Hardy, Charles A., 107
Hawley, Willis C., 41, 171n5
Henderson (GGC supporter), 79
Hill, Howard, 36, 85
hillbilly term, 79
Hoelting, A. R., 93, 96, 115

as term, 4
White settlement in, 5, 6
Southern Oregon Mail (Medford), 12–13, 15, 26
See also *Mail Tribune* (Medford)
Southern Oregon Sales, 24
Southern Pacific Railroad
Ashland facilities, 8
bypass, 40
and Commercial Club, 27
freight rates, 11, 41
Jacksonville spur, 26
and Populist Revolt, 11
promotion of area, 9
railroad-grant lands, 167n5
robbery of, 37
tourism, 23
Stailey, Electa. *See* Fehl, Electa
State of Jefferson movement, 134
Steiner, R. E. Lee, 128
Sterling Mine, 164n20
Sternsher, Bernard, 3
Swedenburg, Francis G., 83, 98, 108
Sweet, L. M., 86–87, 105

Talent
decline of, 25
and Populist Revolt, 10
water and irrigation, 30, 34, 37, 41
Talent Irrigation District, 30, 34, 37, 41
tax-protest groups, 150
Terrill, Charles, 32, 34, 35, 58
Territory of Jackson, 6–7
Thatcher, Jennie, 84
Thomas, Charles M., 34, 35–36
Thomas, Norman, 172n16
Thompson, Dorothy, 2
Tidings (Ashland)
on Banks, 62
and 1932 election, 58, 61
and Populist Revolt, 12, 14, 15
use of in *Daily News*, 64
timber management, 150
tourism, 23, 26, 40
Townsend, Francis E., 132
Townsend Plan, 50, 132, 133, 143
Traffic Association, 44
Train, O. C., 87
Trump, Donald, 150
Tryor, Donald, 66

tuberculosis, 47, 50
Tuttle, Lee, 167n3
T'Vault, William G., 7

Unemployed Council, 84, 173n4
Unemployed Relief Association, 41–42
unemployment. *See* employment
Union Party, 132
US Department of Agriculture, 41, 44, 46

Valley Record (Ashland), 13
Van Hoevenberg, Henry, 89
Van Winkle, I. H., 102, 107
violence
Banks's fears of violence, 63, 88, 92, 98
Banks's incitement to, 62–63, 65–66, 92, 98–101, 103, 112
and Fehl, 92, 98–99
and Good Government Congress, 3, 91, 92, 96–97, 98–101, 105, 111–112
and incorporation and West, 177n40
and modern Far Right, 150
and national tradition of rebellion, 145
and shooting aftermath, 104–106
See also night-riding KKK incidents; Prescott shooting

Wakefield, Ira, 11, 12, 15
Wallace, George, 149
Warren, C. A., 100, 101
water
droughts, 25, 30, 35, 58
supply and politics, 29–30, 34–35, 37, 45, 46, 86, 140
Weaver, James B., 13, 162n27
Weighed in the Balance (Banks), 125–126
West
boosterism in, 144
incorporation and violence, 177n40
Jackson County as Western, 163n7
and tradition of rebellion in area, 143–144
Western resentment and Banks, 48
Western American, 31
White, William Allen, 124
Wilkins, M. O., 60, 61
Willamette Valley, White settlement of, 4–5, 6
Wilson, E. M., 52
wineries, 149
Winrod, Gerald B., 180n38

women
  and backwardness, 79
  and Good Government Congress, 67, 68,
    81–82, 85, 88, 142, 178n52
  and Grange, 161n14
  increase in political activity by, 82, 142
  and KKK, 31–32, 142
  and Populist Revolt, 11, 142
  support for Banks during incarceration,
    88, 142
  and tradition of rebellion in area, 140
  women's suffrage, 27
Women of the Ku Klux Klan, 31
Women's Christian Temperance Union, 27,
  32, 142
Woodville and Populist Revolt, 10
  See also Rogue River (town)

Zorn-MacPherson Bill, 60
Zundell, Lowell, 60, 61, 64